EAST ASIAN SIBERIA

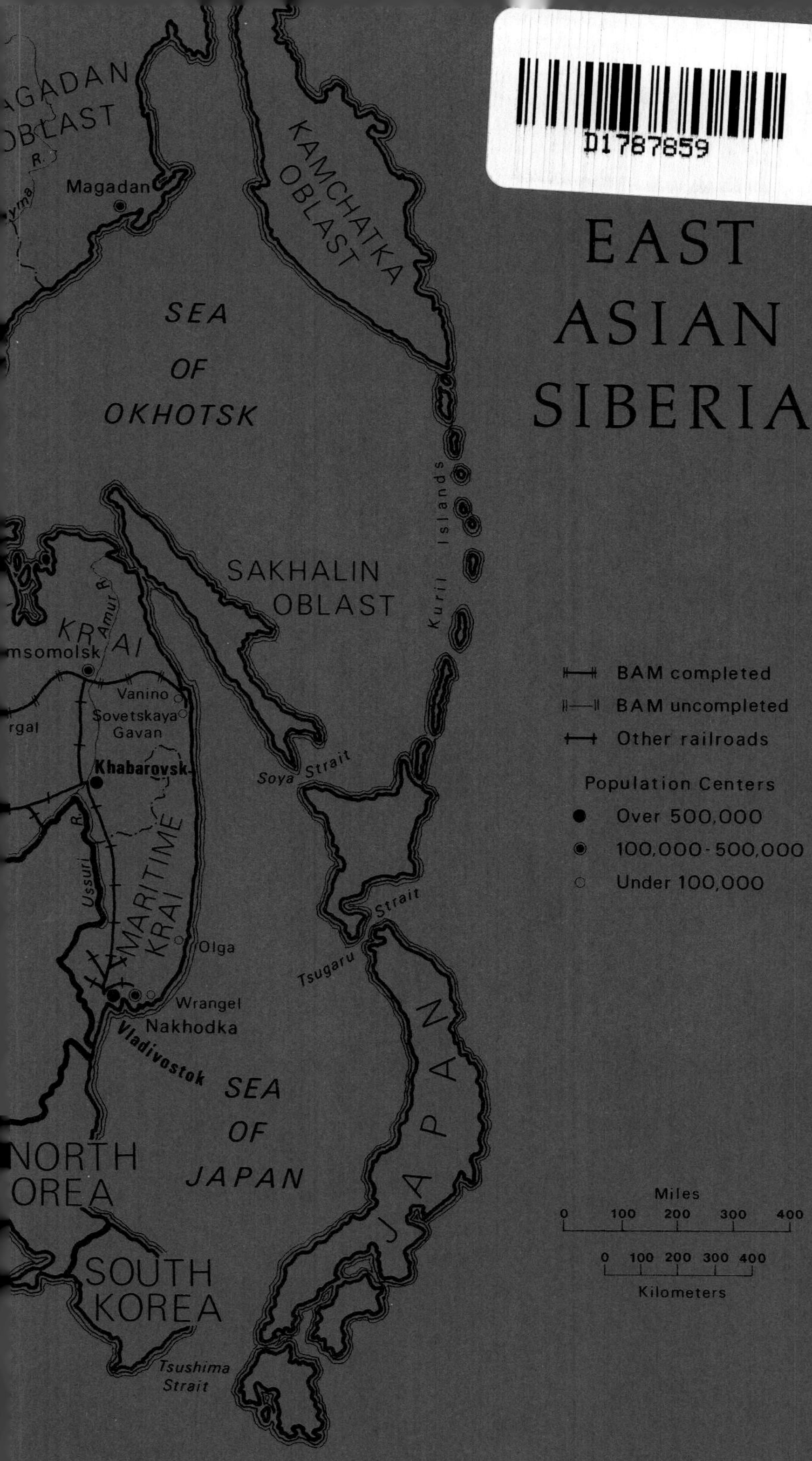

⊢—⊣ BAM completed
⊩—⊪ BAM uncompleted
↔ Other railroads

Population Centers
● Over 500,000
◉ 100,000 - 500,000
○ Under 100,000

LIBRARIES
UNIVERSITY OF MAINE
AT ORONO

RAYMOND H. FOGLER LIBRARY

ORONO

Siberian Development and East Asia

Allen S. Whiting

Siberian Development and East Asia
Threat or Promise?

1981   STANFORD UNIVERSITY PRESS
STANFORD, CALIFORNIA

STANFORD UNIVERSITY PRESS
STANFORD, CALIFORNIA

© 1981 by the Board of Trustees of the
Leland Stanford Junior University

Printed in the United States of America

ISBN 0-8047-1109-7

LC 81-50057

To Knight Biggerstaff and Philip E. Mosely
who started me on this path

Preface

It is literally impossible to acknowledge the assistance of the many individuals and institutions who have helped to make this study possible. The Soviet officials and scholars who patiently answered my questions in the institutes of the Academy of Sciences of the USSR at Akademgorodok, Irkutsk, Yakutsk, and Khabarovsk must unfortunately remain individually anonymous so as to safeguard the integrity of their position, regardless of how my understanding or use of their information may appear in this volume. Nevertheless, I wish to pay tribute to their generosity with their time and their hospitality of spirit, both so essential to the success of my two field trips in 1975 and 1978. Special appreciation is due to Boris N. Slavinsky, deputy director of the Far East Science Center, Academy of Sciences, Vladivostok, whose warm assistance made possible the second trip.

For different reasons, the many Japanese government officials and business executives who gave freely of their experience and views concerning Soviet-Japanese relations, especially as they involve Siberian development, cannot be identified individually. Their continuing involvement in this area of activity precludes associating their names with specific information offered during our successive interviews in 1978-80. The process of gaining access to their insightful and illuminating observations was greatly facilitated by the kind support and guidance provided by Kiichi Saeki, chairman of the Nomura Research Institute and former president of the National Defense College of Japan, to whom I am deeply indebted.

Financial support was generously provided by the Rockefeller Foundation, the Ford Foundation, and the East-West Center (for the year 1978–79). The Academy of Sciences, USSR, provided assistance during both of my visits to the Soviet Union. Repeated trips to Japan and travel within the country were aided by a conference sponsored by the Project on United States–Japan Relations of Stanford University (June 1978), and another was cosponsored by *Yomiuri Shimbun* and the Brookings Institution (October 1978). A third round of interviews was made possible through the courtesy of the Cunard Line (March 1979). Research in Sapporo was carried out while I was lecturing in Japan under the auspices of the International Communications Agency.

In June 1978 the Chinese People's Institute for Foreign Affairs hosted my visit to the Xinjiang Autonomous Region and to Beijing, and in both locations discussion of Sino-Soviet relations and border problems proved informative.

The manuscript was basically written at the Resource Systems Institute of the East-West Center, thanks to the timely invitation of its director, Dr. Harrison Brown. My colleagues there provided endless enlightenment in matters meteorological and geological, and assisted in other disciplines where I trespass with little claim to competence. Without their counsel and criticism, especially that of Kim Woodard, Richard Sheldon, and Martha Caldwell, this would have been a lesser study. At the University of Hawaii, Roland Fuchs deepened my understanding of Soviet geography, and John Stephan proved invaluable as a careful reader and specialist in Russo-Japanese relations, particularly as concerns Sakhalin and the Kuril Islands. Patricia Polansky opened the rich Siberian holdings of the University of Hawaii to my inquiry, and Gladys Wong and Rita Hong at the Resources Systems Institute library sustained the copious flow of documents and articles that is necessary to a multidisciplinary work.

By happy coincidence, I launched my study at the same time that the Association of American Geographers initiated its Project on Soviet Natural Resources in the World Economy. Robert G. Jensen, the director, kindly invited my participation,

PREFACE ix

thereby making available the discussion papers of specialists in various economic sectors and disciplines. The participants' work, especially that of Victor L. Mote, has greatly enriched my own. Another symposium, under the direction of Donald S. Zagoria for the Council on Foreign Relations, focused on Soviet policy in Asia. As a member, I benefited from the contributions and criticisms of this group. The two publications that emerged from these separate projects contain chapters that I drew from this larger work.

By this point it should be obvious that this book is to a considerable extent a synthesis of existing information, albeit scattered widely in different publications and languages. It is for this reason that the material is so heavily footnoted. The average reader need not bother with the references; they contain no substantive information, except in Chapter 6, "The China Factor." However, as far as possible I have tried to provide the specialist with the source for any observation or datum derived from others in order to permit evaluation and further inquiry.

One learns from one's students, and I have benefited from the work and observations of many, in particular Roy Grow, whose insightful research into transnational interactions within the Japan-China-Soviet triangle contributed much to my approach. Research assistance and useful suggestions also came from Eric Jones, James Tong, Yoshihiro Tsuranuki, and Marita Kaw. Their systematic search of Russian, Japanese, and Chinese periodicals provided an invaluable updating of my own research for the period 1979–80. I am deeply grateful to Theodore Shabad, John Hardt, Alan B. Smith, Evelyn Colbert, and Paul Langer, who provided special assistance and helpful comments. None of the institutions or persons identified above bear any responsibility, however, for whatever slips or misconceptions remain.

Last but not least, I wish to thank my wife, Alice, and my two children, Jeffrey and Jenny, who patiently tolerated the months of absence and the trial of living with self-imposed deadlines that truncated weekends and vacations.

A.S.W.

Ann Arbor, Michigan
January 1981

Contents

1 Siberia and East Asia 1

2 The Internal Setting: Quagmire or Bonanza? 19

3 The International Setting: Triangle of Tension 65

4 Siberian Development: The Strategic Implications 85

5 The Japan Connection 112

6 The China Factor 160

7 Soviet Decision Making, Development, and External Influence 182

8 United States Policy Interests 207

Notes 239

Index 269

Abbreviations

ASSR	Autonomous Soviet Socialist Republic
ASW	antisubmarine warfare
BAM	Baikal-Amur Mainline
CCP	Chinese Communist Party
CIA	Central Intelligence Agency
COMECON	organization of the Communist economic bloc
EAS	East Asian Siberia
Eximbank	Export-Import Bank (United States)
GNP	gross national product
ICBM	intercontinental ballistic missile
JDA	Japan Defense Agency
JSP	Japanese Socialist Party
LDP	Liberal Democratic Party
LNG	liquefied natural gas
MITI	Ministry of International Trade and Industry (Japan)
MRBM	medium-range ballistic missile
NATO	North Atlantic Treaty Organization
OPEC	Organization of Petroleum Exporting Countries
PLA	Chinese People's Liberation Army
PRC	People's Republic of China
RSFSR	Russian Soviet Federated Socialist Republic
SALT	Strategic Arms Limitation Treaty
SDF	Self-Defense Forces (Japan)
SLBM	submarine-launched ballistic missile
TPC	territorial production complex

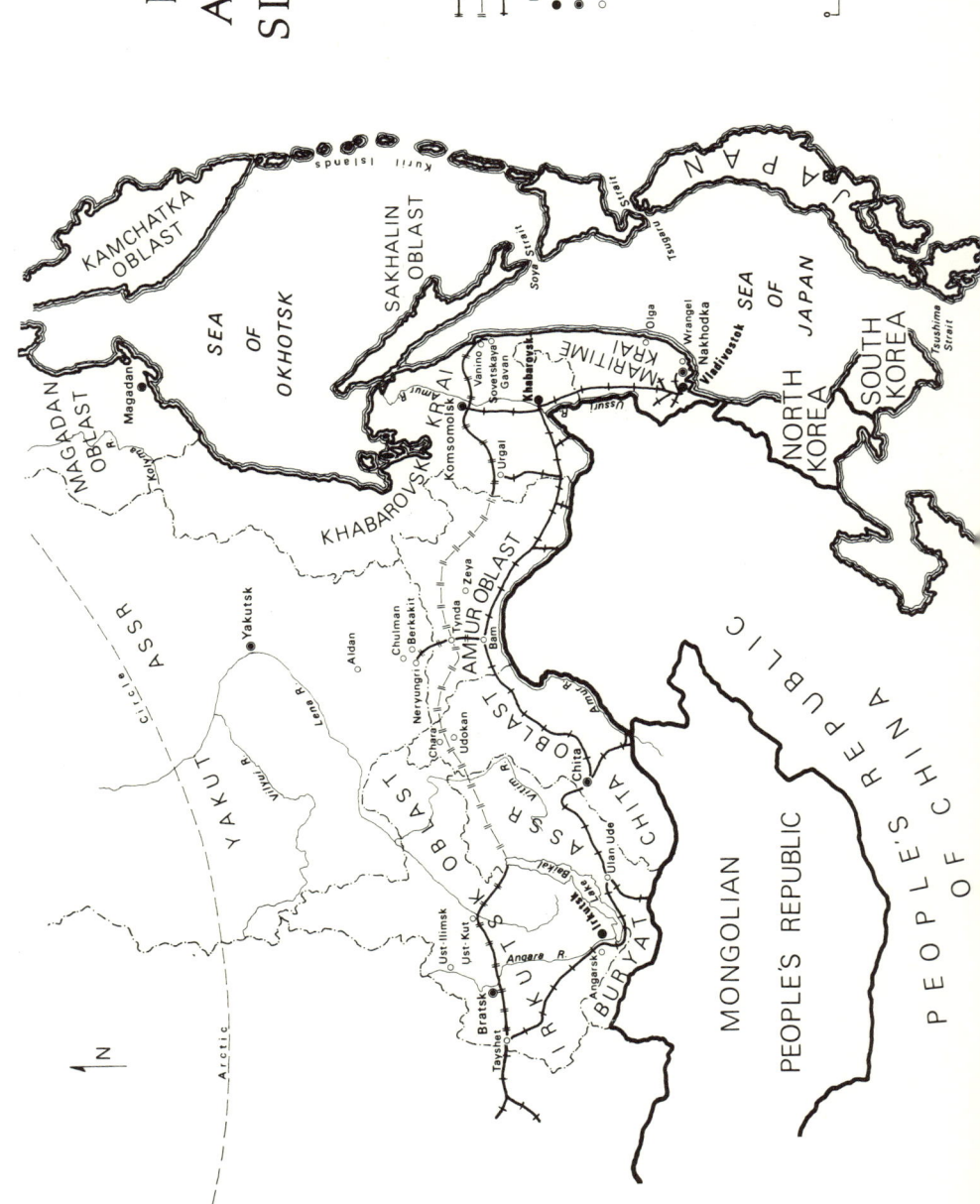

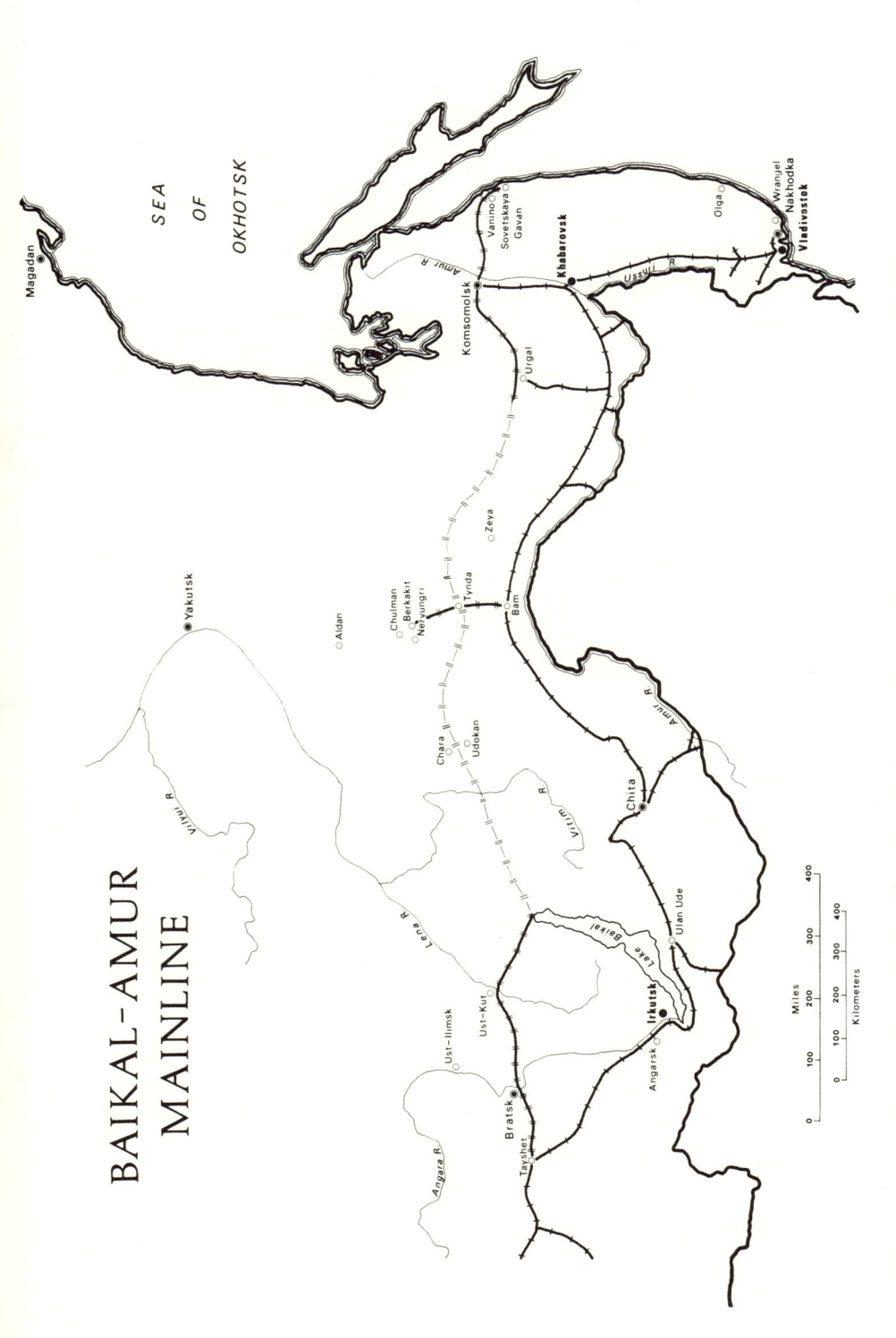

Siberian Development and East Asia

1 Siberia and East Asia

Inception of the Inquiry

The vast expanse of Siberia stretches from the Ural Mountains to the Pacific and from the Soviet border with China and Mongolia to the Arctic Ocean. Traditionally the name has conjured up the image of a windswept, frozen wasteland, destitute of people and civilization except for primitive settlements where banished exiles perished in forced labor. The introduction to a nineteenth-century memoir of an exile's life there put it characteristically: "The subject of the present work is Siberia: a region dreary in nature, and not only in name synonymous, but actually identical with a vast prison—a locality associated in our minds with the most poignant of human suffering."[1]

That this stereotype remains today is evidenced by the typical response to my announced intention to visit the area for research. In 1975 friendly but serious concern greeted my plans for an initial foray with my wife and two small children into the region via the Trans-Siberian Railroad; and my return to Siberia in the fall of 1978 for a three-week stay aroused bemused incomprehension among my academic colleagues. Escape made sense. Going back voluntarily did not.

However, in the 1970's other images began to emerge. On the positive side, West Siberia's newly found bonanza of oil and nat-

2 SIBERIA AND EAST ASIA

ural gas suddenly catapulted the Soviet Union into first place in the world production of these vital energy resources, to the benefit of Eastern and Western Europe. To supplement the Trans-Siberian, a second railroad traversing East and Far East Siberia—the Baikal-Amur Mainline (BAM)—was begun in 1974, opening vistas of further resource exploitation to serve the Pacific market, Japan in particular. On the negative side, as Sino-Soviet relations deteriorated in the late 1960's, Moscow built up its military forces along the 7,500-kilometer (4,650-mile) frontier. This underscored the strategic significance of the region. The simultaneous expansion of the Soviet Pacific Fleet provided another dimension of concern over the Kremlin's renewed interest in developing its long-neglected Asian region.

These more recent images were captured in the hyperbolic prose seemingly inseparable from writings on Siberia. Writing of its Eastern and Far Eastern regions, a French journalist waxed euphoric: "First there is the natural gas, an ocean of gas, one-eighth of the world's known reserves. . . . There is also an ocean of oil—perhaps as much as Western Siberia—the reserves of which are half those of the entire Arab world."[2] Equally extravagant assertions of the area's allegedly unparalleled natural bounty poured from the official Soviet press to mobilize support at home and abroad for the construction of BAM.[3]

On the negative side, alarmist prognostications of a Sino-Soviet war over this underpopulated transcontinental region emerged in 1974 at a conference sponsored by the North Atlantic Treaty Organization (NATO). A noted British scholar specializing in Siberia warned, "'Lebensraum' must be considered in its up-to-date form as a quest of access to raw materials . . . as well as to mere space for the settlement of people. . . . For all of Siberia, the overwhelming, close-looming, gigantic fact and presence, written in huge letters all across the base line of the map is CHINA. . . . The Soviets have left the whole region, by Chinese standards, almost empty of people and almost unutilized."[4] As a final note, he declared, "The third side of the triangle is now—with the virtual withdrawal of basic Western interest in the area—Japan."

This allusion to a Northeast Asian triangle challenged the

SIBERIA AND EAST ASIA 3

dominant triangular concept of the time, which posited the Moscow-Beijing-Washington interaction as determining the policies of each respective power. However, the more circumscribed regional triangle of tension had pitted Russia, Japan, and China against each other through the three-quarters of a century of confrontation and conflict manifest in this brief chronology:

1894–95: Sino-Japanese War
1904–05: Russo-Japanese War
1918–25: Japanese intervention in Siberia and Sakhalin
1929: Russo-Chinese conflict over Chinese Eastern Railroad
1931: Japanese seizure of Manchuria from China
1937–45: Sino-Japanese War
1938–39: Soviet-Japanese border clashes
1945: Soviet-Japanese War
1969: Sino-Soviet border clashes

The contemporary relevance of this historical past became apparent in 1974–75, when Beijing persuaded Tokyo to refuse Moscow's proposal for joint construction of a pipeline associated with BAM to transport oil from West Siberia to the Pacific. Although Tokyo ostensibly reversed its previous interest because of Moscow's reducing the promised supply and increasing the cost, it was Chinese objections to the strategic implications that made broader regional triangular considerations decisive for the Japanese.[5]

These images and assertions raise a host of contradictory propositions that require systematic examination if their diverse policy prescriptions are to be evaluated for possible adoption. What is the actual mineral wealth of East and Far East Siberia, and is it accessible? Does it offer significant relief from eventual shortages elsewhere in the USSR, especially in oil and gas? If so, is it desirable to assist Moscow in exploiting these resources by making credits and technology available from abroad, particularly from the United States? Should this assistance be manipulated in order to influence Soviet policy, whether toward human rights at home or toward intervention abroad?

What are the strategic implications of the Baikal-Amur rail-

4 SIBERIA AND EAST ASIA

road for Soviet military capabilities in the region? How are these implications perceived in Moscow, Beijing, and Tokyo? How do the Japanese view Siberian development? Will interdependency result from Japanese participation? If so, what are the implications for both sides of the relationship? What are Soviet intentions in East Asia? Can they be affected for better or for worse by the presence or absence of foreign cooperation in Siberian projects? What does the opening up of Siberia portend for the Pacific basin and the larger future of global resources?

Conventional wisdom offers ready answers to these questions, but satisfactory evidence is rarely available, and underlying assumptions are seldom questioned. How likely is local or regional tension in East Asia to repeat the major-nation conflicts of the past? What issues remain to be resolved among neighboring regimes? How explosive are they? Is trade and the bartering of technology for resources concessionary or mutually advantageous? What factors impinge on decision making in key capitals? How flexible is policy over time? Can "worst case" and "best case" assumptions concerning the future be balanced in contingency plans that both protect against threat and explore opportunities of promise?

One spur to investigating these questions was the strikingly different postures of Tokyo and Washington with respect to Siberian development. By 1978 the Japanese Export-Import Bank had advanced $1.5 billion in credits to match a comparable amount from private banks for port construction, timber projects, coal mining, and offshore oil exploration. The United States Export-Import Bank, by contrast, was limited by the 1974 Stevenson amendment to a total of $300 million for the entire USSR, of which no more than $40 million was available for energy exploration and research. No Eximbank loans could be used for Soviet energy production and transmission. On top of this came the Jackson-Vanik amendment to the 1974 Trade Act, which prohibited all government credits and investment guarantees to the USSR so long as it denied or obstructed emigration. Last but not least, in addition to these restrictions, in 1978 President Carter temporarily blocked the sale of manufacturing equipment for high-quality oil-drill bits to the Soviet Union in protest over the trial of a noted dissident. This threatened the integrity of American contracts, a threat that was realized to a far greater degree when he imposed a partial embargo on credits and the transfer of technology in the wake of the Soviet invasion of Afghanistan in 1979.

The contrasting postures are particularly striking in view of the contrary bilateral relations of the Soviet Union with Japan and the United States. Moscow and Tokyo have yet to conclude a World War II peace treaty because Soviet forces occupy small islands north of Hokkaido that Japan claims were not ceded with the Kuril Islands by the 1945 Yalta and Potsdam accords. Moscow and Washington, however, held periodic summit conferences throughout the Cold War, and during the 1970's they mutually espoused detente as a framework for greater cooperation. Strategically, Japan's proximity to Siberia and its vulnerability to blockade by the Soviet Pacific Fleet make Moscow's military power in the region a primary concern in Tokyo. Washington's main focus is on the Soviet presence in Europe and the Soviet strategic nuclear threat in the Pacific, and it puts only secondary stress on developments in Northeast Asia. Yet despite its background, Japanese policy toward Siberian development is basically cooperative; United States policy, obstructive.

An added element of paradox in the American posture turns on the question of energy and its future availability. In 1973–74 the Organization of Petroleum Exporting Countries (OPEC) triggered a series of price increases in oil combined with a temporary embargo that induced near panic in West Europe, Japan, and the United States. Then in 1977 the Central Intelligence Agency forecast that Soviet oil production would peak in the near future and by 1985 might force the USSR onto the world market as an importer instead of exporter.[6] In this context the policy issues associated with the exploration and exploitation of Siberian oil and gas take on special significance.

The central point of my inquiry is Siberia itself—or, more precisely, the area that relates primarily to East Asia and that I have termed East Asian Siberia (EAS). The analytical basis for this differentiation and a fuller description of EAS make up the final section of this chapter. It suffices here to note that West Siberia is excluded because it is oriented wholly toward the European USSR, Eastern Europe, and Western Europe as its resource markets. Moreover, West Siberia has won the preponderance of attention among Soviet and foreign analysts, compared with the less studied East and Far East regions.

My experiences during two sojourns in the region extending from the Yenisei River to the Sea of Okhotsk stand in vivid contrast to my contemporary experiences in Moscow. Casual encounters in the intimacy of four days' "hard-class" travel via the Trans-Siberian and evening conversations in the plebeian cafeterias of Irkutsk and Khabarovsk revealed a mixture of frontier openness, pioneering exuberance, and political shrewdness dramatically different from the more circumspect, dispirited, and routine exchanges of the Soviet capital. Hour-long question periods following my lectures on "Post-Mao China" in the research institutes of the Academy of Sciences, whether in the most advanced center at Akademgorodok or the most remote branch at Yakutsk, invariably triggered an outpouring of queries that implicitly rejected the official line of nearly twenty years on the sensitive subjects of China and Sino-Soviet relations. At times the audacity of the questioner made the audience gasp, but he or she would persist nonetheless. By comparison, my similar presentations in Moscow evoked guarded probing at best; more frequently they were followed by ritualistic formalities or simple silence. Only when we were alone and certain that no observation or reporting was possible would individual seminar members raise more heretical matters.

The hundreds of scientists and scholars in the diverse research institutions scattered across East Asian Siberia clearly march to a different drummer than do their counterparts in Moscow. They exhibit none of the tension and inhibition that constrains communication and stifles spontaneity in formal scholarly discussions. The absence of bureaucratic barriers to the sharing of research is a welcome relief after the cumbersome procedures and delays that obstruct inquiry at the center. Differences within and among specialists and institutes are frankly, if not fully, aired with the visitor invited to take part. The men and women engaged in the massive effort of opening this forbidding territory to economic exploitation and industry know they are in the vanguard of a long and arduous effort to transform the last Soviet frontier region. They put professional pride before politics in dealing with the rare visitor who seeks more than a tourist's travelogue view.

Moving among the various institutes and across the country, one soon discerns competing interests and divergent views involving such questions as the proper allocation of capital for Siberian development and the appropriate role of foreign participation. Collectively, the *sibiriaki* ("Siberians"), as the enthusiasts of the region are known, present a common front when demanding more autonomy and larger appropriations from Moscow. Separately, however, the Maritime planners compete with those from Yakutsk and Magadan for a larger share of natural gas. Location of a new metallurgical complex is heatedly debated by partisan advocates representing different sites. Proponents of the extraction of raw material for export vie with those who argue for local processing, each side advancing ostensibly objective economic calculations to prove alleged cost benefits. In contrast with the surface appearance of monolithic unity conveyed by the Soviet media, the refreshingly varied views of specialists in different economic sectors and geographic regions reflect the complex reality confronting the developers of East Asian Siberia.

Japan provided another valuable perspective, but, contrary to expectation, it was not found in academic institutes such as have proliferated in university and nongovernmental centers in the United States. In fact, systematic scholarly analysis of the Soviet Union is relatively rare in Japan, especially in political matters. Except for a small center for Soviet studies in Sapporo, remote from the hub of intellectual and business life in Tokyo, there is no university institute solely devoted to the USSR.[7] Numerous writers on foreign affairs, academic and journalistic, address the Soviet Union from a wide range of political viewpoints, but relatively few base their opinions on a close reading of Russian sources or a lifetime of research on Soviet foreign policy.

Fortunately, this lack is more than compensated by expertise in business and government circles. The umbrella organization for Japanese business, Keidanren, has its own Soviet specialists, as do many of the major firms. The Ministry of Foreign Affairs maintains a highly professional corps of analysts by systematic rotation through the large embassy in Moscow and influential policy positions in Tokyo and a system of academic leave abroad, perhaps at an American university center specializing in Soviet studies. The need for monitoring and analyzing Soviet developments in other specialized official sectors, such as the Ministry of International Trade and Industry (MITI), the Self-Defense Agency, and special research groups, stimulates a variety of perspectives and assessments of particular problems.

The consideration given to Soviet-Japanese relations in these circles is relatively consistent over time and consensual in nature. Basically, relations between Moscow and Japan have been marked by a steady coolness since their reestablishment in 1955, and have experienced neither the emotional euphoria of summitry nor the threatening confrontations of Berlin and Cuba that have evoked extreme change in Soviet-American relations during this time. Some problems have remained intractable, for instance, the disputed islands. Others, such as fishing, have evolved an increasingly relaxed framework of businesslike negotiations. This fairly balanced context has combined with a high degree of informal consultation among interested parties to produce an informed and stable policy. Business and government interests do not always agree, nor are all interests within government necessarily identical. But informal consultation minimizes open confrontation or unanticipated unilateral action so as to preserve a basic consistency in private and official behavior.

It would be wrong either to caricature this process as "Japan, Inc." and thereby imply lockstep unity between business and government, or to idealize it as a flawless process that always produces optimal results. The standard divisions of ministerial authority inhibit the voicing of views that may exceed the area of legitimate concern.[8] Within ministries the geographical division of responsibility limits the degree to which officials other than those assigned to Soviet affairs will express their opinion.

Reservations or differences of opinion may be offered privately in unofficial exchange, but they rarely enter the forum in formal proceedings.

Despite the importance of Soviet-Japanese relations across a broad interrelated network of economic, political, and military matters, and their relevance to the broader framework of Sino-Japanese relations, policy analysis tends to be highly compartmentalized and sporadic. Immediate or isolated issues preempt discussion of overall trends and of how they might be shaped to maximize Japanese interests. This situation is not unique to Japan. It is conventional bureaucratic behavior in most governments. Nonetheless, its limiting effect on policy formulation, and particularly on the projection of alternative future possibilities, deserves acknowledgment at the outset.

Fortunately, this inquiry encompassed a particularly eventful period in East Asian international relations that provided a rich opportunity for eliciting differing Japanese views at the outset and for testing their consistency at the end. Interviews began in June 1978, just as China's withdrawal of economic aid from Vietnam impelled Hanoi to join the Soviet economic bloc organization (COMECON). That August Beijing and Tokyo signed a treaty of peace and friendship that was ceremoniously celebrated during Vice-Premier Deng Xiaoping's triumphant tour of Japan in October. In November Hanoi and Moscow concluded a treaty of friendship and cooperation that included a clause providing for military consultation on threats from third countries. In December Beijing and Washington announced the formal establishment of full diplomatic relations, including the eventual termination of the American defense treaty with the Republic of China on Taiwan. The same month Vietnam invaded Cambodia.

In January 1979 Vice-Premier Deng visited Washington amid a flurry of highly publicized interviews and press statements aimed against the Soviet Union. In February China undertook a limited invasion of Vietnam "to teach it a lesson," withdrawing after three weeks of fierce fighting. As a consequence, Soviet warships and military aircraft gained access to facilities in Cam Ranh Bay, Danang, and other points in Vietnam. Over the year

1978–79 Moscow expanded its military presence on the disputed islands above Hokkaido from a few thousand troops to a full division with airfields, artillery, and tanks. In December 1979 Soviet forces invaded Afghanistan, and Washington, reacting with considerable alarm over the threat to Pakistan and Middle East oil, pressed Tokyo to embargo credits and technology for Moscow.

Finally, the evolution of policy in post-Mao China saw the extreme euphoria that accompanied the announcement of the economic goals in 1978 markedly tempered by reexamination and retrenchment in 1979, a development that sharply modified Japanese expectations of trade and investment in China's highly touted "four modernizations." This put Sino-Japanese relations in more stable perspective as an important aspect of the triangular interaction among Moscow, Beijing, and Tokyo.

The Study in Overview

As already implied, two motivations prompted this inquiry. The first in sequence as well as importance was to assess the implications of Siberian development as it pertains to East Asia. The second was to address the policy issues associated with these implications as they confront the United States and its ally, Japan. Although the two aspects of the study are obviously interrelated, the research and the analysis are presented so as to permit different audiences to address either subject separately. Regardless of how Tokyo and Washington may ultimately determine their relationship with East Asian Siberia, in tandem or unilaterally, the growth of Soviet investment in this region will remain a major phenomenon with far-reaching portents for the USSR, East Asia, and global resources in coming decades. The policy questions may be answered in a few years, but the developmental matters will remain relevant well beyond the year 2000.

In pursuit of its two goals, the study mixes existing knowledge, original research, and speculative projection. It draws from diverse Russian and English materials, integrates these with extensive interviews in the USSR and Japan, and concludes

SIBERIA AND EAST ASIA   11

with an assessment of alternative United States policy options. Chapter 2 details the technical data pertinent to an understanding of East Asian Siberia in terms of resource exploitation and industrial development. Major constraints such as climate and permafrost receive special attention as permanent factors, while demography and infrastructure are examined as reflections of the human response to environmental challenge. East Asian Siberia shares many of the properties and problems of Alaska and Canada, and therefore is not unique as a formidable region for energy resource exploitation. Various aspects of the subject have been superbly covered in the works of Paul Dibb, Violet Conolly, Theodore Shabad, and Victor Mote.[9] This chapter concentrates on extracting the facts that are most germane to subsequent analysis of the strategic implications of BAM and the prospects for Siberia's becoming a major base of Soviet power in East Asia.

Chapter 3 reviews the historical heritage of relations among the three major nations in northeastern Asia: the Soviet Union (or Russia before 1917), China, and Japan. Past wars and betrayed alliances have left scars of hatred and mistrust on the memory of policymaker and public alike in all three countries. This heritage provides a set of preconceptions that shape both expectations and behavior as these regimes address their current agenda of territorial disputes, competition for spheres of interest and influence, and conflicting concepts of national security. This agenda is examined both within the political framework of the 1970's and in the light of prospects for the 1980's, on the assumption that this is the proper context within which economic interactions, present and potential, should be considered.

One of the major questions of the study, the strategic implications of EAS development, is the concern of Chapter 4, which reviews the present structure of Soviet military forces in Northeast Asia to determine what difference such development will make on Soviet capabilities, both real and perceived. Soviet defensive worries over China emerged in the late 1960's, resulting in a major military buildup by Moscow opposite China and intimations on both sides of possible war. In this regard, the chapter examines the vulnerability of the Trans-Siberian Railroad and the military utility of BAM, evaluates supporting developments in East Asian Siberia's economic infrastructure, and briefly summarizes Chinese and Japanese perceptions. More detailed treatment of the China and Japan factors is left for the separate chapters on each country, but the strategic aspects of economic interdependence are assessed in Chapter 4 with special attention to Soviet-Japanese relations.

As already indicated, Japan is pivotal to this inquiry and is extensively discussed in Chapter 5. Because it is commonplace to cite public opinion as "the Japanese view," the chapter examines the intensity and consistency of this opinion, particularly for the degree of Soviet threat articulated in polls. It likewise surveys the media treatment of Moscow's military strength and activity in the area, together with the degree of media emphasis and public sensitivity to the Soviet-Japanese controversy over disputed islands and fishing rights. Reports of change in the Soviet-American military balance, both regional and global, are found to affect public perceptions as revealed by subtle shifts in the public discussion of Japan's defense needs in the 1980's. Moscow's perceptions as evident in propaganda, diplomacy, and military movements are traced for the two dimensions of Soviet-Japanese and Sino-Japanese developments.

The major focus, however, is on the Soviet-Japanese interaction in East Asian Siberia and its policy ramifications as seen from different vantage points in Japanese business and government. The problems of dealing with Moscow's negotiatory style and bureaucratic behavior are weighed against the prospects for political change in Soviet attitudes toward Japan as a consequence of economic cooperation. The various EAS projects, present and planned, are assessed for the degree of dependency they might entail and their relative risk versus gain. The symbolic significance of joint Soviet-Japanese offshore oil exploration near Sakhalin is highlighted, as is the substantive importance of the proposed Soviet-Japanese-American natural gas project in Yakutia. Apparent contradictions between the political and economic aspects of Soviet-Japanese relations and between the public and private views of key sectors in the Japanese body politic are identified and illuminated from the standpoint of participants in the policy progress.

By comparison, Chapter 6 treats the China factor in summary fashion. Beijing's relationship with Moscow has been one of mutual enmity for more than twenty years. The relatively static nature of this confrontation is so well known and so thoroughly examined elsewhere as to require only brief review at this point. Evidence on Chinese perceptions of and attitudes toward Siberian development is surprisingly slight, perhaps because it does not significantly enlarge upon the existing threat to national security. This is in consonance with the findings in Chapter 3. Speculative constructs of alternative future Sino-Soviet relations, however, raise the possibility of a limited reduction of tension that might include a reduction of the military forces presently in confrontation and a resolution of the border dispute. This possibility opens up an entirely different context within which to examine the mutual interest in economic exchange, and even joint projects, evident during the 1950's. Although this assessment is highly conjectural and concerns the remote future at best, it illustrates the role that East Asian Siberia can play in transforming the historical triangle of tension into one of conventional economic competition and cooperation.

The paucity of direct evidence on Soviet decision making constrains the extent of Chapter 7 on the dynamics of interaction between sectoral and regional interests on the one hand and the central organs of policymaking and policy implementation on the other hand. This analysis challenges the concept of Soviet policy remaining fixed over time, immune to external and internal influences other than those operating at the center. It examines concrete instances of lobbying by local Siberian interests as a prelude to projecting the policy changes that may ultimately emerge as a consequence of different types of EAS development, with and without foreign participation. The analysis of sectoral and regional interests in Soviet decision making is still at an early stage, but analogy with large bureaucratic systems elsewhere suggests that this is a promising path for further research. Soviet press reports of debate and criticism over policy implementation in East Asian Siberia suggest this, as do the interviews, although neither provide conclusive evidence of precisely how local interests influence ministries in Moscow. At the very least, however, this analysis serves as a caution against any rigid projection of Soviet policy that ignores the variable inputs, domestic and foreign, that can affect output.

Chapter 8, the concluding chapter, sums up the findings and inferences of the entire study in the context of alternative U.S. policy options. The American debate over the use of export controls and embargoes for linkage and leverage on Soviet policy is summarized, together with pertinent existing U.S. legislation. A survey of East Asian Siberia's potential contribution to Pacific and global needs is perforce speculative in the absence of good data and the presence of many uncertainties in projecting resource supply and demand one to two decades hence. However, this factor, plus the saliency of potential energy resources and the consideration due Japanese interests, combine to justify presidential and congressional action to free Export-Import Bank credits and to liberalize the licensing of technology transfer for EAS development. This would permit the final decision on participation in specific projects to be made by American entrepreneurs on the basis of technical feasibility and economic profitability.

Why "East Asian Siberia"?

Semantic confusion abounds in writing on the USSR. The country and its inhabitants are frequently referred to as "Russia" and "Russians," although the Russian Soviet Federated Socialist Republic (RSFSR) is only one, albeit the largest, of fifteen republics that comprise the Soviet Union. Moreover, Russians constitute a declining majority of the total population as against other fast-growing ethnic peoples, especially in Kazakhstan and Central Asia. Alternatively, the people—and more particularly the leaders—are often termed "the Soviets," although this word literally means "council."

Similarly, the different regions of Siberia appear under a variety of names that at best approximate reality only vaguely and at worst introduce considerable confusion. The general term "Siberia" encompasses the entire area referred to in the opening lines of this chapter. However, most of the recent commentary on Siberia's oil and gas is actually limited to West Siberia, roughly one-fourth of the total area.

Delimiting the subregions of this Eurasian land mass raises problems that transcend mere nomenclature. Erich Thiel, in his classic study *The Soviet Far East*, included under this name "all those Soviet Russian Eastern territories the rivers of which drain into the Pacific Ocean (which strongly influences the climate), and which are separated morphologically from the other parts of the Soviet Union by high mountain ridges."[10] However, he made Lake Baikal the western boundary while admitting that its environs belonged partly to the northward-draining Yenisei and Lena river systems as well as to the Amur. Thiel justified this by noting that "Transbaikalia's communications and economy are much less closely linked with the West than with the East, meaning the Far East in the widest sense of the word." This combination of functional and physical criteria was followed by E. Stuart Kirby nearly twenty years later in his identically titled study.[11]

Soviet terminology coincides only partly with the Thiel-Kirby approach. Moreover, it is inconsistent as between "regions" as defined for planning purposes and as delineated by physical geographers. The entire USSR is officially divided into nineteen economic planning regions, including Siberian regions designated West, East, and Far East. In contrast to Thiel-Kirby, Soviet usage places Transbaikalia under the East rather than the Far East. The last is by far the largest of the three, being five times the size of France and bigger even than Australia.[12]

Soviet geographers, however, although differing on detail among themselves agree that the three planning regions make little sense from either a physical or a functional standpoint.[13] Western geographers concur.[14] For some purposes Soviet planning terminology is convenient, chiefly because it follows administrative boundaries. To the extent that statistics are disaggregated, they emerge within the administrative divisions of autonomous republics, krais, and oblasts. This facilitates a longitudinal economic analysis where administrative boundaries and planning regions remain in constant correspondence. But in 1963 the Yakut Autonomous Soviet Socialist Republic (ASSR) was transferred from the East to the Far East region, thus preventing a simple comparison of regionally oriented data before and after this year.

Moreover, the planning framework has a limited utility for any meaningful projection of economic development. Saushkin and Kalashnikova offered a telling indictment of the earlier East–Far East regional division that may have contributed to the decision on Yakutia:

> The division has Krasnoyarsk Kray, Irkutsk Oblast, and the Yakut ASSR as a single unit. At present the untenability of this union is becoming especially obvious. Powerful territorial production complexes have developed (and are increasing in complexity) in this territory because of enormous electrical power construction. In the southern part of East Siberia there are two such complexes: the first is taking form on energy from the Angara River and on minerals from the Angara region and the Trans-Baikal region, and the second is based on energy from the Yenisei River and the natural resources of the Yenisei territory. The Yakut region stands out quite distinctively in the North, with immense riches and specific ways of developing them.[15]

This critique focuses on economic interaction as the proper rationale for a functional definition of regions. The concept of territorial production complexes (TPC) will be discussed in more detail later. It has evolved considerably since 1959 when this article originally appeared, and its linkage of spatial and economic criteria appears to be a more useful approach to microanalysis and planning than the more cumbersome and artificial definition of macroeconomic regions based on administrative boundaries. Yet so long as the latter approach determines the presentation of official statistics in open sources, Soviet analysis and forecasting must accommodate accordingly.

The problem becomes particularly evident as the emergence of economic activity along the Baikal-Amur railroad recalls the earlier development that followed construction of the Trans-Siberian railroad. Whereas the designated planning regions divide Siberia vertically along north-south axes, the impact of both railroads is on horizontal, east-west lines. Needless to say, the exigencies of administration within the vertical divisions often prevail over economic rationality in policy formation and implementation. Nevertheless, the projection of a region's objective economic potential must rest on a rational and realistic basis, even if this means changing the focus from that offered by the more readily available materials.

A noted Soviet economic specialist on Siberia, Boris Orlov, has called attention to the need for a horizontal as opposed to a vertical approach. Writing on the impact of BAM, Orlov noted it "will mean the creation of a new 'industrial belt' 800–1,000 kilometers to the north of the 'industrial belt' which has been formed along the first Trans-Siberian railway since the 1930s and 1940s. This belt will lie in the so-called Near North of Siberia and in the Far East, . . . a corridor 300–400 kilometers across which stretches along either side of the railway."[16]

As indicated earlier, this study's geographical focus is determined by a figurative economic watershed that orients political, economic, and military outputs toward East Asia rather than westward. This focus parallels the overall proposal of Saushkin and Kalashnikova, which aggregates four suggested subdivisions as alternatives to the existing planning regions: the East Siberian region (Irkutsk and Chita oblasts, Buryat ASSR); the Yakut region (Yakut ASSR); the South Far East region (Amur and Sakhalin oblasts, Maritime and Khabarovsk krais); and the North Far East region (Magadan and Kamchatka oblasts).[17]

This area spans the entire length of BAM and therefore can reveal the full implications of the single most important development project east of the Yenisei. Fortunately, the boundaries of the area coincide with administrative lines. However, it differs sharply from official planning divisions. It omits the Krasnoyarsk Krai and the Tuvin ASSR of the East Siberian region, thereby excluding Norilsk, the Yenisei power projects, the Kansk-Achinsk complex, and Sayan. These points are oriented westward and therefore lie outside our focus. To illustrate the impact of this omission, in 1965 Krasnoyarsk Krai comprised 58.3 percent of the East Siberian territory, 40.3 percent of its population, and 45.5 percent of its industry.[18] The latter two figures are undoubtedly much higher today, considering economic development in the krai as compared with the rest of the region during the interim.

It should be clear by this point that the popular challenge What's in a name? can be highly misleading. True, the economic productivity of a particular piece of territory might remain the same, regardless of its name. But nomenclature can structure perceptions, focus analysis, and affect policy contrary to the economic dictates of that territory. This poses the need to adopt terminology that does justice to the area under review, particularly for the aggregation of data and for broad generalization. "Soviet Far East" is an inadequate term because BAM goes well beyond that area even as defined by Thiel-Kirby. But "East Siberia" includes much economic activity that is wholly or predominantly westward oriented. Combining the two terms fails to solve these problems, and is awkward.

These circumstances explain why this study uses "East Asian Siberia" to designate the territory under examination. The term denotes the criterion of relevance to East Asia with implications for China, Korea, and Japan. It avoids the need to redefine other terminology already in use and clearly excludes West Siberia. Although there is no precedent for this name, it embodies the underlying concept that has guided other works on the portion of the Soviet Union that is oriented toward the Pacific Ocean.

2 The Internal Setting: Quagmire or Bonanza?

Introduction

Reference to Siberia often conjures up hyperbolic imagery, whether negative (the frozen purgatory of political dissidents) or positive (the limitless economic cornucopia). Its political past continues to haunt the present, not always justifiably. To the nineteenth-century exile sentenced to live in isolated hamlets of log huts and mud roads, Siberia could mean a surprising degree of freedom in the environs of lovely Lake Baikal.[1] Explorations in the area by Polish intellectuals banished from European Russia by an autocratic Tsar provided the rudimentary geological information that sparked the initial urge to develop Siberia. Today's visitor to local museums finds their photographs and discoveries prominently displayed, along with reconstructed prison cells where the more severely punished spent years of their lives.

To the twentieth-century victim of Stalin's purges, Siberia could mean a living hell above the Arctic Circle where hundreds of thousands were literally worked to death in the frigid Kolyma gold mines.[2] Magadan became more than a place name, an infamous charnel surpassed in reputation only by Buchenwald and Auschwitz.[3] The vast labor camps were finally closed in 1956, and forced labor was officially abolished. However, Stalin's successors continue to send dissident intellectuals to remote areas where mental and physical deprivation are intended to break their spirit, if not their bodies. In view of this long record, it is not surprising that, for many in the USSR and abroad, Siberia represents the worst oppression in modern Russian history. Despite the obvious truth of this image, it can also distort present reality and obscure perception of the potential future.

East Asian Siberia's economic reputation is similarly subject to journalistic hyperbole, usually without justification. The claim of "an ocean of gas" and "an ocean of oil" was made when only one gas field of moderate size had been proven and virtually no exploration for oil undertaken. But this did not inhibit the official briefer, much less his credulous audience.[4]

An equally extreme example in the opposite direction was offered by a respected American business magazine, which dismissed Siberia as an "economic quagmire."[5] The association of this term with the United States experience in Vietnam was amplified by reference to a "bottomless pit" that was "unlikely to attract foreign capital and technology"; moreover, "seventy million poverty-stricken Chinese face fifteen million Russians in three or four Siberian industrial centers." The article failed to report either Japan's advance of nearly three billion dollars in governmental and private credits for East Asian Siberia or the much larger West European involvement in West Siberia. As for the Chinese "threat," the region holds little to attract a massive migration of farmers, particularly in the absence of enormous infusions of capital and advanced technology. The brutal climate and inadequate soil prevent agricultural self-sufficiency for the existing population, much less for one many times that size.

These extreme images, whether negative or positive, must be modified by reality if we are to assess the possible implications of development in East Asian Siberia, whose basic geographic, meteorologic, and demographic dimensions establish the conditions and the constraints that confront planners in Moscow. Some factors, such as permafrost, are determining. Others are susceptible to change through human endeavor. In combination, they provide the parameters of possibility within which we can project the region's prospects, depending upon Soviet and foreign investment in its resources.

To appreciate the demands on capital and technology imposed by local conditions, the broad parameters should be examined point by point. Microclimatic factors can confront planners with difficult choices if they wish to locate population centers near available food supplies, industry near resources, and transportation near mineral extraction sites. The sharp differences between the climate along the coast and that a hundred kilometers inland, or the greater concentration of permafrost at one latitude compared with another, can spell success or failure for plans drawn up on regionwide dimensions at a great distance from EAS.

As a leading specialist on the region's economy and geography has noted, "The cost of developing the much-heralded potential resources of Siberia is almost prohibitive with standard technology, which is twenty to thirty years behind in the performance and capacity needed to operate in extreme environments."[6] Moreover, even if adequate capital and technology are available, the cost of supporting an expanded work force in terms of building construction, heating, clothing, and food—in addition to the higher wages needed as an inducement to settlement in an isolated and inhospitable environment—raises a major obstacle.[7] Therefore, prior to striking an overall net assessment of the developmental future, a brief introduction to the factual framework is necessary.

Geography and Climate

The conventional stereotype of Siberia envisions an endless frozen wilderness where deep snow, fierce wind, and incredible cold make the region virtually uninhabitable. As with all stereotypes, some truth underlies the image. Siberia is vast, and its winter is extremely cold except in the most southern region. However, relatively little snow falls over much of the area, and there is virtually no wind in the winter. Finally, although the population density is extremely low overall, the presence of more than 11.5 million persons in East Asian Siberia testifies to its habitability. A more detailed examination of these conditions will help to separate fact from fancy.

East Asian Siberia covers 7,766,600 square kilometers (3,100,000 square miles), or nearly one-third of the entire USSR.[8] This is roughly the size of Brazil and only 11 percent smaller than China or the United States. In contrast to the West Siberian plain, which stretches from the Urals to the Yenisei River, mountains and plateaus dominate the EAS landscape, which is only sporadically broken by small areas of lowland. The forbidding terrain is made partially accessible by a network of rivers, mainly flowing north-south, which provide routes of transportation, valleys for agriculture, and power for electrification.

The two principal rivers, the Amur and the Lena, are among the longest in the world. The Amur extends 4,416 kilometers (2,738 miles).[9] It follows the Sino-Soviet border for more than half its length before curving sharply northward to empty at Nikolayevsk, opposite the upper end of Sakhalin. Less well known but equally impressive is the Lena, 4,400 kilometers (2,728 miles) long, which bisects Yakutia on a north-south axis for much of this distance.[10] With a basin of more than 1,950,000 square kilometers (760,500 square miles), its average discharge exceeds 15,200 cubic meters (536,775 cubic feet) per second.[11] North of the mouth of the Vilyui, for nearly a quarter of its length, the Lena's depth reaches 15 to 20 meters (49 to 66 feet).

The region's rivers vary considerably in their potential utility and their hazards. The bulk of the heavy summer rainfall sweeps down the steep mountains, sharply raising water levels, and the Amur has an average annual variance at Khabarovsk of 6.5 meters (21 feet), with the greatest recorded range being 10.6 meters (35 feet).[12] In 1967 its flooding cut the Trans-Siberian Railroad extensively enough to require a special airlift for essential supplies.[13] Further north melting snow in late spring swells the water volume. The Lena's flow varies from 1,170 cubic meters (4,317 cubic feet) per second in March-April to 61,120 cubic meters (2,158,390 cubic feet) per second in June. The Kolyma River in the far northeast has an even greater variance, from 45.6 cubic meters (1,610 cubic feet) per second in March-April to 11,856 cubic meters (418,683 cubic feet) per second in June. In contrast, the Angara River, which falls 375 meters (1,230 feet) in 1,776 kilometers (1,110 miles), has a nearly uniform flow throughout the year, being regulated by Lake Baikal, which

THE INTERNAL SETTING 23

serves as a natural reservoir. These variations affect agriculture and electric power generation as well as river transport.

Winter has a mixed effect. Ice stops shipping in the Amur for 151 days at Khabarovsk and 189 days at Nikolayevsk. But once the frozen surface is strong enough, the Lena and its fellow north-south rivers become vital highways. Spring thaws in its upper reaches, and the ice jams in its lower course that block the increased water flow, cause floods.

Without this network of waterways, the development of resources in the north would be far more difficult, even impossible at some points. Supplies and products from the more industrial portions of the south are shipped north, by boat in the summer and by truck in the winter, to small towns strung out along the river banks. The utility of water transport is illustrated by the supply route from Yakutsk to Ege-Khaya on the Yana River, once a major tin-mining region but now more generally known for zinc and indium.[14] To circumvent the mountains that run between Yakutsk and Ege-Khaya, freight goes down the Lena to the Laptev Sea, above the Arctic Circle, and then up the Yana.[15] Although this requires going more than 2,016 kilometers (1,260 miles) to connect two points only 384 kilometers (240 miles) apart, it provides access to resources that otherwise would remain locked beneath the frozen ground.

The most important factor affecting the flow of rivers and also the permafrost and population patterns is climate. The meteorology of East Siberia has far-reaching implications for its economic prospects, both agricultural and industrial. The huge stationary anticyclone that stands over Siberia in the winter is the major determinant of its weather. It produces frequent calms and temperature inversions that result in extreme cold, light snow, and little wind for all but the coastal regions. Temperature ranges vary widely on both an annual and a daily basis. Within these general conditions, considerable differences exist as a function of latitude, altitude, and distance from the coast. Because of the popular lore about Siberian weather and because of its variable impact on development, some specific statistics bear examination.

Verkhoyansk, near Ege-Khaya, has a population of less than

3,000 and is the coldest inhabited spot at low altitude anywhere in the world. Located above the Arctic Circle at 67.5° latitude and 137 meters (452 feet) elevation, Verkhoyansk endures an average January temperature of −48.9°C (−56.2°F) and has a record low of −68°C (−90.4°F), approximately the temperature of dry ice.[16] Oymyakon, to the southeast, enjoys the dubious distinction of having recorded a greater low, −71°C (−95.8°F), but it is at a considerably higher elevation, 740 meters (2,442 feet).

Although highly publicized abroad, these "cold poles" are atypical extremes and largely irrelevant to the region's future. Much more can be learned from larger centers of economic activity such as Irkutsk (population 550,000, 1979) and Yakutsk (population 152,000, 1979).[17] Irkutsk, near 52° latitude, averages −21°C (−5.8°F) in the winter with temperatures as low as −50°C (−58°F).[18] Yakutsk, at 62° latitude, averages −42.7°C (−45°F) and has hit a recorded low of −69°C (−92.2°F).[19] Summer in Irkutsk is short and cool, with an average temperature of only 17.5°C (63.5°F) and a frost-free period of 94 days.[20] Yakutsk, although much further north, has a higher average July temperature of 19°C (66.2°F), the warmest July in the world at this latitude.[21] Yakutsk enjoys 98 frost-free days, with temperatures occasionally reaching 38°C (100°F). Some inhabitants choose to work at night to escape the heat.

Since they are inland cities, Irkutsk and Yakutsk do not have enough wind in winter to worsen the raw temperature readings. Suslov correctly notes, "The heat loss during a calm with the temperature at −45.5°C (−50°F) is little different from the loss at −19.4°C (−3°F) with a moderate wind or at 0°C (32°F) in a gale."[22] Along the coast, however, the windchill produces situations that rival, and at times exceed, the more celebrated continental climate. Many spots, especially along the northern and northwestern coasts of the Sea of Okhotsk, the Kuril Islands, and the Kamchatka Peninsula, experience winter winds that average 7–8 meters per second (15–20 miles per hour) and go as high as 20–40 meters per second (40–80 miles per hour).[23] The resulting windchill readings of −125°C (−193°F) prohibit all outdoor activity.

Thus, in contrast to many other areas of the world, the coastal climate in East Asian Siberia is not necessarily more moderate than in the interior. Moreover, at the water's edge contact between the warm moist monsoon and air cooled by the adjacent cold marine current causes heavy fogs. Cape Nizmennyy on the Sea of Japan has 26 days of fog each in June and July, while the nearby port of Olga has fog for only 9 to 11 days because of an intervening small wooded mountain.[24] The key naval base of Vladivostok records 20 days of fog in June and 16 in July.[25]

The Amur-Maritime area has a very late spring that is long, cold, and dry, followed by warm, heavy rains. Suslov's graphic imagery tells a depressing tale:

In the second half of June to September, the rain drips, drops, drizzles, and mizzles without pause for ten or 20 days at a time. When the rain stops the sun may still remain hidden behind the clouds: suddenly cold piercing fogs from the sea drift in. . . . At this time of year it rains continuously in the mountains, and when, in the valleys, the rain stops for breath, the sun has his chance to add to the discomfort. The warm air saturated with water vapor reminds one of the atmosphere of a bathhouse or a warm, moist hothouse. Three or four times during the summer there are intense downpours lasting from one to four days. . . . The rivers overflow their banks and cause enormous destruction, washing away buildings near the river banks, destroying young crops, and carrying away harvested hay and grain. In the mountains the downpours erode slopes not secured by forest, remove the soil, wash out forest, undergrowth, dead trees, and branches which form large jams in the swollen mountain streams.[26]

To complicate matters further, this area's annual precipitation varies greatly. Winter snow can range from 0.10 centimeters (0.04 inches) to 18 centimeters (7 inches), while rains can vary in the spring from 0.6 centimeters (0.24 inches) to 39.3 centimeters (15.5 inches), in summer from 6 centimeters (2.4 inches) to 78.7 centimeters (31 inches), and in autumn from 5.3 centimeters (2.1 inches) to 47.7 centimeters (18.8 inches). The total difference in precipitation between two successive years has reached 69.85 centimeters (27.5 inches).[27]

Throughout the interior of East Asian Siberia a general lack of precipitation poses a problem for agriculture. In addition, seasonal variance belies the annual figures, particularly when a thin, dry snowfall leaves little protection against frost and no residue for the spring melt. In the southern portion, the total annual snowfall is only 20 to 25 centimeters (8 to 10 inches). Even at Yakutsk it still reaches only 30 centimeters (12 inches), but it lies on the ground much longer, 205 days as compared with 140–150 days in the south.[28] Coastal snow accumulates considerably more, with an average of 89 centimeters (35 inches) at Nikolayevsk at the mouth of the Amur.

Although attention abroad understandably focuses on Siberian cold, another impediment to human activity is ice fog. Under conditions of extreme cold the breath of people and animals and the by-products of combustion create water vapor that saturates the air, creating a dense fog. The calm that prevails throughout much of the winter traps this fog under the temperature inversion for long periods at a time, and the fog quickly freezes into ice crystals that reduce visibility to three feet or less. Thus, during the few hours of winter sunlight that shines on the northern half of the region, vehicular headlights are required at midday. In December and January Yakutsk lies under this ice fog for sixteen to seventeen days.[29] Elsewhere steam fog occurs where water temperatures fall more slowly than the air above. Because the Angara River rarely freezes, its steam fog shrouds Irkutsk for more than three weeks in December.

Permafrost

A basic problem far more challenging than climate confronts the developers of East Asian Siberia, the phenomenon of permafrost. As the term implies, this refers to permanently frozen ground, and it extends from a meter or less below the surface to depths that range from two to more than four hundred meters. Extending throughout most of the area in either continuous or discontinuous form, permafrost is a critical factor for agriculture and a complicating one for industry. In particular cases it poses severe problems of cost as well as of engineering.

The causes of permafrost are complex, and the consequences vary from one location to another.[30] Its formation is promoted by (1) long periods of low temperature; (2) light precipitation in winter; (3) thin snow cover; (4) an absence of winter clouds, which allows cooling of the earth through radiation; (5) calms

THE INTERNAL SETTING 27

caused by temperature inversion, which result in the supercooling of air in depressions and river valleys; and (6) short, dry, cool summers with cold nights. Altitude affects permafrost distribution and thickness, as does rain.

Permafrost can be solid, or it can be comprised of alternately frozen and unfrozen layers of earth with ground water continuously or periodically circulating through it. It can be continuous or discontinuous, occurring either as a permafrost mass with islands of thawing ground or as thawing ground with islands of permafrost. The continuous permafrost cap extends over the top third of East Asian Siberia. Suslov maps its lower limit roughly along the 63rd parallel, which leaves Yakutsk, Okhotsk, and Magadan in the discontinuous zone. However, the islands of thawing ground are so few near the transition band as to justify placing the line at 60° latitude.[31] As one moves southward through the remaining two-thirds of the region, the balance between permafrost and thawing ground gradually shifts until in the Amur-Maritime area and lower Chita Oblast nearly half the land has islands of permafrost in thawing ground. The only areas wholly free of its effects are the lower half of the Kamchatka peninsula, Sakhalin, the Amur-Maritime sections along the coast, and the area of the Amur and Ussuri rivers.

The soil that lies on top of permafrost is known as the active layer. Its thickness is determined by climate, relief, physical content of the soil, moisture content, heat conductivity, and the kind and degree of vegetative cover. These many factors differ in their importance, but vegetative cover is the most susceptible to human interference and therefore is a key variable to be considered in all economic activity.

The active layer expands as it freezes, creating large mounds and hilly bogs. It decreases in thickness from south to north and on slopes that face north as opposed to south. The soil is deep in sandy areas but shallow under peat. Running surface water will push down the permafrost, but standing water will raise it. The vertical water movement is limited because it cannot go below the permafrost surface, and so the soil just above this point is supersaturated. Capillary action raises the water, moistening the active layer surface.

Not all of the effects of permafrost are bad. It condenses the water vapor, both immediately above and below its layer, thereby benefiting low precipitation areas. In fact, without it much of Yakutia would be an arctic desert.[32] In effect, permafrost creates an auxiliary reservoir. Water from melting snow and late spring rain remains on top of the permafrost to supply vegetation in the first half of summer. Once the rains are past and the snow melt is completed, further thawing of the frozen ground helps the maturing process. By summer's end, the completely thawed active layer can absorb most of the autumn rain, which then freezes and is held in storage until spring, when the cycle begins again.[33]

This is not the only assist permafrost provides vegetation. According to Suslov:

> Under conditions like those on the Yakutian meadow-steppe, easily soluble salts are washed down to the frozen soil by autumn rains and remain there because of the negligible circulation of ground water, which freezes rapidly. The water released in spring and summer by the gradually thawing soil, and the small amounts supplied by precipitation are completely absorbed by the roots of plants before enough accumulates to flow laterally. Thus, soil solutions at any given point are always the same, and no salts are washed out of the soil: the salts that are carried downward in solution collect in big rusty patches and streaks just above the permafrost.[34]

If permafrost is not wholly a liability so far as agriculture is concerned, it is a severe constraint. It slows decomposition, causing the buildup of organic matter and the formation of peat. Peat, in turn, acts as a heat insulator and slows the thawing of the soil. Permafrost also blocks the downward growth of roots, prompting them to spread horizontally. The active layer often is so thin that the shallow roots let the trees be toppled by strong winds. If permafrost is very near the surface, the trees are stunted and twisted through impoverishment, with as many as 86 percent defective.[35] This has serious consequences for the timber industry.

Although its name conjures up a static condition, permafrost exists in a constantly dynamic environment, one that is characterized by melting, freezing, flowing, and cracking. This results from the interaction of above-frost water, permafrost, interfrost water, and below-frost water. The natural variation in thickness of both the active layer and the permafrost is compounded by this interaction to create a special challenge to the engineering of transportation routes and industrial construction. Karsts, sinks, and lakes abound in the permafrost area, and they spread or shrink with time, depending on local conditions.

Forest fires and the felling of trees by storm or human activity enlarge the area exposed to the sun, whose heat will thaw ice seams. Small basins form and fill with water, becoming swamps and then sinkhole lakes. This accelerates the thawing of permafrost because the heat capacity of water exceeds that of soil; under one lake drillers did not encounter permafrost above a depth of 30 meters (99 feet), although along the shoreline it lay only a meter or less below the ground surface. The rapidity of lake formation under these conditions was graphically demonstrated by a cabin that once stood 18 meters (59 feet) from the shoreline; after thirteen years it was resting at the water's edge and beginning to collapse.[36]

Because water expands approximately 10 percent in freezing, the pressure of increased volume moves unfrozen water and quicksand along the course of least resistance, which cannot be downward because of the permafrost. Therefore, it pushes upward against the frozen active layer, raising it perhaps five to 15 centimeters (two to six inches). This buckled and broken layer then subsides in summer, dropping more slowly than it rose. This seasonal "pulsation" can wreak havoc on pilings and foundations.

Water under pressure can actually break through the frozen active layer if it is too thin, flowing into the open air and then freezing. The resulting formations are known as *naledi* or icings. They hang out over railroad bank cuts, covering the rails and blocking drainage ditches; they penetrate tunnel walls and break out under warm buildings to flood basements and lower rooms. Suslov tells of how "one February, water suddenly appeared in the subcellar of a building in Trans-Baikal, burst into the house, poured out of cracks and windows, and froze so swiftly that finally the whole house was filled with ice clear to the ceiling."[37]

Any disturbance of the natural ground cover will alter the thermal and water balance of the soil, thereby changing the permafrost level. Warmth, both transmitted under buildings and created by their acting as windbreaks, will lower this level and produce foundation sag and cracking walls. Such are the estimated geophysical processes associated with permafrost that reinforcement faces a stress factor of many thousands of pounds per square inch.

Frozen soil has a resistance to compression many times that of thawed soil, depending on its mechanical composition, humidity, and temperature. It can be very difficult to work. Frozen clay does not crack or disintegrate when blasted. Drilling is difficult because the heat of the drill transfers to the soil and thaws it, resulting in loss of abrasiveness and in binding of the drill.

Ground ice, common with permafrost, is another hazard. Buildings will collapse and roads sag if built over strata or lenses of ice many meters thick. Frozen sand loam or clay, when thawed, becomes tacky with much water and turns to quicksand that can swallow up roadbeds and vehicles if not properly guarded against. The supplying of water in permafrost areas can also be a problem. Wells are impossible to dig and maintain, and pipes may freeze.

Bridge construction poses particular difficulties, especially when discontinuous permafrost presents differing conditions at opposite ends. Heterogeneous strata in the active layer will expand irregularly in freezing. This can raise individual posts and pilings 20 to 25 centimeters (8 to 10 inches) per year, resulting in a change of 50 centimeters (20 inches) over two to three years. Some pilings may wind up on the river bottom, or actually hang free. Foundations are susceptible to similar elevation.

In this brief survey, it is impossible to do justice to the phenomenon of permafrost and the obstacles it raises to agricultural and industrial activity. We shall be returning to its implications later in our study. It is not an insuperable obstacle, as evidenced by Siberian development to date and similar undertakings in Alaska. However, it does require human ingenuity, technology, and capital beyond that necessary elsewhere. Its implications for the Baikal-Amur railroad are far-reaching, not only for the line's

THE INTERNAL SETTING 31

construction but also for its operation. In short, although the cold is the most widely known constraint on Siberia's population growth and economic development, permafrost poses equally serious problems for Soviet planners.

Demography

Given the inhospitable environment provided by geography, meteorology, and permafrost, it is easy to understand why East Asian Siberia has the lowest population density in the Soviet Union at 0.6 persons per square kilometer compared with 7.9 for the entire RSFSR.[38] Yet as of January 15, 1979, a total population of 11,573,000 was estimated to live in the region. The juxtaposing of these two figures reveals the danger of discussing demographic data in a vacuum, and therefore we must move to disaggregation and interpretation. The population density varies widely from 0.3 persons per square kilometer in Yakutia, the largest administrative division, to 11.9 in the Maritime Krai, the second smallest division.[39] Urban concentration characterizes EAS generally; except for the Buryat ASSR, all ten of its administrative areas have more than 60 percent of their inhabitants in cities, and six have less than 25 percent in the countryside.

Much Soviet and foreign writing on the prospects for Siberian development has emphasized demographic problems as a main obstacle. At least until recently an excessive out-migration, a high rate of labor turnover, and an uneconomic population flow from the countryside into the cities increased the labor shortage. However, two considerations call for a closer examination of the situation to assess its relevance for our inquiry. First, some of this concern, in the USSR as well as abroad, is based on aggregate data for all Siberia in which the western region looms particularly large. But demographically West Siberia differs from East and Far East Siberia in several respects. Second, the pessimistic analysis of trends down to the 1970's must be reviewed in the light of developments during the last decade. Intensive demographic and sociologic research by Soviet scholars has affected both planning and its implementation and is gradually improving the situation over time.

The negative emphasis given to demographic prospects derives from the past failure of Siberia to attract and retain a larger population despite political exhortation and economic incentives. Siberia's share of the total Soviet population has remained relatively constant over the past twenty years, standing at 10.7 percent in 1959, 10.4 percent in 1970, and 10.6 percent in 1979.[40] However, the inclusion of West Siberia distorts the situation to the disadvantage of East and especially Far East Siberia. West Siberia grew by only 8 percent in 1959–70 and 7 percent in 1970–79, compared with 15 and 9 percent for East Siberia and a striking 20 and 18 percent for the Soviet Far East.[41] In 1959–70 the Far East had the highest net inflow of the entire Soviet Union, actually providing the whole EAS region with a slight net migration increase, gaining 143,000 persons while East Siberia was losing 110,000.[42] The 1970–79 increase in the Far East reflected work on BAM and subsidized settlement near the Chinese border, as well as the expanded coastal economy and the better climate relative to the rest of East Siberia.

This breakdown of the aggregate data does not wholly eliminate labor turnover and labor shortage as problems in EAS, but it places them in a less pessimistic perspective than is provided by analysis that includes West Siberia. Soviet awareness of these problems is reflected in an abundance of statistical surveys undertaken in the 1960's. Much of this information pertains to West Siberia, the region of primary economic concern in Moscow—and coincidentally the base of Siberian research, which is headquartered at the Academy of Sciences center in Akademgorodok near Novosibirsk. Nonetheless, some of the conditions examined also exist in varying degree in the East and Far East regions.

For the entire Siberian area during 1959–70, the exodus of persons aged 20–29 was four times that of those aged 30–39, and eleven times that of persons over 50.[43] This loss of the most active and strongest workers threatened economic development with a "premature aging" of the population. The importance of youth in the labor force was shown by data from the Bratsk aluminum plant in 1969, where 76 percent were under 30, and the

Baikal cellulose factory, where 71 percent were in the same category.[44]

The economic costs of migration were suggested by a report that in the Aldan region of the Yakut ASSR 74 percent exited within two years of arrival and another 17 percent within five years, leaving only 9 percent as permanent residents.[45] At the Ust-Ilimsk hydroelectric project only 5.5 percent stayed on, while in Irkutsk Oblast 14.5 percent of the incoming youth remained longer than three years.[46] This constitutes a serious drain on productivity as well as on administrative services. According to one writer, "Every time an employee leaves a job there is, on the average, a 28-day interruption in work."[47] Signing on requires one to two weeks for medical certification, safety instruction, and other items, and leaving may require clearance from a dozen or more agencies and services.

Soviet surveys provide illuminating data on the causes of out-migration. One such study in 1969 queried departing residents of West Siberia as to their reasons for leaving, and as to whether they would have stayed were specific conditions improved. Three items could be selected out of a much longer list, so the total exceeds 100 percent, but a sense of priority nonetheless emerges (see Table 1).

On the positive side for Soviet planners, the low rating given to climate compared with factors more susceptible to human

TABLE 1
Causes of Out-Migration from West Siberia

Cause of departure[a]	Percent citing cause	If improved would stay[b]
Living conditions	43.7%	37.1%
Consumer goods (incl. food)	37.2	27.3
Cultural conditions	34.5	24.4
Pay	18.1	15.3
Climate	17.9	
Other (many listed)	37.1	

[a] B. P. Orlov, ed., *Ekonomischeskie problemy rasvitia Sibiri* (Economic problems in the development of Siberia; Novosibirsk, 1974), p. 121.
[b] *Ibid.*, p. 125; 37.8 percent replied that they would stay under no conditions.

34   THE INTERNAL SETTING

amelioration makes migration a potentially manageable problem, provided that the economic costs and administrative responsibility are accepted. On the negative side, however, the 37.8 percent who unequivocally ruled out staying in West Siberia seem to present an irreducible problem.

The stress on material interests reflected in "living conditions" and "consumer goods" may result partly from disillusionment because of an inadequate anticipation of the true situation. In Irkutsk Oblast, a smaller survey taken at the Ust-Ilimsk hydroelectric project in December 1969 asked arrivals why they had come. Only 17.2 percent replied "material interest," compared with 63 percent who said they had come "to participate in a big, important project" and 33.4 percent who professed "interest in a new place in Siberia."[48] A comparison of the two surveys suggests that the negative impact of reality appears to have radically changed these initial attitudes. Of course, the responses on arrival may not have been wholly frank. Nearly ten years later responses to the same questions posed to workers on BAM showed a shift: 39 percent said they came because of its "importance," and 37 percent alleged interest in "new places," but 25 percent acknowledged "material self-interest" to be their motivation.[49]

Soviet sources provide ample data to justify complaints against living conditions as a cause of out-migration. In the mid-1950's extremely cramped housing characterized East Siberian cities, with the average number of square meters per person listed as 2.8 in Bratsk, 3.7 in Angarsk, and 4.0 in Ust-Kut.[50] By 1960 Irkutsk Oblast could claim six square meters per person, but its target of nine for the mid-1970's would still fall below the 1968 RSFSR average of 10.28 square meters per person.[51] Moreover, because of the climate, more time is spent indoors than in central Russia, making this comparison even less favorable for East Siberia.[52]

Complaints over consumer goods are endemic throughout the Soviet Union. However, the Ust-Ilimsk survey showed particularly negative reactions when the question was raised. Department stores were rated "bad" by 53.7 percent of the respondents, "satisfactory" by 46.3 percent, but "good" by none.[53]

THE INTERNAL SETTING 35

Grocery stores fared somewhat better, with 37.2 percent replying "bad," and 62.8 percent "satisfactory," but still none replied "good." As for cultural conditions, 73 percent rejected "satisfactory." The same percentage reportedly demanded more concerts and plays in Irkutsk Oblast.[54]

This stress on cultural activity is a prominent feature of Soviet society in general and of East Siberian residents in particular. It is attributed in part to the new cities' tending to be dominated by one or two large factories, which gives rise to a desire to go out socially in the evenings. The high proportion of residents under the age of 30, 65 percent in Angarsk and 45 percent in Bratsk, adds to the pressure for clubs, theaters, libraries, and concerts.[55]

Both the poor regional comparison with national averages and the relative cultural poverty of the newer cities highlight the need in this area. In 1970 the entire Soviet Union had 10,170 books and journals per thousand residents in libraries, but East Siberia could claim only 4,200 per thousand. Within the region Bratsk had less than one-third the proportion of Irkutsk, and Irkutsk likewise offered twelve times as many concerts as did Angarsk and Bratsk.

Not all the demand was for cultural activity and entertainment. According to the Ust-Ilimsk survey, 90 percent of 1,500 young workers wanted to use their free time to improve their job skills through technical training.[56] At the Baikalsk cellulose plant, where more than 60 percent had not finished middle school in 1969, the provision of the opportunity for such training won a wide positive response. The high proportion of work done without machines, 37 percent in Irkutsk Oblast, proved demoralizing and lowered the productivity per worker. Soviet analysts consequently urged the expansion and improvement of night schools and on-the-job training so as to increase opportunities for individual advancement and stimulate economic growth.

The upgrading of worker skills can address the problem of labor turnover as well as out-migration. The 1969 Ust-Ilimsk data revealed that 61.4 percent of those discharged or voluntarily leaving jobs were local inhabitants.[57] Moreover, 90 percent left during the first year. These statistics indicate the high degree of dissatisfaction with working conditions, in addition to the other factors that prompt an exodus.

To estimate the degree to which working conditions can be improved requires more detailed information on the particular circumstances that cause disaffection than is available in the published data. An implied preference for "clean" jobs as compared with "dirty" ones is not easily met under the conditions of a newly developing region.[58] Nor is the recommendation that workers be better apprized of the "social significance" of their job likely to eliminate the problem.

The leading Soviet specialist on the demography of East Siberia, V. V. Vorobiev, offers an impressive battery of statistics to show that "the existence of territorial differences in the standard of living" is the primary determinant of migration.[59] He insists that regional comparisons must be based "not on any single factor (for instance, wages), however important it may be, but on the entire complex of conditions which are important for the life of the population." He pointedly notes that despite the absence of any comprehensive and scientific statistical analysis of these regional differences, "practical activity" informs the people and prompts their migratory patterns.

Specifically, Vorobiev cites studies that show that climatic conditions in East Siberia require 15 percent more caloric intake than for comparable work in central regions. But prices for food in government stores were 8 to 9 percent higher and, in the more important cooperative and kholkhoz markets, 30 percent higher than their counterparts in the European USSR. The cost of food for one worker averaged 14.4 percent higher in East Siberia than in the central RSFSR, soaring to 56 and 64 percent higher in Bratsk and Yakutia respectively, according to a 1972 source.[60] The differential between Kiev and Khabarovsk for a family of four reached 400 rubles per year, excluding fruit and vegetables.

Other items showed comparable findings. Clothing ran 16–18 percent higher in East Siberia than in central regions. Moreover, the differences within the region as between northern and southern areas exacerbated the problem. For a family of four, food cost 26 percent, clothing and shoes 47 percent, and housing (including heat) 88 percent more in the north than the south. All this added to the other differentials between the regional average and the European area.

As might be expected, examination of infrastructural aspects revealed another dimension of disadvantage. The transport capacity of an established city such as Irkutsk provided half the service per capita of the central cities. Leisure and medical facilities in Irkutsk Oblast fared only slightly better by comparison.[61] In sum, the cumulative shortcomings of life in East Siberia as against living elsewhere effectively nullified the greater wages allowed in the region as ostensible incentive. Surveys of migrants from East Siberia to the Ukraine disclosed a marked sense of improvement despite the reduction in pay of between 20 and 40 rubles per month.[62]

Difficult as were circumstances in the city, they did not deter migration from the countryside, where the situation was appreciably worse. From 1959 to 1973 the total population of East Siberia grew by 20 percent, but the rural share fell by 11 percent.[63] On a smaller scale, the flow from rural to urban living in Irkutsk Oblast during 1968–69 was triple the reverse migration.[64] This hit hard at agricultural production, which is labor intensive and already far short of satisfying local demand. It also added an unskilled pool of workers to the labor force where they were least needed.[65]

Recent Developments and Future Prospects

The academician A. G. Aganbegyan, head of the Institute for the Economics and Organization of Production in Akademgorodok, noted in 1978 that the East Siberian net out-migration had finally been stopped.[66] He attributed this reversal of the past trend to a host of measures that had reduced the major impetus to depart, while admitting that the exodus had not been eliminated completely. Aganbegyan emphasized the steady expansion of higher salary coefficients for all work in most of the region in contrast with the earlier practice of rewarding only selected branch industries and the northern band of territory. On top of a 1.7 salary coefficient for all but the southern portion, as compared with the European portion of the USSR, annual 20 percent increases could total another 80 percent gain. In addition, eighteen extra days of annual leave and a two-years' pension allotment for one year of work fattened out the fringe benefit package. Moreover, men can now retire at 55 and women at 50, five years earlier than elsewhere.

The chairman of the RSFSR State Labor Committee echoed this positive prognosis, claiming that "the population of the Russian Republic's eastern regions has increased substantially in the past ten years."[67] However, he warned that the overall increase was "still insufficient to fully satisfy the area's manpower requirements.... Concrete steps must be taken to reduce the amount of labor at industrial enterprises and construction projects and to bring living conditions up to a par with those in the country's other regions."

These recommendations responded in word, if not in deed, to an earlier statement from the director of the Economic Research Institute at the Far Eastern Scientific Center in Khabarovsk, who termed the need for labor "a serious problem."[68] He called on the State Labor Committee to "determine long-range requirements for labor" and "to facilitate an influx of new people into the area and their permanent settlement. Among top-priority measures, we could name the institution of preferential rates for transportation and consumer and municipal services, the introduction of wage supplements based on length of time in the Far East, and the acceleration of housing.... Consumer services ought to be improved."

Yet despite the agreement among academic analysts and officials on the need to provide better living conditions to meet the demands of potential workers and their families, press reports continued to detail the inadequacies that plague life in new cities. Three major examples—Tynda, Sayansk, and Angarsk—serve as modest case studies to characterize the situation throughout East Asian Siberia as reflected in the media.

Tynda is called "the capital of BAM."[69] Yet in late 1978 its chief architect admitted that its "haphazard development and the acute shortages of water and heat nullify the advantages of its well-built housing. . . . The lack of social, cultural, and consumer-service facilities, which are not scheduled to be built until after 1980, is causing a high rate of personnel turnover." Feelings ran high at a public confrontation between officials and residents. When the USSR deputy minister of transport construction and director of Glavbamstroi (Chief Administration for the Construction of BAM) declared that all planned facilities had been built as scheduled and disclaimed responsibility for providing maternity hospitals, he was asked, "Does that mean railroad workers find their children under cabbage plants?"[70]

As of mid-1978, after four years of construction, Tynda did not have "a single major cafe, dining room, Palace of Culture, or movie theater."[71] Instead of a central boiler house, 38 small "departmental boiler houses" provided inadequate heat for the city. As a consequence of heat and water shortages, nine-story apartment buildings remained empty. With no dairy section or greenhouse farming, milk and sour cream were shipped in by air. Dust roiled in the streets in the summer because of the absence of hard paving. The writer who had noted the lack of cultural amenities urged, "Tynda is the first city born of the nationwide construction project, and its appearance should be in keeping with the lofty status of BAM's capital."

Sayansk, another new city, won attention in a Pravda report that claimed that "needed people can be retained not only and not so much by 'super-high' pay as by well-appointed housing that is better equipped and more roomy than accommodations in areas where the climate is not so harsh."[72] According to scientists in the Zima Electrochemical plant at Sayansk, although new production facilities would require 150,000 square meters of housing for additional workers, only 36,000 square meters would be ready in 1978. Barely 400 out of 1,000 families on the waiting list could be accommodated. One kindergarten was ready, two more were scheduled, but four were needed. No buildings in the new hospital complex had been built. A makeshift "cultural center" in a dormitory basement offered the only recreational auditorium, and there were no plans for a movie theater or Palace of Culture in the near future.

Angarsk, a city of nearly 240,000 by 1979, had only half of the planned funds for housing allocated over several years.[73] As a result, the electrical machinery plant could not invite enough workers from other areas, and to meet its needs, it raided existing enterprises in the city, "denuding important production sections." As elsewhere, reporters noted "the absence, in places where the plans envisage them, of shopping centers, consumer-service buildings, movie houses, and theaters."

Problems of development are inevitable in regions remote from the center. The transport capacity of the Trans-Siberian railroad is finite, and the competition for materials among simultaneously planned projects, the disruption of construction schedules by adverse weather, and the limitations of inexperienced labor, further weakened by a high rate of turnover, are only a few of the factors that would be expected to confound Soviet planners in executing a massive project like BAM. What, then, of the full agenda of items programmed for East Asian Siberia?

But these problems do not receive the brunt of criticism from local officials and reporters. Instead, the responsibility for serious but consistent shortcomings is attributed to the lack of centralized administration and the refusal of Moscow's ministries to shoulder the collective task of city planning and development. In the case of Tynda "imprecise planning and a failure to coordinate actions" are cited, not "merely growing pains."[74] A plan for its integrated growth was not even ready until the fourth year of construction, and months later no single department had "real responsibility."[75] The deputy minister of railroads and chief of the Board of Directors for the Construction of BAM dismissed Tynda as "merely a railroad junction, . . . no prospects for development," although in 1974 the city's population was already projected at seventy thousand.[76] Moreover, the Ministry's own plan called for a locomotive and railroad car repair center with up to twenty thousand employees.

The Moscow State Design and Surveying Institute for Transport Construction, designated as general designer, was also unwilling to take on this responsibility. We have already noted the disclaimer of the deputy minister of transport construction. The situation was summed up by "one well-known architect" at the public meeting with central officials, who remarked, "Everyone's avoiding the city like the plague!"[77] Finally, the chairman of the USSR State Committee for Civil Construction and Architecture concluded by recommending that all the parties go back to the plan for Tynda's integrated growth and revise its completion schedules. The reporter commented, "What this means is further exchanges of paper among departments and further delays in putting the costly management mechanism into effect."

Sayansk suffered from similar inadequacies, but here blame was put solely on the Ministry of Chemical Industry. In 1974 investigation revealed that no plan provided for such items as "a bakery, a dairy, cultural institutions, and sports facilities, and the putting into operation of stores and consumer-service shops is being postponed."[78] Subsequent detailed construction schedules for these facilities were approved by the deputy minister of the chemical industry. Yet four years later "financing of a number of facilities has still not begun, and in other cases funds have been allocated but the builders have not made full use of this money, doing only the profitable jobs."

The ministry was accused of having relegated housing and related projects to the "second line," which usually lags behind the first line, "the creation of the industrial base." However, the reporter pointed out that the two lines are interrelated. The inadequate living conditions limited the recruitment and retention of workers, which in turn delayed the construction of production buildings, the installation of equipment, and the achievement of full-capacity operation. Thus, "according to the initial plans the combine that is now under construction (mid-1978) should have been producing output as early as 1972."

Angarsk, the most mature of the three cases under review, exemplifies the gap between central ministerial control and local need. The Angarsk soviet executive committee proposed that the municipal economy and all its services be centralized so that the committee could contract for new housing tracts. However, the Ministry of the Petroleum-refining and Petrochemical Industry balked because it held most of the housing stock.[79] This followed the failure of the Ministry of Electrical Equipment to allocate half of its designated housing funds. There is an apt summary of the bureaucratic battle to avoid responsibility for consumer construction, and it deserves quotation at length:

> ... In the past, when the city was small and the Ministry of Petroleum-Refining and Petrochemical Industry was the only organization doing construction work, its funds were used to build institutions of this kind. But then Angarsk became a multibranch center. One would have thought that now the appropriate nonindustrial departments would strengthen the base of social, consumer-service, and cultural-enlightenment institutions.
>
> What has been done for the development of Angarsk by, for instance, the republic Ministries of Consumer Services and of Culture and the Russian Republic State Committee on Cinematography? Virtually nothing. They have not allotted a single ruble from their centralized capital investments for the expansion of the network of institutions under their jurisdiction. The Russian Republic Ministry of Trade has declined all responsibility for serving the residents of Angarsk; this job is handled only by the workers' supply administration for the construction workers, who constitute a tiny share of the population. For this reason, there are gaping holes in the rows of new apartment buildings—the impression is that of a backward child whose teeth have not all come in yet.[80]

As might be expected from the demographic data, fewer problems appear to have arisen in the Far East region. But though it consistently attracted migration because of its comparatively moderate climate, better developed transport system, and larger agricultural base, it continued to give evidence of difficulty in securing the necessary workers to develop its economy. One official in authority addressed himself to the requirement for more technicians from higher and specialized secondary schools. Acknowledging that between 1974 and 1976 between 50 and 70 percent of such local graduates had been assigned in the region, he said "a substantial number of young specialists left for assignments outside of the Far East," while "several thousand [more] have left the territory in the recent past."[81] Moreover, he added that "only 1,000 engineers and technicians graduating from educational institutions in the country's western regions have come into the territory. . . . It is known that a considerable number of specialists assigned to work in the Far East fail to adapt here for various reasons and return home."

In sum, at the end of the 1970's the demographic prospects for

East Asian Siberia as a whole, although considerably better than for West Siberia, remained limited, to judge from press reports. The seeming intractability of the various problems can be traced in part to the refusal of central ministries to make the necessary concessions in funds and authority to allow local planning and management of consumer requirements so that EAS can attract and hold permanent residents. Increased monetary allowances and accelerated investment in housing and associated services brought some relief but were insufficient to change the basic situation. Nor, as we shall see in our later examination of the territorial production complex, was this innovative institution successful in winning the necessary authority to bridge either the gap between central ministries or the gap between the center and the local communities.

Recognition of the obstacles to overcoming these demographic deficiencies contributed to a shift in emphasis from early projections of major EAS population expansion to a more recent focus on minimizing the need for labor and maximizing increases in productivity through technology and mechanization. Addressing this question, Aganbegyan declared that Siberian development would not require a greater quantity of labor as much as a better quality of skilled workers.[82] In this regard, he saw BAM as a massive training program that, when completed, will leave an abundance of competent construction and engineering personnel to tackle subsequent projects throughout the region. In the more rugged northern areas, work can be done in successive shifts by groups that come for limited periods, thus obviating the need for an expensive and extensive infrastructure. Raw material extracted in the north can be processed in the south where living conditions and costs are better for a larger populace. This would permit an 80–90 percent increase in southern output through increased labor productivity rather than through an expanded work force. "Of course," he added, "we must attract new people, but in the thousands, not in the millions."

One of his associates, the academician B. P. Orlov, a noted specialist in Siberian development, calculated that industrial production in Siberia and the Far East should grow 8.5–9 times in the period 1970–2000.[83] But population will increase only 1.6–1.7 times the 1970 figure, an extremely modest projection compared with estimates of a decade previous. As a consequence, output per worker must increase four to five times if the expected growth in production is to be realized. Orlov concluded by calling for a greater rationalization of resources, particularly labor, and a more intensive application of technology.

The original plans for Siberia foresaw an overall economic program that would gradually raise the area through "balanced development" at a rate of industrialization comparable with that of other Soviet regions, as dictated by fundamental Soviet planning philosophy.[84] An alternative approach, more congruent with the demographic situation, will exploit East Asian Siberia's resources for local processing or for processing elsewhere in the country, as well as for export. This plan utilizes EAS's assets while lessening the impact of its liabilities. The greater the use of mechanization in mining and processing, the less the need for human labor. But to assess the potential of this approach, a preliminary survey of the region's mineral wealth is necessary.

The Natural Resources of East Asian Siberia

Against the preponderantly negative factors we have examined thus far, Siberia's natural resources provide a positive balance. Long the subject of speculative Soviet panegyrics, their actual extent still remains to be fully determined. Less than 10 percent of East Asian Siberia has been adequately surveyed.[85] Formidable problems of access and climate obstruct the geological mapping of this vast region. Yet on the basis of what has been determined so far, and by analogy with similar regions elsewhere, there is little doubt that the region possesses an abundance of mineral resources. Moreover, its intrinsic value should increase as other sources of supply decrease both in other parts of the USSR and throughout the world.

Before we take inventory of the EAS storehouse, however, several caveats are in order. First, our brief review must disregard the economics of cost, especially in comparison with alternate sources. Although some general observations can be made, no systematic cost-benefit analysis is yet possible. Too much uncertainty exists with respect to the internal Soviet economic situation and world market conditions ten years hence, especially for hydrocarbon fuels. Both situations are highly dynamic, and thus are unpredictable over a long period of time. We will therefore identify the probable presence of resources, but we will not evaluate their ultimate economic utility.

Second, in the absence of a thorough survey, it is impossible to determine fully the quality or quantity of mineral deposits. Small samples can offer promise, and rough extrapolations can be made, but until the completion of BAM provides better access to the region, most observations must remain preliminary and tentative.

Third, virtually all of our information is based on Soviet sources. One notable exception is the natural gas reserves in central Yakutia, which were surveyed by American geologists in late 1978. But this was a unique instance, a case where Moscow granted outside access because it hopes to engage Japanese and American capital in the exploitation of these reserves. The results of the survey show that Soviet restrictions on foreign inspection do not necessarily vitiate their own claims. Yet so long as the restrictions remain, various reservations prohibit outright acceptance of the claims.[86]

To offset these warnings, it should be noted that the USSR Academy of Sciences has invested heavily in research and planning for Siberian development. Its world-renowned center at Akademgorodok, near Novosibirsk, embraces 23 institutes specializing in biology, botany, chemistry, economics, geology, mathematics, mechanics, mining, physics, seismology, soil sciences, and other disciplines. Three more scientific centers have been established at Irkutsk, Vladivostok, and Yakutsk, with regional research stations sprinkled throughout the area—at Chita, Khabarovsk, Magadan, Yuzhno-Sakhalinsk, Petropavlovsk-Kamchatsky, Ulan-Ude, and elsewhere.[87] There, extremely competent senior and junior scientists live close to their field work and can integrate theory with practical problem solving in relative freedom from the bureaucratic and political atmosphere in

46 THE INTERNAL SETTING

Moscow.[88] Their findings provide a better basis for forecasting than do traditional travelers' tales or the speculative flights of journalists.

As a further observation, past estimates of reserves and potential resources in other countries have generally shown a conservative bias that tends to underestimate the existence and extent of mineral wealth that can be exploited. This is well documented in the case of petroleum. The repeated predictions of exhaustion for world oil reserves that began in the 1950's have proved groundless. Even the presumably more sophisticated and better-informed forecasts of the early 1970's failed to anticipate the major Mexican discoveries later in that decade.

A leading Soviet geologist remarked privately that in addition to their professional scientific conservatism, an additional consideration strengthens the conservative bias among his colleagues: "We are always expected to show increases in our annual discovery rate. Therefore we make certain to fulfill this quota by underestimating the potential reserves at any given time."[89] This problem can be compounded by cautious experts and bureaucrats at the center. Although there is little argument over gas reserves, foreign Soviet specialists have long debated the reliability of oil figures used by central agencies.[90] Two highly placed officials responsible for surveys in the major oil and gas fields of West Siberia complained that local estimates were consistently discounted in the Leningrad Petroleum Institute and in the USSR Ministry of Petroleum Industry.[91] Moreover, "planning agencies often lean toward the skeptics' opinions." The writers offered the data shown in Table 2 to prove their point. They claimed that for 1990 "the disparity for oil is even greater, for gas similar."

Serious consequences can follow from faulty estimates. Planning agencies will commit fewer funds to drilling if estimates are lower, with the result that fewer discoveries are made over time. West Siberian officials reported that a fall in drillings from 500,000 meters in 1967 to 385,000 in 1972 caused a loss of time and workers. Had the more optimistic estimates been heeded, the authors claimed, by 1979 annual drilling would have reached

THE INTERNAL SETTING 47

TABLE 2
West Siberian Oil: Estimates and Output
(Million tons of oil)

Last year of Five Year Plan	Local estimate	Early center estimate	Actual production
1970	30–35	12	31
1975	150	70–80	148
1980	N.A.	240–60	315 (planned)

1.5 million meters, presumably with greater output. A CIA analysis suggests that this larger production would only have advanced the peaking out of West Siberian fields and would not have added to the total flow of oil.[92] In any event, the gap between estimates and actual production illustrates the difficulty in trying to calculate ultimate potential from such scattered sources as are provided in the Soviet literature.

To complicate matters further, the Soviet terminology for reserve and resource estimates differs from that generally employed in the West, where it also varies between governmental and private commercial usage.[93] Without elaborating the highly technical definitions and their various permutations, it suffices to note that Soviet categories are less restrictive as to the certainty of economic utilization, and therefore are viewed abroad with some skepticism. Another variable is the ratio of reserves to recovery, which must be known in order to project production from what is estimated to be in the ground. With oil, for instance, the Soviet use of waterflooding and the extreme depth of the deposits in Siberia can produce results quite different from what would be realized from Middle East fields. A particular complication in the case of oil arises from the fact that Moscow has not published a reserve estimate since 1938; in 1947 oil reserve figures were made an official state secret.[94]

These considerations caution against attempting to forecast the future of East Asian Siberia's mineral production in specific amounts for given commodities. However, this does not preclude identifying those resources that are likely prospects for eventual exploitation. In this regard, it is helpful to recognize the difference between reserves and resources as practiced in official western usage. According to the definition developed by V. E. McKelvey and subsequently widely accepted, "reserves" are identified deposits—whether measured, indicated, or inferred—that can be profitably exploited with available technology under existing economic conditions. If the technology or economic calculations improve, the reserves thereby become greater. The term "resources" includes exploitable reserves and other deposits that may become available at some future time. These deposits may be known but not economically or technologically recoverable at present. Alternatively, they may be hypothetical, that is, undiscovered but in known areas; or speculative, undiscovered but possibly existing somewhere.[95]

Except for gold, the EAS natural resources that hold the greatest promise in value, either for domestic use or export abroad, are those associated with energy. Yakutian gas and coal reserves are already established in major amounts; oil has yet to be discovered in commercial quantity, but is considered likely; and surplus hydro power, actual and potential, exists throughout the area.

Yakutian gas was first discovered in 1936 to the east of the present fields. However, permafrost 1.5 kilometers (0.9 miles) thick impeded exploration.[96] Subsequently the Vilyui River area was tested at various points, with large deposits finally being found in its upper reaches. In the early 1970's negotiations with Japanese and American firms developed interest in joint development, and tentative agreement was reached to schedule deliveries of 10 billion cubic meters of liquefied natural gas (LNG) annually to each of the participating countries. However, before final negotiations could occur, a minimum of one trillion cubic meters had to be proven. By mid-1979 850 billion cubic meters of gas had been identified, and the remainder was expected to be found in the near future.[97] In addition to the annual export schedule, 10 billion cubic meters are to serve Soviet domestic needs each year. The total inferred reserve has been estimated at 13 trillion cubic meters.[98]

Aganbegyan is an avowed enthusiast of the region's potential, and he claims that potentially larger deposits of natural gas exist in the Chukotka Peninsula.[99] This forbidding area astride the Arctic Circle is the farthest possible point from centers of Soviet consumption. Aside from such local use of the gas as might be practicable for power and heat, Aganbegyan envisages its ultimate distribution to North America via a pipeline across the Bering Strait to Alaska, where it could enter the Trans-Canadian pipeline to major markets in the United States.

Both schemes must depend largely on foreign capital and technology if they are to be realized. The export of Yakutian gas requires that it be piped 3,000 kilometers (1,860 miles), liquefied, and shipped in special LNG tankers. This is an extremely costly venture. Coming on top of heavy expenditures for BAM, it is very unlikely that Moscow will make the basic investment in Yakutian gas to serve only local consumption, especially given the abundance of coal and hydro power in the region. As for the Chukotka fields, they have not been proven, and their attraction for American investment is most remote in view of more politically reliable sources on the North American continent, both onshore and offshore.

By comparison with gas, little effort has gone into exploration for oil in East Asian Siberia except for Sakhalin, a well-established source, albeit with deposits of relatively modest extent. However, on the basis of general geological information and analogy with similar areas elsewhere, a consensus of Soviet and western specialists holds that "conditions favorable to large future discoveries of oil exist over much of the Arctic offshore regions, . . . the East Siberian lowlands, . . . and perhaps off Kamchatka and Sakhalin."[100]

The incentive for exploration is low because of the absence of necessary infrastructure and local demand, and the high cost of extraction.[101] The Soviet prognosis for an expanded effort in this direction is pessimistic for the short run, according to the criteria for priority allocations among competing sources of energy, as defined by scientists at the Energy Institute at Irkutsk: (1) economic cost indices; (2) reserve estimates of availability in terms of location, time, difficulty, and depletion prospects; (3) environmental constraints; and (4) technological constraints and

50   THE INTERNAL SETTING

the necessity of foreign imports. These factors determine the availability of funds for the systematic surveys without which analysis must remain largely theoretical.

Within this framework, however, Soviet geologists are cautiously optimistic. They estimate that at least half of Yakutia holds some promise of oil and gas.[102] Problems of permafrost and the depth of suspected deposits have delayed drilling until better technology is available and rigs are released from West Siberian fields. The geological structure in areas tapped so far has not revealed any large exploitable deposits other than those in the Vilyui River region. The region north of Lake Baikal in southern Yakutia is crossed with arcs where exploratory wells have tapped oil in noncommercial amounts, which caused Aganbegyan to lament that "the reserves are great but the structure is more complicated than West Siberia."[103] He calculated that, even with waterflooding and modern technology, oil recovery might still be only 20 percent. However, he was optimistic concerning the prospect of better discoveries in the future, because the structure is largely Mesozoic in formation, the source of half the oil found in the USSR in 1970.[104] Aganbegyan summed up the professional debate: "Pessimists say these are just remnants of oil from an early large deposit. Optimists say the deposit could not have moved and we must find it."

The Soviet technology for geological surveying lags behind that of the West.[105] Equipment deficiencies include quality seismic geophones, digital processing units, powerful drills, and hard bits. Although these can be purchased abroad, their piecemeal acquisition has served higher priority needs in West Siberia. Drilling below 2,000 meters is extremely slow if dependent on locally produced equipment. Transportation also poses severe problems. Helicopters provide the only means of access to much of the region, and they have difficulty coping with the extensive pipe and support structures. Use of rivers in the summer and snow roads in the winter provides a makeshift solution, but the complicated logistics and the vagaries of the weather raise costs and delay operations.

Offshore oil exploration faces equally severe obstacles. No available technology can cope with the pack ice that overlays prospective areas in the Arctic Sea.[106] Ice around Sakhalin prevents drilling in the northeast sector between mid-October and July, and in the southwest sector between December and mid-March.[107] As a result, little productivity is anticipated from the Soviet-Japanese offshore effort before the early 1980's.

Yet assuming the ultimate technological feasibility of extracting such oil and gas as may be discovered in East Asian Siberia, the economic benefit for the region could be considerable. At present the Soviet Far East is deficient in oil and requires costly hauls of over 10 million tons of crude oil and petroleum products a year, the major portion of which enters the Trans-Siberian railroad from the pipeline terminus at Angarsk.[108] Sakhalin's onshore output in 1978 amounted to only 2.25 million tons of crude oil and 800 million metric tons of gas, based on reserves estimated in 1970 to be 11 million tons and 91 billion cubic meters respectively.[109] Two underwater pipelines convey the oil to a refinery at Komsomolsk. Despite forecasts of up to 5 billion tons of oil offshore, Sakhalin will not be of major importance unless actual discoveries greatly exceed the private estimates of Soviet and Japanese specialists.[110]

The uncertainties and problems associated with EAS oil and gas are absent in the case of coal, which exists in abundance and in readily exploitable conditions. Much of it is brown coal, or lignite, and it is mainly used at present for thermal plants located near the mines. But sizeable fields of bituminous coal allow production of excellent coke and high-grade steam coal for export to Japan as well as for local use. Two of the largest such deposits are in southern Yakutia. The first to be exploited, at Neryungri, is estimated to have 500 million tons of high-caloric coal. Its projected yearly output of 12 million tons, 5 million of which will go to Japan annually until 1998, should last at least 40 years.[111] A second area to the north at Chulman adds to the district's total proven reserves of 11 billion tons, three-fourths of which are of good coking quality and are largely available through stripmining. Estimates of the possible resources in the district go as high as 40 billion tons.[112] The "little BAM" already links the Neryungri field with the Trans-Siberian railroad via the Trans-Siberian's northward spur to Tynda and Berkakit. Completion of BAM itself will increase the accessibility of the field, particularly for export to the Pacific.

Soviet scholars express considerable interest in the potential gasification of southern Yakutian coal.[113] This development would utilize Yakutian gas in concert with the vast Chulman coal reserves in support of an iron and steel complex based on the nearby iron ore at Aldan. The direct use of coal in ferrous metallurgy there would risk serious pollution because of the temperature inversion and prolonged calm of the winter. Previous Soviet experiments with coal gasification did not prove economical.[114] However, steadily rising energy costs in recent years have revived interest in this approach, at least in the research institutes.

East Asian Siberia abounds in lignite, fortuitously located in the southern sector where it can fuel thermal power plants without costly and inefficient transportation requirements. It is also used to generate electricity for much of the Trans-Siberian line and for direct consumption on the remaining nonelectrified portion west of Khabarovsk.[115] Most of the deposits are strip-mined, with output ranging from a modest one million tons up to ten and twelve million tons per year. Minehead power stations of 1,200 megawatts provide electricity in the Buryat ASSR and Chita Oblast, while smaller stations are scattered throughout the Amur-Maritime region. Bituminous mines in the northern settlements of Sangar and Zyryanka lie along major river routes, and the mine at Beringovskiy on the Bering Sea also enjoys water transport.[116] They provide fuel for thermal stations in remote areas, as does most of Sakhalin's output of nearly five million tons.

The actual and potential amount of the third energy source, hydroelectric power, justifies the sweeping adjectives associated with Siberia but often dismissed as journalistic hyperbole. At its completion in 1966, the giant station at Bratsk was the most powerful in the world, generating 4,500 megawatts.[117] A second station, farther downstream on the Angara River at Ust-Ilimsk, was scheduled to have a capacity of 4,320 megawatts by the end of 1980. The Zeya River station in Amur Oblast was to have a capacity of 1,290 megawatts by 1980. Further east the Talakan

THE INTERNAL SETTING 53

dam on the Bureya River will produce 2,000 megawatts in the mid-1980's. Meanwhile, in the far north the new Kolyma River station will bring 900 megawatts on line by 1985 to serve the gold-mining operations near Magadan. This impressive battery of dams was built at great expense in extremely difficult conditions over the past 25 years, yet it still does not exhaust the potential of the EAS river network.

The total present and planned hydroelectric power output is far in excess of local need, especially with the widespread thermal plants that can draw on lignite well into the distant future. One possible use is the introduction of industries with a high consumption of energy, such as aluminum, chlorine and caustic soda, calcium carbide, ferroalloys, and electric steels.[118] These "energy-embedded industries" make it economically feasible to ship raw materials from distant points for local processing and reshipment to other points of consumption. The aluminum plants at Bratsk (the largest in the world) and Shelekhov produce 500,000 and 200,000 tons per year, respectively, using bauxite shipped from the distant Urals and abroad. Soviet planners believe this process may prove attractive for Japan if the increased cost and scarcity of energy should eventually make the manufacture of high energy products in East Asian Siberia both profitable and practical from Tokyo's viewpoint.

A second use for the surplus hydro power will be realized when the region is eventually linked to a national power grid sometime in the 1990's. This will permit the transfer of electricity from one area to another according to the changing load required by differential levels of industrial demand and by the different time zones that make for a ten-hour span across the USSR.[119] The transmission of hydroelectric power between East Asian Siberia and the European USSR will provide significant relief from the anticipated shortages of energy. It will also justify the tremendous capital investment in these projects, albeit only after several decades of delay in realizing the return.

The cross-country extra-high-voltage lines necessary for the national grid are expected to require a very large amount of copper. By coincidence copper is one of East Asian Siberia's major resources. The Udokan deposit in northern Chita Oblast, with an estimated 1.2 billion tons of ore, may be the richest in the Soviet Union, which is already second in world production.[120] Lying close to the surface, the ore is susceptible to open-pit mining, and the first pit is expected to yield 20 million tons of 2 percent ore with an annual output of 400,000 tons in refinable copper.[121]

The potential productivity of Udokan exceeds domestic need for at least the 1980's. For more than ten years Soviet officials have tried to interest Japanese investors in the joint development of these deposits, but without success. Discussions have also been held with various prospective West European collaborators, but proximity makes Japan a more logical partner once BAM is completed. The extreme volatility of the world copper market and the uncertainty of future Japanese demand precludes forecasting Udokan's export potential. However, some specialists claim that Moscow will exploit it on a more modest scale if no foreign participation emerges.

EAS iron ore has received less attention, but Soviet geologists hold considerable hope for its availability when BAM facilitates the movement of heavy exploratory drilling equipment into previously inaccessible areas.[122] One such area, estimated to have six to eight billion tons of enrichable ferriferous quartzites, was discovered in the Chara-Tokko region near the trijuncture of the Chita-Irkutsk-Yakutia border.[123] Another promising site at Aldan is convenient to the "Little BAM," already mentioned in connection with the Chulman coking-coal fields. Soviet geologists put Aldan's proven deposits at one billion tons, capable of an annual output of twelve million tons of ore for several hundred years.[124] Two additional mines of high quality in the Amur Oblast and the Khabarovsk Krai together have proven reserves of equal amount.[125] The Amur ore is high grade, mostly of 56 percent iron content.[126] Another deposit in Birobidzhan is believed to have a billion tons, but here Soviet experts cite the need for more complete surveys.

The minerals associated with steel manufacturing are also available in the region. Tungsten exists in "one of the richest deposits in the USSR" near the Ussuri, and another mine is operating in the Buryat ASSR.[127] Manganese is thought to be present in Birobidzhan.[128] Subsidiary commodities such as dolomite, quartz, magnesite, and graphite are scattered throughout the area.[129]

The abundance of nonferrous and rare minerals in East Asian Siberia has prompted local sayings that characterize the almost mystical belief in the region's mineral wealth. Yakutians claim that "when God passed over Yakutia while creating the world, his hands became cold and all the rich minerals slipped between his fingers to the ground below."[130] Similarly, inhabitants of the Soviet Far East declare that "when God's angels were finished making the world, they shook out their bags over the Far East region."[131]

Gold mines in the northern area and diamond mines in Yakutia justify these popular views. Figures on production and reserves remain secret, but both are ranked among the leading global sources. The Mirny diamond-processing plant is alleged to be the largest in the world. It is supplied by an exceptionally rich reserve that has been compared with the famed Kimberley pipes in South Africa.[132] Additional pipes of even better quality lie to the north, providing a wealth of gems and a vast quantity of industrial diamonds. More deposits are expected to be found as prospecting expands over the Yakut ASSR.

Our inventory cannot hope to cover the location, size, and quality of all the EAS minerals. It is sufficient to identify the deposits of major importance in value or amount so as to illustrate the extent to which the region's potential for exploration can profit from further investment, particularly with the increased access and additional transportation to be provided by BAM.[133] Lead, zinc, silver, and tin from the region have long served Soviet needs, and additional mines are being developed. A polymetallic concentration west of Khabarovsk is claimed to have 40–45 percent tin, 20 percent copper, and 20 percent lead-zinc.[134] Rich phosphates with a 40 percent concentrate, a deposit estimated at two to three billion tons, lie 180 kilometers (111 miles) from BAM; they offer a base for chemical fertilizer that may end the need for imports from European Russia.[135]

Antimony and mercury exist in exploitable amounts, as do more exotic minerals important to space and defense activities,

56 THE INTERNAL SETTING

such as tantalum, brucite, columbium, and molybdenum.[136] Large deposits of mica, both phlogopite and muscovite, offer a valuable resource for the electrical industry. BAM will also provide access to the richest asbestos deposit in the USSR. As reported by the chief geologist of the Buryat ASSR, "The content of textile-grade asbestos in the entire country's known deposits is one-tenth that of Molodezhnoye. In addition, the reserves here are equal to the country's four largest deposits put together." [137] Open-pit methods will produce a high-grade ore that is compared favorably with the best long-spinning textile-quality asbestos to be found in Canada.[138]

Timber has traditionally been one of the region's main products for export to other parts of the USSR and Japan. Gross reserve estimates vary widely and can be misleading because of inaccessibility and uneven quality, but at a minimum the BAM zone contains 1.4 billion cubic meters of mature timber.[139] The EAS share of total Soviet roundwood production rose from 16 percent in 1965 to 19.7 percent in 1974.[140] Between 1965 and 1975 there were particularly noteworthy increases in Khabarovsk Krai (108 percent, 5.9 to 12.3 million cubic meters), and Irkutsk Oblast (41 percent, 19.8 to 28 million cubic meters), as against an all-Union increase of only 14 percent.[141] By 1990 the BAM zone alone is expected to yield 10 percent of the timber products in the Soviet Union.[142]

Soviet calculations place the demand for wood pulp in 1990 on a par with that for metals, coal, and oil.[143] This burgeoning industry is accompanied by facilities for plywood, fiberboard, chipboard, and newsprint.[144] In addition to supplying Soviet markets, the expansion of export capacity through the new port of Wrangel (Vostochnyi) is designed to extend sales beyond the main consumer, Japan, to the southwestern Pacific basin and India.

This brief list does not exhaust the natural resources of East Asian Siberia, nor does it reveal what else may be found through systematic exploration, little of which has occurred. A final evaluation requires the careful calculation of costs, depletion rates, and alternative sources of supply in the context of changing technologies and world market conditions. However, the consensus of geologists, geographers, and economists in the research institutes of Akademgorodok, Irkutsk, Yakutsk, Khabarovsk, and Vladivostok foresees a steadily growing exploitation of the region's natural wealth. They firmly believe this will be of inestimable value to the Soviet economy through both direct domestic utilization and export.

BAM and Soviet Investment Policy

It is clear from our repeated references that the Baikal-Amur Railroad is essential to any significant development of East Asian Siberia or exploitation of its natural resources. According to the USSR minister of geology, "The extraction and processing of highly important minerals was a basic stimulus to the construction of BAM, and the location of the largest resource combinations predetermined the selection of its route."[145] By the end of 1978 some 20,000 "workers and specialists" from his ministry were involved in exploration and prospecting in the BAM zone.

Foreign opinion has questioned the likelihood of BAM's being completed, especially should Brezhnev's successors reorder economic priorities for planning regions and economic sectors. With only 45 percent of the line finished by the end of 1979, BAM's original target date of 1983 is clearly in jeopardy.[146] Soviet specialists speak privately of 1985–86 for full operational capability.[147] In addition to this extended schedule, the original cost estimates of eight billion dollars will also be greatly exceeded, with foreign estimates ranging as high as fifteen billion dollars.[148] Last but not least, BAM was at first justified economically on the basis of export shipments of West Siberian oil to Japan. According to an authoritative Soviet article, "Most of the freight movements on the BAM (70 to 75 percent of the ton-kilometers) will be made up of West Siberian crude oil for the Far East. . . . The second most important commodity in BAM freight operations will be timber (10 to 18 percent)."[149] Written in 1974, this analysis received economic corroboration from another author, who argued on the basis of computations "by an expert commission of Gosplan USSR, together with the Institute of

Complex Transport Problems and with the Transportation and Oil-Gas Industry departments of Gosplan USSR," that the combined pipeline-railroad shipment of oil from West Siberia to the Far East would be "more economical" than using a large diameter pipeline exclusively.[150]

However, CIA estimates claim that by 1985 West Siberia will be doing well if it manages to meet the combined demand of European Russia, East Europe, and West Europe, in view of declining production in the old fields and the failure to discover any new ones comparable to Samotlor.[151] This will leave little oil, if any, for the Soviet Far East and Japan. Perhaps for this reason, in 1979 a Gosplan analyst, flatly contradicting the earlier economic computations cited above, suggested that the original rationale for BAM was no longer valid: "The BAM is supposedly being built mainly as a transit route with crude oil expected to be one of the main commodities moving over the railroad. It seems to us, however, that such a one-sided approach to the use of the railroad is not justified. . . . The overall pipeline transmission costs for crude oil turn out to be half of the transport cost of an equivalent amount of oil by rail."[152] Behind the juggling of statistical calculations, the detailed bases for which were not given, this article implicitly questioned the utility of pushing BAM to completion.

Cancellation of the remaining portions of BAM, among which are the most difficult and expensive, would carry an incalculable political cost. The Soviet regime has committed its domestic prestige to BAM, in effect making it a test of the country's ability and will to recapture the fervor that marked its early days of reconstruction more than half a century ago. Hundreds of thousands of young people have been recruited through the Young Communist League for the most arduous labor under conditions of extreme vigor. Many cities and towns have pledged support to new sister cities and stations on the BAM line. Media attention to BAM has rivaled the earlier publicity for space achievements. As the subject of film, theater, books, and countless articles, the railroad's imprint on Soviet consciousness is indelible, at least for present generations.

It is difficult to capture the full scope of the project in a limited

THE INTERNAL SETTING 59

space.[153] A Soviet official claimed in 1978 that its cost was running at two million rubles per kilometer or 0.5 percent of the USSR's total capital investment.[154] An earlier foreign estimate put both figures twice as high.[155] The gross statistics, as summarized by Victor Mote, tell the story in more vivid terms:

> The roadbed will consist almost exclusively of road-metal ballast, which will be supplied at the rate of 400,000 tons per year. Other annual building material requirements are 80 million bricks, 11 million cubic feet of rock, and 40,000 tons of lime. Heavy equipment needs are: 1,200 excavators, 435 bulldozers; 320 graders; 835 cranes; 72 mine-loading machines; 60 rock crushers and sorters; 950 mobile compressors; 7,440 eight-ton trucks; 310 tractors; 100 1,200-horsepower switching locomotives; 1,550 dumper cars; and 300 4-axle flatcars.[156]

For the Soviet Union, BAM truly appears to justify its title, "The construction project of the century."

The geographic, meteorologic, and permafrost conditions we surveyed earlier add a qualitative dimension to these quantitative indicators of BAM's magnitude. Of the 3,145-kilometer (1,965-mile) distance between Ust-Kut and Komsomolsk, 1,192 kilometers (745 miles), or more than one-third, were "designated as endowed with conditions that are unsatisfactory for engineering."[157] We will examine these in greater detail later when we analyze BAM's strategic implications. At this point, it suffices to highlight the most serious hazards. According to a Soviet seismologist, "Along the 1,100-kilometer (682-mile) segment from Kunerma (in the Baikal range) to Tynda, up to 90 percent of the area is highly prone to earthquakes of eight or more on the Richter scale."[158] Flooding, landslides, mudflows, avalanches, and icing combine to present year-round threats.[159] Tunnels pose a special challenge; they will have a total length of 24 kilometers (15 miles). One will run 15 kilometers (9 miles) and another 6 kilometers (4 miles). Several pass through the most seismic area. As a further complication, Soviet scientists are acutely aware of ecological factors and seek to minimize environmental damage during the building of BAM and its subsequent operation.[160]

Even under the best of circumstances no project of this scope and difficulty could be expected to go precisely according to plan. However, our survey of the problems associated with new cities revealed how Soviet bureaucratic practices often complicate matters beyond the natural. Such has been the case with BAM. There is no need to recapitulate the entire record of blunders, because *Pravda* conveniently selects a few illustrative examples for attention in its annual review of BAM's progress. For example, in July 1978 it reported that only 60.3 percent of the 1977 tunnel construction plan was fulfilled.[161] As originally planned, freight was to have been shipped by rail to the port of Baikal, where part would be ferried across the lake in large tankers and barges. "In reality, gasoline trucks deliver fuel, of which the tunnel construction sites burn about 100 tons every day. The roads near the railway route are no good at all. Vehicles take five days to cover the 400-kilometer distance across Buryatia. The road is narrow. . . . The almost 280 bridges on the gasoline-truck road are not sturdy."

As usual, bureaucratic behavior allegedly accounts for the inadequacies that caused the shortfall in tunneling. The Ministry of Transport Construction failed to provide the necessary resources to the organization given the jurisdiction for road building. The Siberian State Design and Surveying Institute did not specify an adequate carrying capacity for "what are practically 30-ton trucks hauling cast-iron tubing." The Ministry of Railroads exercised inadequate supervision, and the USSR State Planning Committee was called upon to "act more efficiently in resolving questions of the planning and financing of BAM's construction." In short, there was enough blame to spread around so that no single target needed to feel the burden of responsibility.

It would be easy to recapitulate similar shortcomings in the planning and implementation of BAM. However, undue emphasis on the negative aspects, readily documented from the Soviet press, would obscure the true achievement represented in BAM's construction. One such instance is the extraordinarily long tunnels being blasted through permafrost. Before the main hole can be bored, a drainage tunnel, often as large as the Moscow subway, must be dug 300 meters ahead to test for problems.[162] As one official curtly noted, "Accidents happen." Although he did not elaborate, more than one hundred fatalities are rumored to have occurred in a single instance. Understandably, the human cost of BAM is never included in Soviet press accounts.

Another problem plaguing construction is the frequency with which bridges, some more than 90 meters (297 feet) long, must rest on ground with different thicknesses of permafrost. This places a different seismic stress on each section of the bridge, challenging the designer to safeguard the builders as well as the eventual users.[163] The available technology is nearly a century ahead of that which built the Trans-Siberian railroad, but the engineering problems in the BAM zone are far more severe.

Of course, BAM is not an end in itself; it is only the means to one of several ends, strategic as well as economic. We will assess its military implications later. As we have already seen, its economic payoff has been a subject of debate in Soviet circles almost from its inception, particularly with respect to the goals of external export versus internal development.[164] Put most simply, external goals aim at maximizing exports to earn the hard currency necessary to pay for imports of technology and grain. Internal goals aim at the balanced development of economic regions so as to reduce costly interregional exchange and to have reasonably equitable living standards throughout the country.

Although these alternate sets of goals are not necessarily incompatible, they can result in different investment priorities. For example, the exploitation of Yakutian natural gas has greater returns externally than internally, and its heavy cost could preempt funds that otherwise might go toward an iron-steel complex to serve local needs. Within the choice of internal goals are conflicting priorities, for instance, as between balanced economic development among regions and regional specialization. The higher costs engendered by pay incentives, complex infrastructure, and specialized equipment necessitated by the geographic, climatic, and demographic problems in East Asian Siberia pose economic problems for advocates of capital investment there rather than in more cost-effective areas.[165]

As a final observation, regardless of the problems of choice between external and internal goals or among competing internal goals, development of the region will require a continuous heavy investment of capital long after the completion of BAM. Moreover, the returns on such investment will not be realized quickly. BAM may be the "construction project of the century," but its ultimate economic utility is not likely to be ascertained until well after the end of the century.

Concern over Moscow's failure to resolve these questions and to allocate an overriding priority to the region was reflected in the writings of the late G. Tarasov, director of the Economic Research Institute of the Far Eastern Scientific Center in Khabarovsk. He acknowledged that because of "harsh natural and climatic conditions, additional outlays are necessary here for capital and housing construction, for the creation of social, cultural, and service facilities, utility lines and transportation services, and an increase in the wage fund," yet "a number of ministries approach problems of developing the Far East from the standpoint of recovering their investments in the shortest possible time." In addition, "The methods that the USSR State Construction Committee and a number of ministries now use for the technical and economic substantiation of the designing and construction of complexes in eastern regions . . . do not reflect the effectiveness of certain outlays . . . and do not take some resources into account—for example the land and water resources that are major advantages of the new regions."[166]

Tarasov challenged the conventional approach in Moscow, which combines the branch-level calculation of operating costs, including normal depreciation, with the regional-level calculation based on the ratio between the national income, or gross product, and investment.[167] He argued that the indices should allow for the lack of infrastructure, for remoteness, and for climate. More fundamentally, he called for an overall revision of the "effectiveness index" throughout the Soviet Union to show "the limited nature of water, land, power, and other natural resources or expenditures on environmental protection . . . [that] would significantly increase the outlays on comparable projects in the western regions and raise the effectiveness indices of development of production in the eastern region, especially the Far East." As an example, he cited the fact that the Far East has

THE INTERNAL SETTING 63

the highest amount of water per capita in the USSR (250,000 million cubic meters) and 27 percent of the country's timber (22.3 billion cubic meters).

Tarasov directly addressed the question of a delayed return on investment, admitting that in some instances this will take 20 to 30 years and violate standard cost-accounting procedures. Directly addressing critics of BAM, he declared, "When BAM is opened for operation the return will be considerably less than prescribed by the effectiveness normatives. However the opening-up of vast areas in which, thanks to BAM, . . . profitable products will be obtained will make it possible to recoup all outlays on BAM's construction with money to spare."

Tarasov showed no confidence in existing procedures and institutions, instead calling for "an all-Union specific program" focused on the social and economic development of the Far East. He claimed that, despite the plan compiled by the State Planning Committee's Council for the Study of Productive Forces for the development of major national economic complexes up to 1990, "the detailed working up of specific questions is not always adequate to implement specific plans." The methods used by design institutes to recoup capital investment by periods were inadequate, and "special research to determine effective systems for settlement" was needed. He implied that without such steps the controversial concept of territorial production complexes would fail to remedy the situation.

Although Tarasov's analysis was directed specifically at the Far East planning region, it applies equally well to all of East Asian Siberia. Moscow's apparent inability to resolve these long-standing problems by reorganizing at the center and allocating greater authority to regional and local levels cautions against any expectation of drastic change in the planning and implementation of programs. The leadership's reluctance to increase the area's share of capital investment, which has remained roughly the same in recent years, and the slowdown in overall economic growth and state revenue are further obstacles to drastic improvement. Before BAM was begun, the portion of total Soviet capital investment that went to all of Siberia was 15.2 percent in 1966–70, and it increased only from 15.7 to 16.1 percent during 1971–74.[168] If West Siberia were subtracted, the EAS share would be sharply reduced.

These considerations increase the importance of external factors in two ways. First, Moscow may be unable or unwilling to allocate sufficient investment to insure the maximum exploitation of the region's resources. If so, foreign capital might provide the necessary supplement. Second, internal demand may be insufficient to absorb the optimum output. If so, foreign markets might take up the balance. At a minimum, these markets will be necessary to pay for capital and technology through compensatory deals that offer resources and products instead of hard currency, which is likely to remain in short supply for the USSR.

This closes the circle, bringing together the question of external versus domestic goals in Siberian development. The problem of differing priorities remains, but the choice is between overlapping rather than mutually exclusive programs. We know too little of present decision-making processes in the Soviet Union, much less those that may obtain over the next decade, to forecast what will determine the outcome, although further consideration will be given to this problem in Chapter 6. We also will examine external factors as they exist in each of the three concerned countries, Japan, China, and the United States. At this point we only need to recognize the variable as opposed to the fixed factors in the internal setting, and to indicate the prospects for development or exploitation that ultimately must depend upon decisions in Moscow and their implementation in the EAS region.

3 The International Setting: Triangle of Tension

The Historical Heritage

It is impossible to understand the dynamics of international relations in East Asia without reference to the past century of interaction among the three major states—China, Japan, and the Soviet Union, plus their predecessor regimes.[1] The record is indelibly, if differentially, written into the memory of present-day elites and their maturing successors both as first-hand experience and as knowledge acquired through nationally oriented histories, textbooks, and mass media. This mental framework predisposes policymakers to certain attitudes. It also influences their expectations of what to prepare for or defend against in the behavior of other states.

At the very least, the past is prologue to a continuous drama of which the present decade is only an intermediate act. Whether the past determines the present depends upon the degree to which preconceptions condition behavior. The "self-fulfilling prophecy" that arouses hostility by assuming malevolent intent in the other party is a familiar pattern of human interaction. Governments are no less prone to this pitfall than are individuals, as is clear from such phenomena as arms races and the spirals of escalating tension that come from mutual misperception.

But, as prologue or precedent, the past hundred years in East

Asia have produced such a seedbed of potential conflict that the prospects for economic cooperation would seem slim indeed if assessed solely from the historical perspective. Beginning in the mid-nineteenth century, the three major nations engaged in a triangle of shifting adversary and alliance relations, the kaleidoscopic record of which deserves brief review if we are to appreciate the framework of perceptions within which the present interaction of Moscow, Beijing, and Tokyo takes place.

The Moscow-Tokyo side of the triangle has been dominated by conflict, although cooperation has occurred from time to time. In 1904–5 Russia and Japan fought over spheres of interest in northeastern China (Manchuria) and Korea. Then from 1909 to 1916 they joined hands in open and secret agreements to exclude others, especially the Americans, from this region. In the space of a half decade the two nations had moved from enemies in combat to virtual allies. However, after the Bolshevik revolution of 1917 Japan sent its armies into Siberia to support anti-Bolshevik forces. The prolonged intervention in Siberia did not end until 1922, and the occupation of northern Sakhalin continued until 1925.

Following their seizure of northeastern China in 1931, local Japanese commanders provoked a series of incidents along the Soviet and Mongolian borders. These actions grew increasingly aggressive until finally, in 1938 and 1939, the Red Army successfully smashed Japanese attacks in full-scale battles. Eventually Tokyo moved to settle the border dispute and concluded a five-year neutrality treaty with Moscow in April 1941, although, unbeknown to the Japanese, Hitler was planning to invade the Soviet Union within two months. As a consequence, the treaty provided valuable insurance to Stalin against the prospect of a two-front war.

The neutrality pact unfortunately proved less reliable for Japan. In April 1945 Moscow informed Tokyo that the agreement would expire at the end of its initial five-year term in 1946. In August the USSR entered the Far East war, the treaty's continued validity notwithstanding. Soviet troops quickly defeated Japanese forces in northeastern China, Korea, southern Sakhalin, and the Kurils. This action climaxed four decades during which Russia and Japan fought two major wars and numerous border clashes of varying size, in addition to having confronted one another in the Russian civil war. In this same period Russia and Japan both cooperated and competed in sharing the spoils of imperialism in China. Although they concluded formal agreements foreswearing any hostile acts, the accords were eventually betrayed by one side or the other as opportunity and advantage permitted.

The Russo-Chinese relationship was no more consistent. However, here cooperation prevailed over conflict. In 1896 the two neighbors were allies in protecting the crumbling Qing empire from Japanese expansionism. Nevertheless, St. Petersburg exploited Beijing's weakness to extract concessions in northeastern China, and after the anti-foreign Boxer riots in 1900, Tsarist forces occupied the entire area. Their hold was broken by the Japanese attack in 1904, but a few years later, as we have noted, Russia and Japan collaborated in the joint exploitation of the region without regard for Chinese claims of sovereignty.

The Bolshevik revolution added a new dimension to Russian policy. In 1919 Moscow renounced its extraterritorial privileges in China, thereby becoming the first country to withdraw foreign troops from concession areas. In the 1920's Moscow provided money, munitions, and advisers to the Kuomintang forces of Sun Yat-sen, who were in South China seeking to overthrow the official government in Beijing with whom the USSR enjoyed official relations, but in 1927 Chiang Kai-shek ousted the Soviet advisers amid charges of a subversive plot to put the Chinese Communists in power. In 1929, when a local Chinese warlord moved against Soviet rights in the Chinese Eastern Railroad, Moscow responded with force, restoring the status quo ante after brief but bloody fighting.

Yet in 1937 it was the Soviet Union that provided the major source of trucks, weapons, planes, and pilots to China when it was reeling under the Japanese onslaught. This assistance continued until Germany attacked the USSR in 1941. Eventually the European and Asian wars coalesced to join the Soviet Union and China with the United States and Great Britain as the "Big Four," but in February 1945 at Yalta Stalin persuaded Roosevelt and Churchill, behind Chiang's back, to grant the USSR the former Tsarist concessions in northeastern China in return for joining the war against Japan.

With the establishment of the People's Republic of China on October 1, 1949, a common Marxist-Leninist ideology promised to cement Sino-Soviet unity once and for all, and the Treaty of Friendship, Alliance, and Mutual Assistance concluded on February 14, 1950, pledged the two states and peoples to unity for at least thirty years. But in 1960 the alliance came under severe strain when mounting political differences prompted the sudden withdrawal of all Soviet economic assistance and advisers. Tensions escalated until in 1969 bloody clashes at widely separated points on the 7,500-kilometer (4,650-mile) border threatened major war. Finally, in 1979 Beijing gave formal notice of the treaty's termination one year before its automatic renewal in the absence of such an act. This act of state recognized the existence of the armed confrontation that was already manifest in the more than two million troops of both sides arrayed throughout the border region.

Sino-Japanese relations provided the most consistent side of the triangle: conflict predominated down to 1945. The Sino-Japanese war of 1894–95 cost China its island holdings of Formosa and the Pescadores, together with its "suzerainty" over Korea. Although Beijing and Tokyo were formal allies in World War I, the Japanese continued their pressure for sweeping concessions in China through secret negotiations whose revelation at the Versailles peace conference in 1919 triggered the first major expression of modern Chinese nationalism in the form of student demonstrations and public appeals, precursor to the May Fourth movement.

Japan's seizure of northeastern China and its establishment there of the puppet state of Manchukuo in 1932 was followed by penetration into Inner Mongolia and northern China. Open invasion in 1937 led to the quick conquest of most of China's main agricultural and industrial regions. By 1940 Tokyo's troops occupied the heavily populated plains and lowlands extending from Beijing in the north to Canton in the south. But Chinese resistance in the hinterland and Japan's enlargement of the war

THE INTERNATIONAL SETTING 69

to include the United States eventually led to Japan's defeat in 1945. This ended five decades of Japanese expansion at China's expense.

The triangular power relationship intermittently involved a fourth country, the United States, but mainly as a political and not a military actor. Not until World War II did American power determine developments in East Asia, and only after 1945 did Washington play a sufficiently constant role to become a regular fourth weight in the regional power balance. Nevertheless, American intervention was sufficiently frequent and influential to be perceived by each of the other countries as potentially inimical to its interests, and unpredictable over the long term. In 1905 President Theodore Roosevelt's mediation of the Russo-Japanese conflict aroused an outcry in Japanese public opinion for allegedly denying a sizeable indemnity believed justified by the costs of victory, although the government was ready to end the war. The American intervention in Siberia, primarily aimed at limiting Japanese activity there, left a legacy of bitterness in the Soviet Union. In 1933 Japanese resentment smoldered over Washington's refusal to accept the puppet Manchukuo regime. Finally, American obstruction of Tokyo's ambitions in China and its march into Southeast Asia in 1941 led to the Pearl Harbor attack. On the other hand, Chinese frustration over Washington's dilatory response to Japanese aggression in 1937–40 was exacerbated by the secret sellout of China's interests at Yalta.

At minimum, the history of international relations in East Asia induces an attitude of distrust in each nation against the others. This can turn into bitter hatred, depending upon how external developments are experienced and reacted to by domestic leaders or how internal situations are manipulated by regimes. This situation is not unique to East Asia, but it deserves attention at the outset as a framework preconditioning the response of national elites and mass publics to their neighbors.

Nothing in this record precludes the possibility of cooperation when interests are mutually seen to be advanced thereby. The 1904 Japanese attack at Port Arthur and the subsequent destruction of the Russian navy in the Far East was followed by nearly a decade of collusion between St. Petersburg and Tokyo.

Since World War II, despite Pearl Harbor and Hiroshima, the Japanese-American alliance has survived thirty years of drastic change in the respective economic and political roles of Tokyo and Washington.

But the heritage of broken agreements, hostile alliances, and military attacks can feed suspicion of intent. This is particularly true for perceptions of threatening coalitions and for the attribution of offensive motives to defensive measures. The professed Sino-Soviet fear of an American-Japanese alliance in 1950 was based less on an objective appraisal of actual military power than on the subjective recall of past Japanese aggression coupled with an exaggerated image of prospective "U.S. imperialism." Similarly, Beijing's alarm over an alleged "anti-China Holy Alliance" and "superpower collusion" in the mid-1960's was misplaced, as was Moscow's concern over a "U.S.–China anti-Soviet front" in the mid-1970's. Setting aside the hyperbolic nature of Communist propaganda, these images nonetheless are rooted in beliefs based on extrapolation from the past as well as evidence from the present.

The Issues and Stakes

It would be wrong to attribute all actions to persistent repetition or to subjective perceptions that in turn reinforce patterns of behavior. Objective circumstances and real issues that have aroused conflict in the past continue to endure in East Asia. Problems of territorial change, competition over spheres of influence, and conflicting concepts of security exist throughout the world, yet they seem to pose a more serious obstacle to regional cooperation within the Moscow-Beijing-Tokyo triangle than is true for nations of comparable political development elsewhere.

One universal cause of conflict is a loss of territory, whether through military defeat or diplomatic bargaining. A change in boundary lines may be short-lived or reasonably permanent, depending upon the balance of power between neighboring regimes. If the balance shifts in favor of the loser, irredentist claims can fuel political or military confrontation. If the balance remains constant, either adaptive acquiescence or repressed resentment can produce radically different attitudes toward the stronger regime, depending on which posture emerges. Alternatively, regimes can adopt either posture as a temporary expedient and later move to mobilize public opinion for internal or external reasons. In this case, the objective facts of territorial transfer or the actual power balance may be disregarded in the rhetoric of nationalistic passion.

Northeast Asia is a patchwork of superimposed and reversed territorial changes, large and small, that have occurred within the last 125 years. The treaties of Aigun (1858) and Beijing (1860) established the Amur River as a boundary between Russia and China, formally separating Far East Siberia from the Qing empire. They also extended Russian rule over the strategically important territory between the Ussuri River and the Sea of Japan, where St. Petersburg established its primary Far East port and naval base, and then added insult to injury by calling it Vladivostok ("Ruler of the East").

These territorial cessions resulted from a sudden assertion of Russian power coinciding with the rapid decline of Beijing's ability to protect the area of its traditional domain. Except for the relatively brief interregnal civil war that dominated eastern Siberia from 1918 to 1922, the subsequent power balance has precluded China from forcibly contesting Russian control. Nevertheless, both Nationalist and Communist textbook maps identify this area as "lost territory," implicitly nurturing anti-Russian resentment. In 1964 Mao Tse-tung explicitly claimed that a future "accounting" might be required of Moscow. After border clashes broke out in 1969, Beijing officially denied any intention of demanding the return of this vast region, but insisted that Moscow acknowledge that it had been acquired through "unequal treaties." Thus, regardless of the realities of past history and the subsequent power balance, more than a century later the territorial changes of 1858–60 became a major polemical issue in Sino-Soviet relations that seriously aggravated feelings on both sides.

The island of Sakhalin has had such a checkered existence that it has been dubbed "East Asia's Alsace-Lorraine." Its modern diplomatic history began somewhat ambiguously in the Treaty of Shimoda (1855), which declared Sakhalin a joint possession of Russia and Japan to be finally disposed of later. In 1875 the Treaty of St. Petersburg formalized an exchange whereby Japan agreed to renounce its claim to Sakhalin and Russia to withdraw its claim to the Kuril Islands. Although Sakhalin's size and its economic and strategic importance outweighed the scattered barren Kurils, which extend from Hokkaido to the Kamchatka Peninsula, the exchange was not made under duress. Nevertheless, Japanese public opinion regarded the agreement as a humiliating defeat.

Japan's victory in 1905 promised to remedy the loss, since Sakhalin had been successfully invaded in the last stage of the war. But the Treaty of Portsmouth (1905) partitioned the island at the 50th parallel and prohibited military fortifications throughout the territory. Riots in Tokyo and other cities protested the half-loaf settlement, which the Japanese government had accepted because continuation of the war would put a heavy strain on the country. The later discovery of oil in the northern half justified the public anger post hoc.

World War II turned the clock back fifty years. As spoils of war, the Yalta agreement promised Stalin southern Sakhalin as part of an overall package described as comprising "former rights of Russia violated by the treacherous attack of Japan in 1904." Actually, Japan's legal sovereignty over this territory, initially established by the Portsmouth treaty, had been reconfirmed in the Soviet-Japanese Convention of Beijing (1925) and the Soviet-Japanese Neutrality Treaty (1941). Nevertheless, Yalta transferred southern Sakhalin to Soviet rule.

The Kuril Islands also passed to Soviet control in 1945, although unlike Sakhalin their ownership had never been determined as the result of war. Instead, the northern and central portions of this extensive island chain had been ceded to Japan after prolonged contention in the negotiations of 1875. The southernmost sector, however, had not been contested then or at any other time, and therefore was indisputably Japanese. History notwithstanding, all three sectors were seized by Soviet forces.

THE INTERNATIONAL SETTING 73

This loss of territory aroused bitter resentment in the context of Moscow's violation of the Neutrality Pact by its attack on Japanese forces in northeastern China. Moreover, this surprise assault came only six days before Emperor Hirohito broadcast his surrender to the Allies in response not only to the Soviet action but more basically to the series of shattering defeats inflicted on the Japanese army and navy, climaxed by the American atomic bomb raids on Hiroshima and Nagasaki. As a final grievance, hundreds of thousands of Japanese prisoners of war suffered for years in Siberian labor camps, where many perished.

Except among extreme nationalists, Sakhalin did not become an issue in Japanese politics. However, the southernmost Kurils, known as "the northern territories," remained so acute a matter of public controversy as to prevent conclusion of a Soviet-Japanese peace treaty. Although some groups still demand return of all the Kurils, Tokyo officially remains firm only on the southernmost islands. Nevertheless, the overall situation contributes to an anti-Soviet feeling that is clearly reflected in public opinion polls and to a persistent media orientation that favors Beijing against Moscow. Irredentism is not a serious pressure, but its indirect effect on Japanese-Soviet relations cannot be ignored.

These larger territorial issues coexist with far smaller points of geographical controversy whose political importance sometimes rivals the more celebrated cases of boundary change. For example, Damansky Island (Zhenbaodao) in the Ussuri River was the scene of bloody clashes between Soviet and Chinese troops in March 1969, despite the fact that it is under water at flood tide and has no strategic or economic value at any time. At issue, however, was the wider question of whether the boundary alignment runs along the west bank of the Ussuri, as contended by Moscow, or through the main channel, as claimed by Beijing. This difference, in turn, affects a host of questions associated with use of the river, such as transport, fishing, and maritime patrol.

Somewhat different circumstances attend the argument over a large uninhabited island at the point where the Amur and Ussuri rivers separate. China claims that the channel lies to the east, which places the island in its territory. The Soviet Union insists that the channel is on the western edge of the island, an understandable position, since the island not only commands a critical transport juncture for the Soviet Far East but also looks out on Khabarovsk, a major industrial city and port.

Perhaps the most miniscule territorial issue of exaggerated political import involves the Senkaku Islands (Diaoyudao). This cluster of uninhabited rocks lying between Taiwan and the Ryukyus is patrolled by the Japanese navy but claimed by Beijing and Taibei as well as Tokyo. Except for possibly providing access to oil in the continental shelf through slant drilling, the Senkakus have no strategic or economic value. Moreover, the oil prospects are wholly unproven. Yet despite Beijing's desire to keep Tokyo favorably inclined toward China and opposed to the Soviet Union, Vice-Premier Deng Xiaoping refused to sign away the claim in concluding the Treaty of Peace and Friendship in 1978. Earlier that year a sizeable flotilla of armed fishing boats had sailed around the islands for a week, bearing signs affirming China's claim. No explanation as to who authorized this demonstration ever appeared, but it seriously embarrassed Prime Minister Fukuda, who had already committed himself to negotiating the treaty.

Territorial disputes are highly variable in their consequences. The controversy over the northern territories did not prevent Soviet-Japanese exploration for Sakhalin offshore oil nor did the Senkaku situation block similar Sino-Japanese cooperation in the Bohai Gulf. However, the 1962 Sino-Indian war illustrates the risk of local incidents triggering more serious fighting. The danger lies in the possibility of such disputes being exploited by governments or inflamed by public opinion so that politics come to govern economics because of the arousal of nationalistic passions.

Competition for spheres of influence and patron-client relationships present less volatile hazards but can fuel controversy and impede cooperation. One such case is Mongolia. This landlocked country offers a potential buffer zone between Russia and China. Its own interests would be enhanced if Mongolia could play one neighbor off against the other in a balance of competitive assistance. Instead, because of its sparse population, it has often been a helpless pawn in the game of big-power politics.

During the Russian civil war, anti-Bolshevik forces aided from abroad used Mongolia as a base. In the 1930's Japanese expansionists tried to penetrate Mongolia politically while they tested its defenses militarily. After World War II, Stalin utilized Soviet domination there to attempt the separation of Inner Mongolia from Chinese rule. In the 1950's Mao wanted to reimpose Chinese control over Mongolia, but Khrushchev refused. Finally, in the 1960's Moscow concluded a formal defense treaty with Ulan Bator and moved armored and missile divisions into Mongolia for possible use against China.

In similar fashion, Korea became the subject of Russo-Japanese rivalry at the end of the nineteenth century, slowly slipping out of the sphere of Chinese "suzerainty." Its complete colonization by Japan lasted from 1910 to 1945, but its liberation after World War II did not end the contest of outside powers for control of the peninsula. Its demarcation at the 38th parallel, initially to define zones of occupation by the Soviet and American armies, led to permanent division. The Korean War of 1950–53 further froze the situation, inter alia bringing Chinese and American armies into prolonged conflict for the first time in history. Although North and South Korea enjoy full formal independence, their respective security is ultimately dependent on their separate relations with the major powers. The problem of Korean unification therefore is linked to the larger regional and international relationships. As a further complication, North Korea is also the subject of competition for influence between Beijing and Moscow.

Historically, northeastern China (formerly known in the West as Manchuria) and northwestern China (Xinjiang) were cockpits of conflict, directly or indirectly contributing to confrontation among the major powers. At the start of this century, as we have noted, Russia and Japan experienced both confrontation and cooperation in their effort to exploit Manchuria economically and to control it politically. In the 1920's a local warlord managed to preserve some semblance of Chinese authority, but the founding of Manchukuo in 1932 established Japanese rule there until 1945. Then the Yalta agreements facilitated Soviet penetration of this important industrial region despite its return to the formal control of China, at the time an ostensible ally of the Soviet Union.

In Xinjiang local revolts by Turki and Chinese Moslems in the mid-nineteenth century invited Russian and British intervention, with St. Petersburg taking a slice of the westernmost area in return for helping Beijing to suppress the rebels. During the 1930's Xinjiang became a virtual Soviet satellite when the local Chinese warlord permitted Moscow's secret police and its military and economic agents to operate there without permission of the central government. In 1944–45 Soviet subversion of local rebels divided the western portion from Chinese rule as a so-called East Turkestan Republic. The communist victory in 1949 ended this effort at extending Soviet influence. Instead, joint Sino-Soviet stock companies were set up in the area, and the two sides began work on establishing a direct link between them by means of a railroad that would traverse Xinjiang to join up with a new line from Alma-Ata in Soviet Central Asia. But a cooling of the relationship halted Chinese construction at the capital of Urumchi, far short of the frontier. Then in 1962 the disastrous consequences of Mao's Great Leap Forward triggered a mass exodus of more than 80,000 Uighurs and Kazakhs in search of better economic conditions across the Soviet border. This prompted Beijing to close all Soviet consulates in China and to accuse Moscow of a deliberate effort to separate Xinjiang from the People's Republic.

Above and beyond these specific issues of territorial boundaries, patron-client relations, and spheres of influence, less concrete but larger stakes also arouse contention as a function both of the imbalance of power between and among the three major countries, and of changes, real and perceived, in power relationships. For Moscow as for St. Petersburg, the Far East poses serious security problems. Siberia's population is too small and scattered to defend the area against a threat from China or Japan. Siberia is also remote from European Russia and has logistical and communications lines that are too weak to allow easy or quick reinforcement. The Trans-Siberian Railroad is overburdened and vulnerable to interdiction, especially along the last stretch from Khabarovsk to Vladivostok, where it runs within 15 kilometers (10 miles) of the Chinese border for much of the way. The absence of a warm-water port places critical reliance on Vladivostok, whose access to the Pacific Ocean is not only impeded by ice three to four months of the year but can also be thwarted in the various straits that surround the adjacent Sea of Japan. Last but not least, the long sea runs from Leningrad and the Black Sea to the Far East pose problems of time and risk, as was dramatically demonstrated in 1905.

These conditions have proven remarkably unsusceptible to change, despite the transformation of Tsarist Russia into a Soviet superpower and the intervening technological revolutions of this century. The reality of a Japanese threat from 1904 to 1945 has been replaced by the perception of a Chinese threat since 1965. The growth of Soviet naval power and the strengthening of Siberia's civilian and military infrastructure has been accompanied by the steadily growing capability of a virulently hostile China with one billion inhabitants. Among officials responsible for defense of the USSR, past preoccupations understandably persist into the present.

But protecting security for one country may be seen as creating insecurity for another. Unfortunately there is often no absolute difference between defensive and offensive preparations. Moreover, the watchword for military analysts is a potential enemy's capability, not his intent, and increases in Russian power inevitably arouse concern in China and Japan. Tokyo's insular position has never been seriously threatened by Russian invasion. However, Japan's imperialistic mainland position, whether comprised of political influence in Korea or economic interest in Manchuria, stood to suffer if Tsarist power expanded unchecked. The Great Power game in China was as real and tangible a stake for Japan in 1895–1919 as was its subsequent industrial and colonization program in Manchuria in 1931–45. From this perspective, the concept of security can embrace wider concerns than simply safeguarding territorial integrity against invasion, as can be seen today in Japan's dependence on lengthy sea routes that are vulnerable to hostile interdiction unless adequately protected by American power.

For China the basic problem of insuring the country against attack has been of primary importance from the Opium War of 1839–42 down to recent years. Somewhat less urgent was the problem of foreign economic and political penetration protected by nineteenth-century concessions that had often been wrested from China at gunpoint. Not until World War II were the last vestiges of extraterritoriality, the guarantee that foreigners would not have to stand trial in Chinese courts, abandoned by her allies. Only in 1955, when Moscow returned Port Arthur to Chinese control, did the last foreign military forces finally leave Chinese soil. As recently as 1969 Beijing had reason to fear that the Soviet military buildup in Central Asia, Mongolia, and Siberia foreshadowed either an attack or armed intervention in Chinese politics.

The imperatives of policy confrontation have differed from one nation to another and from one time to another as among economic, military, and political factors, yet as this brief survey suggests, there is considerable continuity. This is particularly striking in the case of Russia and China, despite their common ideological framework after 1949. The persistence of behavioral patterns, issues, and stakes throughout a century of interaction presents some formidable preconditions to international relations in East Asia. Given the opportunity, factions in each nation will define situations in terms of past experience. They will argue against the assumption that other nations can change, and to the extent that policy is so determined, it can have the effect of a self-fulfilling prophecy, inhibiting change in the opposite side.

This calculus of confrontation is not wholly subjective or quixotic. Objective circumstances confront policy elites in Moscow, Beijing, and Tokyo with agendas of problems similar to, if not identical with, those of one or more generations previous. Viewed from China, Tsarist military superiority has been succeeded by Soviet technological dominance. Viewed from the Soviet Union, China's superiority in population continues to threaten Moscow's sense of security. Japan's sudden emergence

THE INTERNATIONAL SETTING 79

as a military power strong enough to defeat China in 1894–95 and Russia in 1904–5 began a march that ended only in 1945; it could be resumed at short notice and so constitutes a concern for both of its neighbors. American policy was an obstacle to mainland China's acquisition of Taiwan down to 1980, although the United States seemed inclined to favor Beijing against Moscow in the 1970's. Intervention in Chinese domestic politics continued while Washington played a balance-of-power game in the region, and policy analysts in Beijing consequently could interpret these moves as characteristic of "U.S. imperialism" in their argument over reliance on Washington in the triangular game of power politics.

We will address the contemporary relevance of these behavior patterns and perceptions more fully in the chapters devoted to each of the countries, since they relate to or may affect the development of East Asian Siberia. At this point we must advance our survey of the international context so as to encompass more recent developments. We will also outline likely alternative futures within which questions emerge to focus our subsequent inquiry.

East Asia in the 1980's

The decade of the 1970's closed with a series of climactic developments that cast the mold for international relations in East Asia for the following decade. In August 1978 China and Japan concluded a Treaty of Peace and Friendship that formalized a new relationship already signaled by Tokyo's granting full diplomatic recognition of Beijing six years previously. In December 1978 Beijing and Washington announced the final agreement on regularizing diplomatic relations that was foreshadowed by President Nixon's historic trip to China in February 1972. Twenty-five years of formal American defense commitment to Taiwan ended on January 1, 1980. Coincidental with these developments was the Soviet-Vietnamese treaty of November 1978, which contained a clause on military consultation and cooperation against threats from third powers. This was followed by Vietnam's invasion of Cambodia, which in turn triggered

China's more limited invasion of Vietnam. Last and least, Beijing announced in April 1979 that it would not renew the 1950 Sino-Soviet treaty of alliance at its specified time of expiration one year later.

The four principal actors—China, Japan, the USSR, and the United States—had basically assumed their respective foreign policy postures over the previous years. However, in each instance these new developments eliminated ambiguities and narrowed the range of uncertainty. Only in the case of Indochina did events unfold with surprising speed and with substantive consequences that could not have been anticipated with confidence a year or two earlier. This added another dimension of tension to Sino-Soviet relations, although it did not change them qualitatively.

The general content of relations in the 1980's is fairly clear. Moscow and Beijing regard each other as potentially deadly enemies but do not anticipate war in the near future. The extension of their rivalry into Indochina's internal conflict between Hanoi and the former Pol Pot regime in Cambodia was made worse by Beijing's short-lived but bloody invasion of Vietnam. China's reported admission of twenty thousand casualties in seventeen days of combat suggests the degree of bitterness engendered on both sides by this war, and its exacerbating effect on Sino-Soviet relations.

In marked contrast, Sino-Japanese relations have never been better in modern history. China's modernization program is heavily dependent on Japanese technology and trade. Beijing also seeks to worsen Tokyo's relations with Moscow by exploiting various points of potential friction and fostering the image of a Beijing-Tokyo-Washington anti-Soviet axis. However, for its part Japan has eschewed any such alignment in the hope of mitigating Soviet hostility. Japan's "tilt" toward China remains a dominant feature of economic policy, but politically Tokyo has avoided taking Beijing's side in its disputes with Moscow and Hanoi. Instead, Japan has sought to balance its primary role in China's economic development with cooperation in the Siberian projects that serve Japan's need for energy resources and for timber, wood products, and fish. The absence of a peace treaty because of the northern territories issue has not been an obstacle so long as cooperation is handled on a businesslike basis by Moscow.

Meanwhile, Soviet concern over Sino-Japanese collusion remained acute, and was further intensified by a suspicion of American encouragement behind the scenes. Having failed to realize a post-Mao reconciliation, Moscow continued its effort to encircle China in South and Southeast Asia. However, in Northeast Asia it can look for little more than a competitive position in Pyongyang and Tokyo. To what extent Soviet policy is prepared to make substantive economic or political concessions to improve its position in Japan remains to be seen. In the past Moscow has miscalculated Japan's need for resources, as with the abortive 1974 proposal to link a pipeline with the construction of BAM while raising the cost and lowering deliveries of oil to Japan; and in 1978 Moscow miscalculated Japan's vulnerability to pressure and failed to frighten Tokyo out of signing a treaty with Beijing that included a clause against "hegemony," Beijing's code word for Moscow. The Soviet record of diplomatic insensitivity and shortsightedness does not augur well for a better relationship.

Beyond these general postures, problematic aspects of the relationships deserve contingency analysis. For example, the border confrontation between Moscow and Beijing has subsided into a stalemate. No significant changes have occurred in their respective military forces over recent years to threaten the existing power balance, and China's seventeen-day invasion of Vietnam did not provoke a Soviet attack, although Beijing reportedly evacuated border towns in Xinjiang to safeguard against this contingency. A qualitative improvement of Soviet forces is matched by an increase in China's retaliatory missile capability, but neither evidence nor logic posits these developments as foreshadowing a deliberate attack by either side.

Whether the Sino-Soviet border conflict will intermittently simmer or be peacefully settled by a negotiated compromise cannot be predicted, but the possibility of settlement outweighs the likelihood of major war. Only small amounts of territory are involved. Except for the island opposite Khabarovsk and a small area in the Pamir mountains, no strategic points are at stake. This is in contrast, for instance, to the Sino-Indian frontier, where a vital road links Xinjiang and Tibet by way of the Aksai Chin plateau, which is claimed by New Delhi but controlled by Beijing. It also differs from the southernmost Kurils, which provide access to the Sea of Okhotsk, a secure haven for Soviet submarines whose missiles are presumably aimed at American targets.

Thus Beijing and Moscow could settle their border differences easily if they both wished. The practical impetus to do so is mutually advantageous. Settlement would reduce the risk of war and thereby permit a drawdown of military forces on both sides. The result would be a far cry from the wholly demilitarized U.S.-Canadian border, but it could still result in an appreciable saving in manpower and military cost, items of economic importance to both countries.

Against these practical considerations stand bureaucratic interests that gain from continued confrontation. Military budgets in Beijing and Moscow profit from the need to guard against the possibility of attack. Political careers may be jeopardized by a move to soften a hard line inherited from the past and mirrored in opposing propaganda postures. Finally, both governments are highly centralized authoritarian regimes whose inertia and inhibitions against dissent limit flexibility. The path to a Sino-Soviet detente is far more rocky and hazardous than the long series of steps that led to Sino-American detente.

Yet the possibility cannot be excluded that in the 1980's some alleviation of the Sino-Soviet dispute may occur. This would stop short of a full rapprochement, much less renewal of the 1950 alliance. Neither side will again link its national security to the other party. Mutual denunciation in world forums is likely to continue, as is competition for influence in third countries. These pressures could be particularly acute in Asia as Moscow and Beijing vie in aligning neighboring capitals on either side of the Sino-Soviet dispute.

But the bilateral confrontation may ease, resulting in expanded economic interaction and reduced military tension. This possibility suggests examining the implications of future Siberian development in a contingency framework that includes not only the existing perceptions of threat on both sides but also the alternative of a border settlement and drawdown of forces. In the latter case, East Asian Siberia may offer mutual benefits for both countries.

Soviet-Japanese relations lack the conflictual potential of Sino-Soviet relations, and therefore they have a narrower range of likely alternative futures. No outstanding issue seems sufficiently serious to provoke a war. An attack on Japan is inconceivable as long as the American defense commitment remains. Even in its absence there is no plausible case for a Soviet seizure of Hokkaido, the most proximate point to the USSR. Yet while war remains unlikely, so does a completely harmonious relationship. Moscow's retention of the northern islands and its burgeoning military presence sharply constrain the Japanese willingness to conclude a treaty of peace and friendship similar to that signed with the People's Republic.

Nevertheless, as we have noted, political differences need not exclude the possibility of economic cooperation, and this cooperation may in time have a positive impact on the political side. This requires a careful assessment of the prospects for and consequences of interdependence between Japan and the USSR in association with Siberian development. Third countries must also be considered. China's opposition or acquiescence can affect Japanese support for Soviet projects. Where large amounts of capital and technology are required, American resources can be the determining factor.

American policy is considered last because the United States has a lesser stake in the consequences of Siberian development than do any of the three contiguous countries. As our historical review suggests, Washington had relatively little involvement with the triangle of tension in Northeast Asia prior to 1941. President Theodore Roosevelt's mediation at Portsmouth did not project American power into the region, as proved by the subsequent inability of American banking interests to secure concessions in Manchuria. President Woodrow Wilson's intervention in Siberia had no lasting effect on the local balance of power, although it may have limited the extent and duration of

Japanese intervention. President Franklin Roosevelt's refusal to recognize Manchukuo angered Japan but did not reverse the situation.

Seen in this perspective, the United States is less encumbered by its heritage than are China and Japan in responding to Siberian development. Moreover, it has no territorial conflicts with any nation that might inhibit or impel policy. But against these two points of potential flexibility stands the overriding confrontation between the United States and the Soviet Union. In the final chapter we will examine to what extent this limits the options of Washington and of its ally, Tokyo. Basically, however, the United States is less central to the developments, present and potential, in Northeast Asia than are the three major powers that have traditionally dominated the area.

4 Siberian Development: The Strategic Implications

Introduction

In conventional usage the term "strategic" usually refers to the potential military capability available for combat. When applied to one's own country, this capability is presumed to be for defense against attack. The strategic capability of other countries, however, is usually assumed to have an offensive role.

The tendency toward unilateral justification of military strength is a natural concomitant of nationalism. It also derives from the difficulty—indeed, the near impossibility—of distinguishing defensive from offensive intent by analyzing the nature of particular weapons. Most weapons can be employed in both capacities, although not necessarily with the same effectiveness. Therefore, prudence as well as politics argues for assuming a potential opponent to be arming for attack. It safeguards against unpleasant surprises while justifying one's own military expenditures.

Unfortunately, this practice can lead to misperceptions and arms competition when the strengthening of defensive forces in one country is seen abroad as posing an offensive threat that necessitates a strengthened defense in response. The response may in turn be viewed with alarm, prompting further military expenditures that set off another mirrorlike reaction. The result is the familiar mutual escalation of armaments.

This phenomenon complicates our inquiry. From Moscow's vantage point East Asian Siberia requires protection against a possible attack by a numerically superior China, now armed with a growing nuclear missile capability. This perceived threat is rooted in the extremely thin and dispersed population of the area compared with that of its immediate neighbor. It is heightened by heavy dependence, of the region in general and the naval base at Vladivostok in particular, on the Trans-Siberian Railroad, which runs within easy reach of the Chinese border. As a final concern, Soviet access to the Pacific Ocean via the Sea of Japan is by way of straits that can be readily blocked by Japanese and American power, joined in alliance since 1951.

Conversely, Soviet military deployments in East Asian Siberia and the northwestern Pacific Ocean tend to be viewed in China and Japan as posing a threat, albeit in somewhat varying degree depending upon the composition of the forces and their location. In this regard, the United States has relatively little interest in Soviet land-based strength except for intercontinental missiles (ICBM), but it must monitor the Soviet Pacific Fleet both as a regional threat to Japan's sea routes as an economic lifeline and for its contribution to the global strategic threat directed at the United States.

Our historical review showed how a triangle of tension has dominated relations in northeastern Asia over most of the past hundred years. This heritage of mutual suspicion, and at times hatred, prompted each nation to strengthen its defensive capacity against the others while viewing their military efforts as offensively motivated, regardless of the role defensive impulses may have played. Sometimes subjective perceptions accorded with objective reality, as when the Soviets and Chinese feared Japanese militaristic expansion in the 1930's. But sometimes misperception prompted moves that triggered conflicts that might otherwise have been avoided, as when the Chinese and American interaction in 1950 led them into battle on the Korean peninsula.[1]

A full analysis of strategic implications must embrace both reality and perception to the extent possible. We will begin by surveying the present disposition of Soviet military forces in the

EAS region. This will provide a base against which we can assess the probable impact of Siberian development on future military capability. Finally, we will touch on how this may be seen from various capitals, leaving a fuller examination of the perceptual phenomena to the subsequent chapters on each country.

The two central questions at issue are, first, what differences will Siberian development make in Moscow's precombat preparations and posture? Second, once hostilities have begun, what differences are discernible in the Soviet capacity for fighting, and how do these vary according to whether the war is short or long, nuclear or conventional, and local or global? Alternative warfighting scenarios and their various mixtures offer a multiplicity of possible developments that cannot be examined in detail here, but some of the more salient aspects of the most important of them deserve at least cursory review within our framework of inquiry.

In addition to military capability, economic factors can also have strategic implications. Where Siberian development requires foreign capital and technology for which repayment is in local resources, either party in the relationship may enjoy a strategic advantage, depending on the circumstances. At the outset, the Soviet ability to exploit such resources will require continuous access to foreign technology until production is under way, and in some instances afterwards. During this time such leverage as may exist will lie with the foreign source of aid. However, once production begins and payback provides a needed resource in the form of export, the foreign consumer may be at the mercy of Moscow, at least in the narrow, immediate sense. Alternatively, Moscow may need foreign markets to recoup its investment in the specific resources, thereby providing leverage to the consumer.

As an example, gas and oil development in East Asian Siberia is likely to remain dependent on foreign cooperation for the remainder of this century, yet delivery of these energy resources to Japan could be of considerable importance to one or both parties. Later we will examine this aspect of the Soviet-Japanese economic interchange from Tokyo's perspective. In this chapter, it will receive brief analysis for its strategic implications.

Soviet Land-based Military Capabilities

It is impossible to pinpoint with precision the exact time and size of Soviet military deployments on the basis of foreign intelligence estimates, which are released selectively through various sources. Nevertheless, such figures provide a guide to the rough order of magnitude and period of changes in Soviet force levels, one that must remain general but that is sufficient for our purpose.

According to CIA estimates, 675,000 to 725,000 military personnel were assigned in 1978 to missions directed against China.[2] This number included army, air force, and missile units. On the ground, 43 divisions, nearly one-fourth of the Red Army, faced the People's Republic.[3] Twenty were deployed near the Sea of Okhotsk, mostly in Maritime Krai; 8 stood along the Trans-Siberian between the Amur's eastern bend and Lake Baikal, for a total of 28 divisions in EAS.[4] Another three were in Mongolia, east of Ulan Bator, with the remainder in the Central Asian republics. Together with 10,000 medium tanks and 75,000 border guards, they offered an impressive array of power, which was compounded by a crescent of nuclear missiles targeted on China. However, the defensive utility of the force far outweighed its offensive potential if one compares it with China's 3.6 million troops.[5]

This massive military confrontation stood in sharp contrast to the "monolithic unity" of the heyday of the Sino-Soviet alliance, a ritualistic formula intoned by both countries during the 1950's. At that time Moscow provided Beijing with a jet air force of thousands of planes, laid the foundations for a coastal navy and submarine fleet, and modernized its army with tanks and artillery.[6] The industrial base for future production also came through Soviet aid. Least publicized but most far-reaching in importance was a brief but relatively generous nuclear assistance program that equipped China's scientists with the essential training and technology to produce atomic weapons.[7]

This cooperation ended in 1960 when Sino-Soviet differences prompted Nikita Khrushchev to withdraw all economic and technical aid. But despite the ensuing polemics, the relationship did not appear threatening to Moscow until 1964, judging from the fact that only fifteen divisions, or 12 percent of the Red Army, stood opposite China.[8] That year, however, two events occurred to arouse Soviet anxiety. In July Mao remarked to a visiting Japanese Socialist Party (JSP) delegation, "A hundred years ago they [the Russians] incorporated the territory to the east of Lake Baikal, including Khabarovsk, Vladivostok, and the Kamchatka Peninsula. Those accounts are difficult to settle, and we have not settled these accounts with them."[9] Mao supported the demand that Moscow return the Kuril Islands, and his statement suggested that he would lay claim to 1.5 million square kilometers (585,000 square miles) of Siberia and Central Asia that the Qing (Manchu) rulers had ceded to Tsarist Russia. Coming after an upsurge in incidents along the 7,500-kilometer (4,650-mile) border—more than 4,000 allegedly occurred in 1963—his words carried ominous implications.[10]

After nearly two months, *Pravda* replied with its editorial "In Connection with Mao Zedong's Talk with a Group of Japanese Socialists":

It could be expected that Beijing would refute this report, but no denial was forthcoming. . . . The Soviet representative in Beijing asked the P.R.C. Deputy Minister of Foreign Affairs Wang Pingnan for an explanation and the latter declared, "If Mao Zedong said that, I agree with him." On August 1, the Japanese newspaper *Asahi* published a statement by Zhou Enlai [which] actually contained the same ideas as Mao's interview. Consequently no doubt was left that the Japanese press was reporting a true statement of the CCP Chairman. . . . He is not only claiming this or that part of Soviet territory, but is portraying his claims as part of some "general territorial question." We are faced with an openly expansionist program with far-reaching pretensions.[11]

The editorial recapitulated various maps published in China after 1949 that purported to show "lost territories" taken by Tsarist Russia, and charged that "Chinese representatives recently began mentioning with increasing frequency hundreds of thousands of square kilometers of Soviet territory which allegedly belong 'by right' to China." It also noted that "the recent issue of the Beijing magazine Lishih Yanjiu (Historical Studies), No. 4, 1964, contends that Russia actually 'captured vast lands to the north of the Amur River and to the east of the Ussuri River and annexed at various times vast territories in Xinjiang and the northwest area.'" Following a full quotation of Mao's remarks, *Pravda* conceded that "the Czarist government carried out a predatory policy, just as the Chinese Emperors carried one out themselves to the extent of their abilities." But after citing various Soviet gestures at reversing Tsarist practices, such as extraterritoriality, the editorial pointedly quoted Lenin: "Vladivostok is far away but this town is ours."

On October 16, 1964, China detonated its first atomic bomb. Shortly thereafter Premier Zhou Enlai flew to Moscow for discussions following Khrushchev's ouster, but no reconciliation resulted. In February 1965 Premier Kosygin visited Beijing for an equally fruitless meeting with Mao. The Chairman remained implacable on all aspects of the dispute.

These developments apparently prompted the decision to bolster Soviet military defenses against China. Between 1965 and 1969 ground forces in Siberia and Central Asia more than doubled, from 15 to nearly 35 divisions.[12] New airfields, including several in Mongolia, and medium-range missiles encircling northeastern China extended Soviet striking power against key populations and industrial centers.[13]

Speaking on the fiftieth anniversary of the October Revolution in November 1967, Soviet Communist Party General Secretary Leonid Brezhnev warned that any attempt at a surprise attack against the USSR, "wherever it may come from—the north or the south, the west or the east—will encounter the all-conquering might of our glorious Armed Forces."[14] His blunt words placed Beijing in a more hostile role than had previously been depicted at an authoritative level.

The paroxysm of xenophobic violence unleashed by the Red Guards at the height of Mao's Cultural Revolution in 1967 gave cause for heightened Soviet concern. Dissension at the highest policy levels and disruption throughout China's urban centers coincided with violent demonstrations in foreign capitals.[15] The British embassy in Beijing was sacked, and bombings in Hong Kong and violence at the nearby border put the colony's fate in serious doubt. With anarchy seeming to threaten China, the

STRATEGIC IMPLICATIONS 91

possible spillover effects on the Sino-Soviet frontier could not be ignored in Moscow.

Finally, in March 1969 the first major armed clash between Soviet and Chinese troops occurred at the island of Damansky (Zhenbao) in the Ussuri River. The preponderance of indirect evidence suggests to most observers that the Chinese side initiated the incident.[16] By Beijing's own account Moscow had previously warned that further encroachments on the disputed island would be met with force. The People's Liberation Army (PLA) prepared for this contingency with concealed deployments that inflicted heavy casualties on the Soviet border troops.[17] Tension increased that spring and summer with a Soviet retaliatory blow at Damansky and further fighting elsewhere, especially on the Xinjiang border. Statements in Moscow focused on China as a direct threat to the USSR.[18]

Beyond the sequence of events that prompted Soviet defensive concerns, additional offensive motivations may have entered into Moscow's calculus by mid-1969. That June Soviet bomber units deployed from East Europe to Central Asian bases and flew mock exercises against targets in northwestern China.[19] Soviet diplomats made low-level probes through their foreign counterparts concerning possible reaction to a "surgical strike" against China's nascent nuclear production facilities.[20] At a minimum, the show of force and threat of war could have been aimed at forcing a border settlement on Soviet terms. At a maximum, Moscow may have seriously contemplated an attack on Beijing's nuclear weapons facilities.

But regardless of whatever offensive goals may have been weighed in 1969, the timing, context, and nature of the previous military buildup seems to have been basically prompted by defensive preoccupations. Moscow's concentration of ground and missile units opposite northeastern China is readily understandable. The Trans-Siberian Railroad provides the only lateral land route around this 2,400-kilometer (1,500-mile) frontier and terminates at the major naval base of Vladivostok. In its final north-south run the line comes within 2.5 kilometers (1.5 miles) of the border at Ebergard, near the Ussuri. Further north, from Dormidontovka to Lesozavodsk, a distance of 280 kilometers

92 STRATEGIC IMPLICATIONS

(174 miles), much of the track lies less than 16 kilometers (10 miles) from Chinese territory.[21] Moreover, the intervening terrain is largely flatland with no natural defense points other than the river itself. By comparison, the much longer east-west run that parallels the border from Khabarovsk to Mogocha is less accessible to ground attack. Its nearest approaches to China, approximately 15 kilometers (9.3 miles), occur at only two points.[22] The remainder is generally twice this distance or further, with the broad Amur River providing a natural barrier.

Interdiction of the Trans-Siberian would cut the one overland supply route to Vladivostok and interrupt the main source of petroleum from West Siberia. The next alternative freight link with the European sector of the USSR is the long sea line to Leningrad and ports on the Black Sea. But this 10,000-mile route transits the Suez Canal and is not reliable in wartime, a factor that compels recourse to the even longer run around the Cape of Good Hope. Under the circumstances, the strengthening of Soviet military defenses in the area, given the events of 1966–68, reflected prudence more than paranoia.

By 1990 East Asian Siberia will be served increasingly by a new sea route through the Arctic Ocean. In 1978 a nuclear-powered icebreaker accompanied a Soviet merchant ship from Murmansk to the Bering Strait extension of the North Pacific in only eighteen days. Soviet sources claim that new nuclear merchant ships will make the Arctic run in 1985, with year-round traffic anticipated later. Until that time, however, overland transport will remain the lifeline for supplies to EAS.

Viewed objectively, the military situation does not pose the nightmare sometimes conjured up by journalistic visions of massive Chinese armies overrunning empty Siberian territory. In contrast to the Soviet side of the border, no lateral railroad traverses northeastern China's frontier region. Instead, eight spur lines terminate at widely separated intervals across this extensive area, in most cases stopping 65 kilometers (40 miles) short of the actual border.[23] The thin road network encounters heavily forested mountains in the northwest and swampy lowlands in the northeast. This inhospitable terrain also inhibits settlement. Although Heilongjiang province has a total popula-

STRATEGIC IMPLICATIONS 93

tion of more than 31 million, the density in most of the frontier area is less than one person per square kilometer (0.39 square mile).[24] By comparison, Soviet territory adjacent to the Amur is much more settled and developed in the lowlands and foothills because of the presence of the Trans-Siberian Railroad.

Yet this objective view is not shared by some sectors of Soviet society, where the crude image of one billion Chinese confronting thinly populated Siberia arouses widespread apprehension. This sinophobia is rooted in historical accounts of the Mongol invasion, which has come to be blended with the perceived Chinese threat into a seamless "yellow peril." Thus, in March 1969, following the clash at Damansky Island, the celebrated poet Yevgenii Yevtushenko exploited this linkage in lurid imagery, referring to "the Chinese God-khan" and more specifically to "Vladimir and Kiev," who "see in the smoking twilight the new Batu khans, bombs rattling in their quivers."[25] His allusion to these classic cases of Mongol pillage struck home. Conversations with Soviet academicians other than China specialists echo the sinophobia encountered more casually in hotel and taxi.[26] A curious exception occurs among residents of Khabarovsk and Vladivostok, which suggests that this fear may increase with distance from China; it is most evident in Moscow.[27]

Whatever the shadings of public opinion, Soviet military planners apparently hold a more rational and relaxed view of the Chinese threat. After the initial bolstering of their capability to defend East Asian Siberia in 1965–69, the pace of deployment slowed. Many divisions are combat ready, but nearly half are at one-third strength or less.[28] More advanced weaponry comes to the area only after its delivery to Warsaw Pact armies. A qualitative upgrading of weapons has improved firepower without significantly expanding the size of local forces, but the overall disposition of strength is more suggestive of precautionary moves than of preparation for actual combat.

Because the military high command in Moscow has long been sensitive to the logistical weaknesses of the Trans-Siberian Railroad, it undoubtedly supported the decision to build BAM as a second route further removed from the Chinese border. Aside from the danger of hostile interdiction, the Trans-Siberian poses

94 STRATEGIC IMPLICATIONS

problems of a more mundane nature. It is vulnerable to flooding, on one occasion requiring a prolonged airlift in order to carry supplies to cut-off areas.[29] In addition, it has had to struggle under the burden of steadily growing freight resulting from an expanding civilian economy, heightened military traffic, and increased use of overland transshipment from the Pacific coast to Europe. This has resulted in a 50 percent expansion in the freight load every five years, making bottlenecks and breakdowns more frequent and more difficult to cope with.[30] We will examine BAM's prospects in the next section, but it deserves mention at this point because its emergence as a major project resulted in part from the Sino-Soviet difficulties of the late 1960's.

Soviet Sea-based Military Capabilities

By comparison with deployments on land, Soviet naval activity in the Pacific is less susceptible to analysis of its implications for northeastern Asia. Because of their mobility, large naval units offer a greater flexibility of mission and deployment than do land-based armies. The same ships can serve various functions as well as move in and out of the area. The analytical problem is exemplified by the fact that the Soviet Pacific Fleet is also responsible for the Indian Ocean. Thus, in 1977 it registered 5,800 ship-days in the Pacific and 6,200 in the Indian Ocean.[31] Multiple missions preclude an accurate calculation of the number of ships of different types that would be available in the West Pacific at any future time.

Vietnam became another responsibility during the American mining and bombing of Hanoi and Haiphong in 1972, when the first major Soviet naval contingent positioned itself in the South China Sea.[32] This activity expanded significantly in 1979 when China invaded Vietnam, and it has continued since. Yet as long as Hanoi does not grant the full use of Cam Ranh Bay as a permanent base, Vladivostok must serve this function.

Finally, and most important, the strategic mission of the Soviet Pacific Fleet is part of the global confrontation with the United States. Defensively, it must protect the homeland against

STRATEGIC IMPLICATIONS 95

TABLE 3
Soviet Pacific Fleet Combat Force Levels
(Percentages are % of total Soviet fleet strength)

Type of vessel	1968		1973		1978		1979
	No.	Pct.	No.	Pct.	No.	Pct.	
Submarines[a]	100	27%	101	30%	113	32%	105
Major surface combatants[b]	58	29	58	27	67	29	78
Minor surface combatants	NA[d]		135	22	113	22	131
Amphibious ships[c]	NA		18	25	18	22	17
Mine warfare craft	NA		NA		110	25	70

SOURCES: The figures for 1968, 1973, and 1978 are from Donald C. Daniel, "The Soviet Navy in the Pacific," *Asia Pacific Commentary*, Summer 1979, p. 69; they reflect a reconciling of data from a wide variety of unclassified American, British, German, and Japanese sources, although the totals for 1978 are almost exclusively from the United States Defense Intelligence Agency, *Unclassified Communist Naval Orders of Battle* (DDB-1200-124-78; Washington, D.C., 1978), pp. 1-4. I have added figures for 1979 as compiled in Research Institute for Peace and Security, *Asian Security 1979* (Tokyo, 1979), p. 52.
[a] Includes ballistic missile, cruise missile, and attack boats.
[b] Includes cruisers, destroyers, and frigates.
[c] Includes medium and tank landing ships only.
[d] Not available.

attack from aircraft carriers and nuclear submarines with ballistic missiles. Offensively, its ballistic missile submarines are targeted against the United States. These strategic units are based in the main ports of Vladivostok, Sovetskaia Gavan, and Petropavlovsk, with ancillary facilities at Nakhodka and Magadan.[33] However, forces earmarked for defensive or offensive strategic engagement with the United States lie outside our focus on East Asia.

It is worth noting the relationship of the Soviet Pacific Fleet to global considerations as viewed from Moscow. This is apparent in the degree to which the general expansion of the Soviet navy is proportionately reflected in an increased Pacific presence. Table 3 illustrates this phenomenon, the percentages indicating the Pacific share of the overall navy. This breakdown shows the relative consistency of smaller allocations to the Pacific Fleet, except for the steady increase in submarines, which strengthens the Soviet strategic capability against targets in the United States. As another indication of its lesser status, the Pacific Fleet is the last to receive more modern equipment. For example it did not receive its first *Kara*-class cruiser until 1979, although these ships had appeared in other fleets in 1972.[34]

The dual mission, global and regional, of the Soviet Pacific Fleet was amply demonstrated in April 1975 during the worldwide Soviet naval exercise Vesna (Okean II). Four task forces ranged widely in the Pacific Ocean. One grouped 400 kilometers (250 miles) east of Shanghai and moved on station south of Taiwan. Another covered the North Pacific. A third was positioned 480 kilometers (300 miles) east of Japan. The fourth remained near the Tsushima Strait.[35] Their varied activities included antisubmarine warfare, amphibious ship exercises, convoying in the Philippine Sea, and sea-lane interdiction east of Japan. This was an impressive display of power compared with what would have been possible a decade previous. It attracted understandable attention and comment, all adverse, in both Beijing and Tokyo, coming as the final collapse of South Vietnam appeared to symbolize the decline of American power in the West Pacific. Yet it was largely geared to missions outside the immediate area under review.

Narrowing the focus to northeastern Asia, an authoritative naval analyst concludes, "As it has always been for the Soviet Pacific Fleet, the primary mission must be to secure the regional waters that wash Soviet Siberia, particularly the Sea of Japan. The numerous small combatants assigned to the Pacific fleet would be good for little else."[36] This cautions against simply juxtaposing ship totals in the Soviet and American fleets to measure their relative combat effectiveness.

One major problem is securing access to the Pacific Ocean. Three potential choke points confront Soviet naval commanders. The southern route via the East China Sea transits the Tsushima Strait between Korea and Japan. The most direct passage to the Pacific passes through the Tsugaru Strait between the Japanese islands of Honshu and Hokkaido. Further north the Soya (La Perouse) Strait between Sakhalin and Hokkaido links the Sea of Japan with the Sea of Okhotsk, from which the Pacific can be reached through the Kuril Islands. The only alternative to these vulnerable points of passage is the very narrow and shallow Strait of Nevelskoi between Sakhalin and the Siberian mainland. From here ships must cross the Sea of Okhotsk, a distance of 1,280 kilometers (800 miles), which is blocked with

STRATEGIC IMPLICATIONS 97

ice for up to six months a year.[37] Considerable time and fuel are additionally required for this route.

Except for the Tsushima Strait, where swift currents impede their use, mines can block movement from the Sea of Japan. Soviet ships could deploy to blue water before a pending crisis erupted into conflict, but they would still need to return to mainland bases for fueling, resupply, and repair. This explains why one-fifth of the fleet consists of minesweepers. Should the choke points be closed, the long route to Vladivostok via the Strait of Nevelskoi could be bypassed in favor of Petropavlovsk, which lies on the Pacific. However, it lacks the facilities of mainland ports, its access is ice-covered from November to April, and it has no rail supply line.[38]

Moscow faces further complications in the need for merchant shipping to supply the Soviet Far East. Enemy submarines could exact a heavy toll along the lengthy route across the Indian Ocean, the East China Sea, and the West Pacific. A revealing statement by Admiral Sergei Gorshkov stressed the limited effectiveness of Allied antisubmarine warfare (ASW) efforts in World War II, warning, "If ASW forces which were so numerous and technically up to date (for that time), possessing a vast superiority, turned out to be capable of only partially limiting the operations of diesel submarines, then what must this superiority be today to counter nuclear-power submarines?"[39]

Any assessment of the actual power of the Soviet Pacific Fleet requires examination of varied combat scenarios, depending on whether the war is limited to East Asia or global in extent and whether it is of short or long duration. This is essential in order to evaluate the American navy's potential role, alternate missions elsewhere, and possible redeployment to the West Pacific. But our brief survey highlights the defensive tasks in northeastern Asia that are an important factor in determining the strength and composition of the Soviet ships in that area.

As for the fleet's ability to support offensive activity, such as an invasion of Japan, the sea power in hand consists of eighteen amphibious ships and two naval regiments totaling 4,000 troops.[40] Shore bombardment would depend largely on air attack, since the growth of missile-equipped ships has reduced the number of gun-carrying ships available for this purpose. However, any action beyond the range of land-based aircraft must come from the single carrier *Minsk* that is presently in the Soviet Pacific Fleet. Its twelve aircraft and twenty helicopters are basically for antisubmarine warfare.[41] All things considered, Hokkaido faces a far less serious threat than one might judge from its relative proximity to Sakhalin.

In the absence of actual hostilities, the Soviet fleet plays an important political role in projecting an image of power that is heightened in Japan by media attention. This traditional use of a navy to "show the flag" is manifest in the recurrent passage of Soviet ships near Tokyo's territorial waters. More than 300 Soviet naval ships traverse the three major straits of Tsushima, Tsugaru, and Soya each year, and an intelligence ship is stationed in the Tsushima Strait most of the time.[42] In June 1978 a Soviet task force of *Kresta-II*-class missile cruisers and destroyers moved from exercises between Okinawa and Guam to take part in an airlift and amphibious ship operation in the southernmost Kurils that involved the disputed islands of Etorofu and Kunashiri. Again in 1980 small flotillas of Soviet ships transited the Tsugaru Strait between Hokkaido and Honshu as part of the buildup of forces in Shikotan and the Habomais.[43]

The heightened visibility of Moscow's fleet contrasts with the reduced profile of Washington's naval presence in the area. The number of ships assigned to the U.S. Seventh Fleet declined precipitously during the decade 1969–79, as the gradual winding down of the Vietnam war led to mothballing or reassignment of vessels elsewhere; in 1969 it had 225 ships; in 1970, 145; in 1971, 95; and in 1978, 50.[44] In simple aggregate numbers, as of 1978 the Soviet Pacific Fleet totaled 550 ships to the U.S. fleet's 50, displaced 762,000 tons to 503,000, and had an average shipage of nine years as compared with fifteen.[45]

The key comparisons depend on whether a war is global or regional. In peacetime, however, public perceptions do not turn on a sophisticated analysis of combat capabilities, missions, and technology. Instead, they tend to rest on a simplistic juxtaposition of aggregate numbers and hypothetical "worst-case" scenarios. This tendency is reinforced by the parochial interest of

STRATEGIC IMPLICATIONS 99

military bureaucracies in enlarging their budgetary allocation by emphasizing another country's apparent strength. Thus, the Japan Defense Agency's White Paper of 1977 declared that the "buildup of the Soviet Navy cannot be simply ignored since it has ramifications for the region. In particular the advance of the Soviet Navy into the open sea has further heightened the relevant countries' concerns for their security, especially Japan which is positioned close to the straits through which the Soviet Navy passes for its access into the oceans." [46] This overstates the case somewhat, as will be evident when we focus on Japanese perceptions in greater detail later. However, it is worth noting as an illustration of some of the strategic implications of Soviet naval activity in peacetime.

Siberian Development: What Difference?

At the outset of this chapter we defined our problem in terms of the difference in military capability that is likely to ensue from Siberian development. In this regard, the best point of departure is BAM, since it is the most strategically important project currently under way.

Russian military performance in the Far East reflects credibly on the capacity of the Trans-Siberian Railroad to meet military needs, at least up to the present. In the 1904–5 war with Japan, although the Tsarist navy met defeat, an army of approximately 250,000 troops fought fiercely enough to force Tokyo into seeking American mediation.[47] At the time this was an impressive logistical achievement since it was accomplished far from European Russia against an enemy so proximately located. Three decades later—in 1938 at Changkufeng (Lake Khasan) on the Manchurian-Soviet border and in 1939 at Nomonhan (Khalkin-Gol) on the Manchurian-Mongolian border—the Red Army inflicted heavy casualties in division-size engagements with local Japanese units.[48] Japanese intelligence claimed that Soviet strength grew from 20 divisions in 1937 to 30 divisions by 1939, or from 370,000 to 570,000 troops.[49] Although the celebrated commander of the Soviet forces, Marshal G. K. Zhukov, acknowledged transportation problems in his memoir, he singled out the Trans-Baikal military district for special commendation.[50]

Perhaps the most remarkable logistical feat was the massive movement of men and material from the European front to East Asian Siberia in order to attack Japan within the three months of the defeat of Nazi Germany, as agreed upon at the Yalta Conference. According to an authoritative Soviet history, in May 1945 a bare 40 divisions equipped with obsolete tanks defended the whole Far East region.[51] By August this force had grown to "eleven field, one tank, three air, and three air-defense armies . . . with over 1,500,000 officers and men, more than 26,000 guns and mortars, and more than 5,500 tanks and self-propelled guns."[52] The feat entailed redeployment over distances ranging from 9,000 to 12,000 kilometers (5,580 to 7,440 miles), as well as interfront and innerfront regroupings of up to 1,500 kilometers (930 miles) between Blagoveschensk and Maritime Krai. The main body of troops actually came from beyond the Soviet frontier in Europe. Altogether some 136,000 railroad cars were involved; during June and July, between 22 and 30 trains per day ran east of Lake Baikal.

The more recent military expansion opposite China pales by comparison in terms of both the much smaller deployment and the longer time involved. Nonetheless, the doubling of armed strength in Central Asia and Siberia from 15 to nearly 35 divisions between 1965 and 1969 proved the system's ability to meet a sudden military demand, although the movement may well have entailed considerable disruption of normal civilian traffic.

This impressive record notwithstanding, Soviet defense officials undoubtedly were acutely aware of the Trans-Siberian's vulnerability to disruption by human and natural causes. According to an authoritative Soviet source, "The idea of building BAM first arose in 1932" after the Japanese seizure of Manchuria.[53] The result was a spur line running north to Komsomolsk from Volochayevka, west of Khabarovsk. When Japanese pressure erupted in full-scale battles along the border in 1938–39, further work progressed on "the alignment . . . between Tynda and Sovetskaia Gavan, [which was] determined in 1938–42." By extending the line east from Komsomolsk to Sovetskaia Gavan and Vanino during World War II, the Soviets provided

STRATEGIC IMPLICATIONS 101

themselves with an alternate route to Vladivostok via the Sea of Japan in case the Trans-Siberian was disrupted below Khabarovsk, where it paralleled the Manchurian border.[54]

After the war, construction on BAM stopped because of the greater priority given to rebuilding the devastated portions of the Soviet Union, but in the 1960's a coincidence of factors revived Moscow's interest in BAM. We have already noted how Chinese statements and behavior heightened the sense of perceived threat, particularly during the Cultural Revolution. In this regard, a Soviet statement to the effect that it was "possible in 1967 to resume design work on the BAM project in light of improved engineering conditions and devices" is highly suggestive.[55] Of course, the completion of reconstruction in the war-torn areas did gradually free more funds for less developed regions, among which Siberia had long held a special attraction for economic planners.

This attraction was strengthened by postwar surveys and studies that had revealed a wide range of natural resources to be available for exploitation if access and technology could become available. The latter factor, in turn, prompted the decision to involve foreign governments and companies in Siberian development as a means of acquiring the capital and the technology necessary for such a costly and difficult venture.

BAM promised to serve both economic and military needs. In 1974 the massive project was officially launched amid nationwide fanfare. In strategic terms BAM offers more than adequate assurance against interdiction by ground attack. Its closest approach to the Chinese border leaves it almost 200 kilometers (125 miles) away. Much of it lies between 250 and 270 kilometers (155 and 170 miles) away, and the remainder is even more distant.[56] Moreover, although the Trans-Siberian frequently parallels the Amur and Ussuri rivers on fairly flat ground, BAM is separated from China by mountainous terrain. Should the Trans-Siberian's north-south line to Vladivostok be cut, BAM could still supply the main naval base through Vanino and Sovetskaia Gavan.

The more likely threat of attack by aircraft or missiles is not so drastically reduced. Allowing for the necessity to site Chinese

102 STRATEGIC IMPLICATIONS

bases well behind the border, the consequent distance of 500 kilometers (310 miles) to BAM offers no decisive advantage for its defense. In addition, the 3,145 kilometers (1,965 miles) of single track between Ust-Kut and Komsomolsk offers numerous potential choke points. Approximately 3,700 bridges and culverts will span bogs and rivers, many of which swell with water from thawing snow and summer rains.[57] More than 140 of the bridges exceed 90 meters (300 feet) in length, and three are 1,365 meters (4,500 feet), 490 meters (1,620 feet), and 412 meters (1,375 feet) long.[58] These offer attractive targets for air attack. Less vulnerable, but more disabling if damaged, are the BAM tunnels, which total 24 kilometers (15 miles), including one of 14.4 kilometers (9 miles) and another of 6.4 kilometers (4 miles).[59]

Most of the line passes over permafrost that is unevenly distributed in location and thickness.[60] Here the track must be elevated on a berm of wood or gravel to a height of two meters or more (six plus feet) to guard against the effects of heat and thaw on surface ground.[61] Bridge pilings frequently must be individually designed for depth and stress to allow for the varied subsoil conditions.[62] These factors complicate the maintenance of BAM in wartime. The situation is worsened by the weak infrastructure of service roads, warehouses, and repair stations that would be needed to speed the restoration of traffic following an attack.

An additional vulnerability lies in the plan to electrify the western portion of BAM so as to exploit the large surplus of cheap hydro power available throughout the region and to minimize pollution. Because of the permafrost, lines and installations will be above ground, which increases both their exposure to attack and the cost of protective shelters. The destruction of power lines and stations would paralyze movement until diesel equipment could arrive or the damage be repaired.

Beyond these specific wartime hazards, a host of natural phenomena make BAM a high risk railroad with uncertain reliability.[63] East of Lake Baikal it traverses one of the most active seismic areas in the USSR. Nearly 30 earthquakes of 6 points or greater on the Richter scale have been recorded in the BAM ser-

STRATEGIC IMPLICATIONS 103

vice area with a periodicity of one every fifteen to twenty years. The effects are worsened by permafrost, which heightens the acceleration of transverse waves by a factor of two or more, resulting in greater ground flow, rock debris movements, liquefaction, and mudflows. The concentration of tunnels in the seismic area poses special problems in their alignment and reinforcement.

Landslides and mudflows occur with particular frequency in the central BAM area. Avalanches pose an additional hazard. Icing is a major problem in hundreds of places along the route, with active zones ranging from one thousand to over a million cubic meters. Cumulatively, these phenomena pose a threat of interrupted service that could cut freight shipments for weeks at a time, depending upon the origin, severity, location, and timing of the event.

North-south links between BAM and the Trans-Siberian provide alternate routes to bypass afflicted portions, but these are few in number and widely separated. As already noted, service roads and storage points for emergency equipment will be inadequate for many years because of the slowness in developing ancillary facilities, especially in the most hazard-prone sections. Soviet engineers and planners are fully apprised of these problems and have made every effort to anticipate them. Nevertheless, the supply of human, fiscal, and technological resources is extremely limited by comparison with the magnitude of the task.

Taking these various factors into consideration, BAM would appear to have more military value in a precombat situation than in an actual war. It provides a major logistical supplement to the Trans-Siberian for strengthening Soviet forces throughout the area, and facilitates the stockpiling of supplies, including ammunition and petroleum, to sustain prolonged fighting on land and sea. It also provides access to additional territory for the stationing and dispersal of military personnel and installations.

These advantages enhance Moscow's ability to prepare for war in East Asia. Once war begins, however, BAM's liabilities may outweigh its assets. Much depends on the specific circumstances, of course. It can make a considerable difference wheth-

104 STRATEGIC IMPLICATIONS

er the war is of short or long duration, whether it is fought with conventional or nuclear weapons, and whether the enemy can target with sufficient accuracy and damage to keep BAM inoperative. Regardless of the scenario, the reliability and vulnerability of BAM under conditions of modern warfare remain open to question.

It may be this uncertain prospect that prompted a high Soviet official to remark privately, "Don't overstate BAM's military importance. In the next war, it won't be a question of moving lots of troops over long distances. In the first hours, missiles will be flying and many people will be killed—on both sides."[64] It is impossible to know the degree to which this view is shared by military strategists. A major portion of the labor for BAM's construction was provided by railroad engineering divisions from the Soviet army.[65] It is doubtful that so costly a project, consuming nearly one percent of the annual USSR investment budget, could be undertaken against military opposition.[66]

Yet BAM does not receive the priority in funding of a project that is primarily seen as having strategic importance. Four years after its start, the State Planning Committee had cut the 1978 financing 30.6 million rubles below the previous annual expenditure, and 1979 was still lower.[67] Reporting this, *Pravda* remarked, "Evidently the Ministry of Railroads and Ministry of Transport Construction have still not argued for an intensive work program." The goal of completion by 1983 seems unlikely to be achieved. Soviet officials informally suggest 1985 as the earliest year to begin test runs over the entire line, and perhaps another two years will be needed before BAM can be fully operational.[68] This stretched-out schedule implies more than a decade of investment before the returns can begin to be realized. It also implies that Soviet strategists have realistically assessed BAM's limitations, and that they do not envisage the line as improving their Far East capability sufficiently to justify a more accelerated effort.

Whether a similar perception will prevail in Beijing once BAM is completed remains to be seen. Beijing's propaganda, always ready to exploit evidence of a Soviet threat to Japan as well as China, has paid relatively little attention to BAM. A rare refer-

STRATEGIC IMPLICATIONS 105

ence in early 1978 reviewed the overall effort to develop Siberia east of the Urals, including "construction of the Baikal-Amur Railway," but placed major emphasis on the line's strategic implications for NATO. The commentary claimed the Kremlin's design is to "make the east the rear of its western front" and "to support its major contention in Europe."[69] Japanese firms engaged in engineering projects on BAM experienced no Chinese pressures to desist, and one of the largest companies subsequently won a major contract in the PRC.[70]

For its part, Tokyo shows no sign of giving BAM the strategic significance that was attributed to the Trans-Siberian Railroad at the end of the last century. Although the competition between Russia and Japan for spheres of influence in Korea and Manchuria was the basic cause of conflict in 1904–5, the war's timing was in large part determined by apprehension that completion of the transcontinental line would permit St. Petersburg to strengthen its military power in the Far East.

No such worries appear to concern officials today.[71] On the contrary, BAM is viewed as advantageous for the exploitation of Siberian resources, particularly timber and coal, to meet Japan's needs. Japanese Export-Import Bank loans are not involved, but the close consultation that takes place in Japan between business and government on such matters makes it likely that official approval underlies the involvement of Japanese firms in BAM's construction. This would not be the case were the railroad seen as significantly increasing the Soviet threat.

In sum, the strategic implications of BAM vary considerably, depending upon whether it is assessed in a precombat or combat context and whether the point of assessment is Moscow, Beijing, or Tokyo. BAM clearly enhances the Soviet ability to strengthen and supply forces in East Asian Siberia and the West Pacific. It also offers defense in depth against a ground invasion that might interdict the Trans-Siberian Railroad. But to what extent these attributes heighten or lessen the likelihood of tension and conflict will depend on specific situations.

For example, if Soviet military planners are more relaxed about the consequences of incidents, escalation, or surprise attack cutting the Trans-Siberian because of BAM's fallback capacity, they might be less likely to unleash a preemptive attack in a Sino-Soviet crisis. If, on the other hand, Chinese military planners anticipate another major expansion of Soviet forces as a consequence of BAM's completion, they might press more vigorously for countervailing measures that would accelerate a local arms race.

On balance, BAM's strategic implications for East Asia are worth noting, but without exaggeration or undue emphasis. By comparison, of much greater interest to Japan and the United States is the effect of Siberian development on Moscow's maritime presence in the Pacific. The most relevant project is the new port of Wrangel. Located across the bay from Nakhodka, by 1990 Wrangel will be able to handle 40 million tons of cargo a year.[72] This will make it possible for many more Soviet merchant vessels to serve the area. Together with BAM, the ships can appreciably augment the logistical flow to meet military needs.

In addition, these ships can perform multiple tasks of intelligence collection and can accomplish the clandestine transport of weaponry.[73] During a conflict, their preplanned conversion to military support roles will offer a valuable auxiliary fleet for the Soviet navy. Wrangel can also relieve congestion at military bases for refueling and repair, depending on the nature of hostilities in the area.

Beyond the direct contributions to military capability offered by BAM and Wrangel, indirect contributions can emerge through the expanding economic infrastructure that will be a consequence of Siberian development. This could result in an enlarged population base and skilled labor force, an improved transportation network, a modern metallurgical industry, and the general upgrading of locally manufactured products. None of these factors are of significance in themselves, but taken together they contribute to the efficiency and effectiveness of a fighting force that is held in place against a distant future contingency. Besides reducing dependence on remote sources for supplies and spare parts, the general development of the region can eventually change the human environment within which the armed services, particularly the army, function.

But this will be slow in coming. The constraints on growth are

STRATEGIC IMPLICATIONS 107

severe and will remain so. The BAM zone produces only one-third of its present food requirement.[74] The severity and vagaries of local climatic conditions, the effects of permafrost, and the scarcity of arable land combine to prevent the region from becoming self-sufficient in agriculture. As a result, long-distance hauling from more fruitful areas of the USSR raises prices and reduces variety. The cost of living is further increased by the greater expenditure for construction, maintenance, heating, and clothing necessitated by the harsh environment.

These circumstances inhibit migration into the BAM zone. They also induce planners to cluster support services such as hospitals, schools, cultural activity, and entertainment in existing population centers. Yet the continued growth of a few very large cities could pose a risk in wartime. Enemy missiles need only hit Vladivostok, Khabarovsk, and Irkutsk to endanger roughly 15 percent of the population and a much larger proportion of the industry of East Asian Siberia. All three targets lie within easy range of possible launching sites in northeastern China.

The effect on Soviet strategic thinking is problematic. The vulnerability of these nodal points in the region's economy places a premium on preempting a perceived threat of attack. However, in time defensive concerns should be alleviated to the extent that population and industry can be more widely distributed, as is envisaged for the next decade. Soviet economic analysis suggests that cities of approximately 100,000 persons are optimal for this region, being large enough to justify the necessary services without requiring an excessive network of transportation, supply lines, and sewage disposal facilities.[75] In addition to reducing the problem of defense, the proliferation of new cities would improve the support environment for military units scattered throughout the area.

Economic development will also improve the transportation system throughout the region. This should enhance military logistics in terms of mobility and reliability. In addition to BAM's lateral route, its possible northward extension to Yakutsk will open up previously inaccessible areas for the exploitation of local resources. Maintenance will improve as the necessary manpower and equipment become available. River use may increase with more icebreakers and dredging.

A modern metallurgical industry would also be helpful from a military point of view. The only existing steel works, at Komsomolsk, are inadequate for more than local requirements of low alloy steel.[76] Large deposits of iron ore located near good coking coal offer an attractive base for further development in southern Yakutia, and it seems likely that a major metallurgical base will eventually be built in the region to meet the growing local need and to exploit local resources. This will enhance self-sufficiency, but it may not make it complete. Moreover, all of the prospective sites lie within range of potential Chinese missiles. Reliance on a single point of production could invite a crippling attack. As in other areas, a precombat increase in capability may be offset by wartime vulnerability.

Viewed overall, Siberian development offers only a limited increase in Soviet strategic military capability beyond that already in existence in the area. Its greatest contribution is in its strengthening of the region's logistical and support capacity before hostilities begin. Once a war starts, however, the defensive liabilities appear to outweigh the offensive advantages.

Economic Leverage and Strategic Implications

The exercise of economic leverage on an importing country is a familiar phenomenon in East Asia. Prior to World War II, the United States embargoed the export of strategic goods to Japan—first scrap iron and then oil—to dissuade Tokyo from further aggression. Beginning in 1950 Washington imposed a total embargo on American trade with the People's Republic of China and a strategic embargo on selected items traded by its allies with Beijing. Although the total embargo was lifted at the time of President Nixon's trip to China in 1972, the strategic embargo persisted well after the "normalization" of relations in 1979 in the form of controls exercised by NATO and Japan.

Siberian development offers Japanese access to energy resources—coal, gas, and oil—as well as such less essential items as timber, asbestos, and copper, which play an important role in the economy. To what extent might Japanese dependency on the Soviet Union for such commodities present a risk in terms of Moscow's ability to manipulate supply for political purposes in peacetime or for military ends in war? As a rule of thumb, Japanese officials indicate a willingness to rely on Soviet supplies for up to a fifth or so of their import total of particular items, but not to go much beyond this limit.[77] Thus, in 1977 the Soviet Union supplied 23.9 percent of Japan's imported asbestos and roughly 20 percent of its imported nickel.[78]

According to one official estimate, if the Yakutia natural gas project comes to fruition, the USSR could supply nearly 20 percent of Japan's total LNG consumption by 1990.[79] However, it is calculated that LNG will contribute less than 10 percent of the overall energy need.[80] Therefore, the potential Soviet leverage, although it may be pinpointed on certain sectors of the economy, will be minimal for the country as a whole.

South Yakutian coking coal is anticipated to meet from 7 to 10 percent of Japanese consumption by 1985–90. With 40 percent coming from Australia, 25 percent from the United States, and 15 percent from Canada, the Soviet potential for leverage will be relatively small. Steam coal will account for only 4 percent of the total energy requirement in 1990, thereby permitting a somewhat greater increase of such imports from the Soviet Union. Sakhalin oil will amount to only 1 percent of total petroleum imports, a wholly expendable amount that can be supplied elsewhere.

The combined impact of all four commodities being cut off by Moscow would cause short-term dislocation in selected areas and industries. However, there would be no long-term impact, assuming that other suppliers could increase their deliveries. Japan's various trading partners in the Pacific Basin appear more than capable of filling gaps that might arise from a Soviet embargo on energy exports, although a brief interval might be necessary to increase production and reorient transportation. This fact is so obvious that it presumably would deter Moscow from any such threat, much less action.

Timber is a less critical item, but it looms somewhat larger statistically, 28.4 percent of Japan's 1977 imports coming from the

USSR compared with 63.7 percent from the United States.[81] Moreover, the higher grade softwoods are North American while their hardwood counterparts originate in Southeast Asia. As with other items, the Soviet supply is useful, but not essential to the economy.

Conversely, the degree to which any such embargo or attempted leverage would hurt the Soviet economy varies from one commodity to another and from one point in time to another. Where the export is in repayment for already acquired capital and technology, Moscow has the advantage, but where it earns foreign exchange needed to pay other bills, for instance, for grain imports, the embargo would inflict a cost on the Soviet economy. In the case of natural gas, Japan will provide the only foreign market other than the United States. There is not likely to be sufficient domestic demand to take up the slack in distribution of output. This in turn would reduce the return on Moscow's original investment. These calculations reveal the symbiosis that characterizes the relationship of the two countries to Siberia's development.

Soviet involvement in the world economy would raise risks on other fronts if Moscow were to apply economic pressure against Tokyo. Reneging on energy exports as payment for acquired technology in Sakhalin and Yakutia would jeopardize the Soviet ability to acquire oil and gas equipment elsewhere. This could paralyze its effort to exploit offshore oil, a vital need in the 1990's.[82] In addition, Washington could support Tokyo with a retaliatory embargo against grain sales to Moscow. Depending upon the availability of alternative supplies, this could hurt, given the chronic vulnerability of Soviet agriculture to bad climate and its continuing inability to raise output.[83] In short, the backlash from singling out Japan for economic leverage could be severely damaging.

Economics aside, it is difficult to define a plausible situation in which Moscow might be tempted to apply such pressure. It would be wholly inadequate for a major goal such as forcing Tokyo to renounce the American alliance or to exclude American bases. It would probably boomerang as an effort to reduce Japanese defense expenditures or to brake a growing Beijing-

Tokyo entente. It certainly would not silence public opinion on such issues as the northern territories and fishing incidents, and once such leverage was attempted, no further Japanese cooperation in Siberian development would be likely. This would leave much of the program without hope of realization in this century.

This does not exhaust the examination of the strategic implications for East Asia that may flow from EAS development. In this chapter we have focused primarily on likely military and economic consequences, not on Soviet behavior and the factors that may affect it. To gain a fuller appreciation of alternative future prospects, we must examine in more detail the specific national relationships and perspectives that both affect and are affected by Soviet strategy in the region, i.e., those involving Japan and China. Decision making in Moscow must be forecast in terms of alternative assumptions that posit, on the one hand, future foreign participation in the development of East Asian Siberia and, on the other, a basically unilateral Soviet program. The availability or lack of EAS resources must be weighed in the context of the larger Soviet economy and of global resources in order to evaluate their full strategic significance.

In general terms, East Asian Siberia is likely to be more of a defensive liability than an offensive asset for Moscow during the balance of the twentieth century. It will remain remote from the center of Soviet power. Its logistical vulnerability and environmental constraints will combine to leave the area relatively weak and undeveloped compared with China, a hostile and unpredictable neighbor. Nothing in the anticipated development of EAS will overcome these deficiencies, although some problems may be ameliorated.

5 The Japan Connection

The Critical Variable

Japan must weigh heavily in Moscow's decisions on the development of East Asian Siberia. Japanese capital and technology are essential to attaining the desired goals of resource extraction and economic expansion. Japan also offers the only market of significance for exports like timber, coal, and gas. Without that market the products of EAS have little chance of earning foreign exchange to serve the overall Soviet economy. Japan thus occupies a central position in Moscow's calculations, in inputs as well as outputs.

Japan is also important for American policy in the area. As the major U.S. ally in East Asia, Tokyo has a claim on Washington's deliberations concerning its interests. But beyond the basic responsibility owed an ally, the view from Japan deserves attention on its own merit. It is not encumbered by such emotional and propagandistic biases as those China derives from the Sino-Soviet dispute. This permits the Japanese greater objectivity in their assessments of Soviet intentions. Soviet capabilities and behavior are also better assessed in the light of practical Japanese experience over the past decade. On this point, one Soviet official privately admitted that the best research and data for the Yakutia natural gas project is to be found in Tokyo, not Moscow.

THE JAPAN CONNECTION 113

As a final factor, Washington's interest in EAS development is secondary and distant whereas Tokyo's is primary and immediate. On the positive side, Siberian gas, and possibly oil, can lessen dependency on the Middle East. The supply of coal, timber, copper and other nonferrous metals is less critical, given alternate sources that are more accessible and reliable. Nevertheless, proximity becomes an increasingly important consideration, especially for bulk commodities, as higher transport costs are generated by rising fuel prices.

On the negative side, Tokyo is sensitive to any strengthening of Moscow's military power in the region. We have seen how nearly half a century of intermittent conflict provides an uneasy background for Soviet-Japanese relations. This is accentuated by the "northern territories" dispute and the recurring intrusion of Soviet military planes and ships in and around Japanese air and sea space. Meanwhile, future uncertainty attends the growing Soviet naval presence in the West Pacific and its import for Japan's economic lifeline to the world. These issues will, for the most part, evolve independently of Siberian development, but the implications for them of Japanese involvement in EAS require assessment, as does their impact on Japanese attitudes toward such involvement.

What may be peripheral or equivocal for U.S. interests can be central and compelling for Japan, whether in calculating potential gain or potential risk. This argues for examining Japanese views and interests as a prior condition for U.S. policy toward East Asian Siberia. These views vary widely over time and among different sectors of society. They also are subject to change, depending on the larger context of Japanese relations with China as well as with the Soviet Union. However, they provide the essential framework within which Tokyo's policy of limited participation in Siberian development has evolved to date.

Images of the Soviet Union: How Threatening?

It is commonplace to summarize Japanese images of the Soviet Union as negative. This statement, though it is correct, does not define the relevance of negative images for policy. Neither

114 THE JAPAN CONNECTION

does it reveal the strength of these images, their determinants, and their susceptibility to change. Last but not least, it does not differentiate images found in public opinion polls, in the mainstream of mass media, and among policy elites in business and government.

We will address these various dimensions of imagery for their relevance to the presence or lack of constraints on Japanese cooperation in EAS projects. Causal linkages between media imagery and public opinion or between public opinion and government policy are difficult to prove, and we will not make the attempt. It is useful, however, to explore the similarities and differences that are subsumed under the rubrics "Japan" and "the Japanese" in describing attitudes that are presumed to filter through the political system and thereby affect foreign policy. Especially important for our purpose is the degree of specific threat read into Soviet behavior, and any recent shifts or trends in such perceptions, at least to the extent that they can be established.

Japan abounds in polls. In one twelve-month period some 75 national surveys were available to policymakers, 29 of them sponsored by government agencies and 27 by newspapers.[1] Unfortunately, they often lack consistency in wording both among simultaneous surveys and over time in individual polls. They nonetheless offer an adequate basis for tracing continuity and change in general attitude and images concerning the Soviet Union.

Despite the historical record of conflict and the consequent sense of hostility and distrust toward the Soviet Union, Japanese opinion has exhibited significant shifts in the last two decades. A *Jiji* press survey made in 1962, for instance, showed that the Soviet Union was "disliked" by nearly half of the respondents; ten years later this group had shrunk to less than one-fourth.[2] Subsequent developments reversed public opinion once more, so that in August 1979 the annual poll by the Prime Minister's secretariat revealed more than three-fourths of the respondents to have "no friendly feelings" toward the USSR.[3]

These wide swings in attitude suggest that communism per se plays little if any role in shaping Japanese views. This is corroborated by the fact that "dislike" of China in the *Jiji* surveys ranged from 40 percent during the high point of Cultural Revolution violence in 1967–68 to only 8 percent following Prime Minister Tanaka's visit to Beijing in 1972.[4] Moreover, although 77 percent professed "no friendly feelings" toward the USSR in 1979, 71 percent felt "friendly" toward China, an impressive jump over the already favorable 62 percent of one year earlier.[5] The leap in Beijing's popularity reflected expectations of greatly increased trade, together with the highly publicized "China fever" attending Vice-Premier Deng Xiaoping's visit in October 1978 to celebrate the conclusion of the Sino-Japanese Treaty of Peace and Friendship.[6]

These simple popularity contests only provide a starting point of analysis. They measure surface attitudes that may be acted upon by governments, national or foreign, through word and deed. More significant, however, is the perception of threat. Here public opinion is surprisingly relaxed when placed against the past history of Soviet-Japanese interaction and the present disparity of power between the two neighboring countries. For example, in August 1979 only 17 percent of those who saw the relationship as "not good" explained this in terms of Soviet military strength posing a threat to Japan.[7] This was a particularly revealing response, coming as it did after a flurry of attention earlier that year to a new Soviet military buildup on the disputed northern islands.

The low public perception of a Soviet threat corresponds with general attitudes on the question of security needs and national defense. Polls taken in December 1978 and March 1980 showed a consistent 58 percent majority for maintaining Japan's Self-Defense Forces (SDF) at existing levels, despite intervening developments on the northern islands and in Afghanistan.[8] These events more visibly affected the minority percentage in favor of increasing the defense budget, which moved from 14 to 25 percent during this period, with a corresponding diminution of the "don't know" respondents.

Media images are less easily and precisely measured. However, an informed Japan Defense Agency (JDA) official noted that by 1978–79 it was no longer difficult to persuade newspapers to publish photographs and stories concerning Soviet air and ship violations of Japan's territorial sovereignty. In fact, he remarked jokingly, the press sometimes provided better photos than did the government.[9]

The increased press attention to Soviet military developments is partly in response to perceived changes in the superpower balance in the West Pacific. In March 1979 *Yomiuri* devoted a full page to a forthcoming visit by JDA Director Yamashita to Washington under the headline "To Search for Response to Soviet Far East Forces."[10] Predictions of the *Minsk* aircraft carrier and the Backfire bomber being deployed in the area in the near future prompted detailed analysis of the added capability this would provide. *Yomiuri* quoted unnamed JDA sources as fearing that "it [Backfire] may impede the U.S. aircraft carrier groups' advance into areas around Japan." The writer included a statistical comparison of the American and Soviet naval forces in the Far East based on JDA estimates showing purported Soviet superiority in all categories except naval aircraft.

Another stimulus to heightened press attention to Soviet power in 1979 was provided by Moscow's military buildup on Kunashiri and Etorofu, two of the islands comprising the "northern territories" held by the USSR since 1945 but claimed by Japan. First detected in May 1978, the initial activity was variously interpreted by defense analysts as a landing exercise or alternatively as the deployment of material and manpower for permanent assignments.[11] No official information was released at that time, however. When *Sankei Shimbun* featured the story that September, government officials refused to comment. They apparently feared that the imminent arrival of Vice-Premier Deng would provoke sufficient resentment in Moscow without inviting a still greater reaction by sensational media coverage of military moves in the "northern territories."

Finally, in January 1979 the JDA confirmed the presence of one brigade of 5,000 troops on the two islands, together with three airfields, several dozen tanks, and ten cannon of twenty-kilometer range. Although this was still well below the pre-1960 deployment of a division and a brigade, it was considerably more than the 2,000 border guards stationed there since.[12] In addition, the fact that the cannon range exceeded the distance of seventeen kilometers between Kunashiri and Hokkaido provided a potential basis for alarm.

However, no alarm was sounded in the press. In fact, little was made of what this development might portend for Japanese security. Instead, most analysis speculated on the probable role of Kunashiri and Etorofu in protecting access to the Sea of Okhotsk as a sanctuary for submarine-launched ballistic missiles (SLBM) targeted against the United States.[13] Only *Nihon Keizai* sounded a concerned note, calling for more vigorous defense preparations against a possible Soviet threat.[14]

The media posture of relative unconcern paralleled official reaction. Foreign Minister Sonoda tactfully suggested that "it will not be wise to fan anti-Soviet sentiments and the Japanese-Soviet confrontation unnecessarily."[15] This was consistent with the overall policy of avoiding any appearance of collusion with Chinese attacks against "the polar bear seeking hegemony." Accordingly, the foreign office formally adopted a "low posture" by limiting itself to an oral protest. It stressed the territorial issue alone, avoiding any implication of a perceived threat in the buildup. Declaring that "the deployment of military power and the construction of facilities . . . on Kunashiri and Etorofu . . . run counter to the spirit of an early and peaceful settlement of the northern territories," the statement expressed "deep regret" over "these new military measures of the Soviet side" and "strongly" requested that the forces be "quickly retracted."[16] The same sentiments were echoed in a Diet resolution, and in mid-March the press reported that the four SDF divisions in Hokkaido were being reorganized with more armored strength and artillery. The timing of these last developments proved helpful, perhaps by design, in eliciting Diet support for a slight increase in the defense budget.

This did not end the matter, however. In October JDA revealed that the buildup had spread to the third island of Shikotan and included helicopters as well as medium-range air defense missiles.[17] Previously, JDA had explained the development as defensively motivated. Now it would no longer exclude the possibility of offensive intent, although as before official and unofficial comment tended to minimize the security implications for Japan.

The winter of 1979-80 provided new cause for concern. In December Soviet forces invaded Afghanistan. In January JDA briefings claimed that the buildup in the northern islands had reached a full division. Pressure from Washington for a greater contribution to Japan's defense coincided with the deployment of the only American aircraft carrier in northeastern Asia to the Indian Ocean. By April 1980 a poll of Diet members in the lower House found that 73 percent of the respondents agreed that Soviet military forces in the Far East posed a threat to Japan's security, although only 23 percent believed this raised the prospect of possible invasion.[18] In close parallel with public opinion, the perception of increased threat did not lead to a willingness to increase the defense budget beyond its established ceiling of 1 percent of GNP. Of the Liberal Democratic Party (LDP) respondents, 59.3 percent held to this limit as against 19.5 percent who advocated going higher. All the others, save one, wanted to maintain the limit, while the Socialists argued for lowering the ceiling further.

This seeming paradox reflects a basic ambivalence toward military strength coupled with contradictory explanations of what motivates Soviet military moves. The general Japanese antipathy against the armed forces derives from traumatic and shattering defeat in a war that was prompted by military expansionism. It is symbolized by the express constitutional provision in which Japan renounced the right to use force in foreign affairs, which in turn explains the euphemism "Self-Defense Forces." The specific revulsion against nuclear weapons as a result of the American bombing of Hiroshima and Nagasaki is reflected in the signing of the nonproliferation treaty and the prohibition against such weapons being deployed in Japan, as well as against their production or acquisition.

Yet in recent years there has been a growing willingness to consider defense matters, especially in the public media and in Diet debates. Explanations for this development vary. *Nihon keizai*, a conservative newspaper, saw its 1980 Diet poll as evidence of an emerging consensus among the three main parties concerning the Soviet threat and attributes the shift to the general

THE JAPAN CONNECTION 119

Soviet buildup in East Asia; the deployment of Backfire bombers, SS-20 missiles, and the carrier *Minsk* to the area; the appearance of amphibious landing craft in the Sea of Japan; and the northern islands buildup.[19] *Asahi*, however, offered a different point of emphasis in the front-page series on defense that it ran subsequent to that of *Nihon keizai*. Concerning the virtual unanimity of business leaders for an increased defense capability, *Asahi* quoted Kiichi Saeki, head of the Nomura Research Institute, who explained it solely in terms of the need to satisfy Washington's demand for a greater Japanese contribution to the alliance.[20] It later expressed editorial concern over reports that U.S.-Japanese military planning for a hypothetical attack on Hokkaido was being handled secretly without cabinet review and proper civilian oversight.[21]

Thus, on the one hand, prominent Japanese who call for a stronger defense do not necessarily articulate this need in terms of a perceived Soviet threat. On the other hand, Diet members who do articulate such a perception do not in general support a larger defense budget. Policy elites outside the government do not depict the USSR in benign terms, but neither do they stress its belligerency.[22] Typical of the restrained tone of analysis is that offered by the Research Institute for Peace and Security, headed by Masamichi Inoki, former chief of the Defense Agency:

Soviet policy toward Japan has four goals. The first is to cut the military tie between Japan and the United States, so that U.S. influence in the Western Pacific can be reduced. The second is to discourage Japan from becoming a powerful military nation, since if this happens, it would only add in Asia a further threat to that of China. The third is to prevent Japan and China from forming a close alliance, not only militarily, but economically and politically as well. The fourth is to harness Japan's economic and industrial potential in the development of Siberia and the Soviet Far East. In a sense these are all subordinate aims: the ultimate purpose is to bring Japan into the Soviet sphere of influence.[23]

In contrast with his more militarily oriented statements as head of JDA, Inoki's analysis stresses the noncoercive side of Soviet policy, including its defensive as well as offensive goals. Moreover, in July 1980 a national security advisory group appointed by the late Prime Minister Ohira and led by Inoki recommended a 20 percent increase in military spending, but this would only amount to 1.07 percent of GNP, compared with the 0.9 percent proposed for the new five-year plan.[24] By comparison, NATO countries spend between 3 and 6 percent of GNP on defense. One notable exception to this moderate position is Shinsaku Hogen, formerly a diplomat in Moscow and vice-minister of foreign affairs. As a renowned specialist on the USSR for more than forty years, Hogen's views command a limited following among older, conservative groups. In a lengthy interview he focused on past Russian perfidy and pressure in the contemporary context of steadily expanding military power, warning, "Russia is by nature expansionist. . . . They really want Hokkaido."[25]

However, Hogen's explicit concern was not echoed in interviews on Hokkaido at the time.[26] A high-ranking military official there acknowledged marked improvements in Soviet capabilities manifested in the more rapid deployment of new weaponry to the area compared with the past delay of three to four years after deployment to the European theater.[27] Speaking personally, however, he saw this as part of an overall change in strategic doctrine and not as narrowly aimed at Japan. He rejected any basis for the proposed use of the term "Sea of the Soviet Union" for the Sea of Japan, a rhetorical device used by the Democratic Socialists in arguing for stronger defense measures.[28] On the contrary, he said, "The U.S. Seventh Fleet together with the narrow straits for exiting to the Pacific leave Soviet forces severely handicapped, so that I'd rather have my problems than theirs."

Two years later a conference on "Hokkaido in the 1980's" heard an LDP member from the island attribute Soviet behavior to an increased feeling of isolation as the result of closer relations among China, Japan, and the United States.[29] This implicit denial of a real threat was explicitly echoed by his LDP colleague from the Hokkaido provincial assembly, who agreed there was no likelihood of an invasion.

Yet at the official level the Defense Agency's annual White Paper evidenced a steady increase in the articulation of potential threat, albeit cast in temperate language, as shown in the following excerpts from successive years:

[1976]
Particularly noteworthy is the increase in nuclear and naval power by the Soviets since the late 1960's. . . . The U.S. is attempting to maintain a viable nuclear potential, while increasingly relying on key allies for conventional military capabilities.

[1977]
During the past decade there has been a marked expansion of Soviet forces, in striking contrast to a quantitative decline in the previously overwhelming American posture. . . . This has been a significant factor in the recent world military structure, and great attention has been focused on the possible outcome of this trend and its potential effect upon the specific military environments for the security of the West.

[1978]
There is reason to conclude that [the U.S. Seventh Fleet] lacks sufficient capabilities for the protection of large numbers of merchant vessels. It will therefore be difficult to counter completely the Soviet capabilities for severing the sea lanes of communication.[30]

[1979]
The Soviet Union has consistently increased its military spending since the 1960's and is now strong enough to compete with the United States in nuclear capability and military posture in Europe and the Far East. Furthermore, as a result of increased naval and air power, the Soviet Union has made it difficult for the U.S. to secure sea lines of communication between the U.S. forward deployment areas and the U.S. mainland. The Soviets have also developed the capability to intervene in local areas considerably removed from Russia.[31]

This evolution of thinking parallels that presented in American commentary of the time, including the annual posture statements from the Secretary of Defense.[32] It also reflects the impact of events elsewhere in the world, beginning with Angola in 1974 and culminating with Afghanistan in 1979. However, the 1979 White Paper was unprecedentedly specific in itemizing developments of particular significance for Japan:

In the event of deployment of high-performance bombers [Backfire] in the Far East, it would be necessary to focus attention on air defense measures and securing maritime communication in waters surrounding Japan.

Since any military presence in such an area [the northern islands] is of great concern to us, it is necessary that we continue to maintain close vigilance over Soviet activities.

122 THE JAPAN CONNECTION

Naval vessels and aircraft have been advancing into open waters, and Soviet activities around Japan have been intensified.

Japan is concerned over Soviet utilization of airfields, ports and harbors, and other facilities in Indochina.[33]

The cumulative effect of external events and domestic politics was evident in 1980. For the first time a Japanese foreign minister explicitly voiced the need "to bring Japanese defense capability to a level where Japan can make other countries recognize that invading Japan costs considerably."[34] The Ministry of Finance reportedly reduced its traditional resistance to Defense Agency pressure for increased expenditure as the two groups explored prospects for accelerating the new five-year defense program.[35]

The parliamentary problem remains, however, as long as Diet members balk at exceeding the 1 percent of GNP ceiling. Resistance to a major increase in defense expenditure comes from more than antimilitary sentiment, strong as that is among older groups. In essence, credibility for the defense need is difficult to achieve on two dimensions: a feasible deterrent posture and a demonstrable enemy threat. The first question was graphically addressed by a JDA official discussing Japan's vulnerability to air attack, especially by nuclear weapons:

With a land mass of 142,726 square miles—a little smaller than the state of Montana—and a 16,470 mile long coastline, no point in Japan is more than 75 miles from the coast. As of December 1970, the Japanese population was heavily concentrated around Tokyo (24 percent) and the Osaka-Kobe area (12 percent). . . . Located close to the continent of Asia, the entire archipelago is within the range of TU-16's, not to mention MRBM's and the northern part can even be reached with MIG 21's or IL-28's. . . . Particularly in the urban areas, there is no popular support for a forward defense (a theoretical necessity for a country with virtually no strategic depth). . . . Japan has no plans for precrisis dispersal and shelter.[36]

In addition to the dilemma of how to provide deterrence to supplement that provided by the American defense commitment and capability, Japanese authorities have the problem of giving credibility to the possibility of a Soviet attack, which lacks acceptance among policy circles.[37] The Soviet forces are prepon-

THE JAPAN CONNECTION 123

derantly concentrated in Europe or targeted against the United States. Their secondary line of deployment is against China. These responsibilities preempt the bulk of Moscow's military strength, leaving little for Japan. JDA officials speculate on the possibility of a tunnel or bridge link between mainland Siberia and Sakhalin that would permit a rapid deployment of forces presently arrayed against China, but until better evidence of such a link is available, this contingency is not taken seriously, even within the Defense Agency.

Despite the Soviet capability, specialists in the foreign ministry profess to see no plausible cause for conflict.[38] In the past Japan and Russia clashed over issues and interests on the Asian mainland, but Japan no longer has a presence there. Disputes over fishing and disagreement over the "northern territories" are insufficient to spark a war. Moscow may worry over Tokyo's possible participation in a Beijing-Washington entente, but any exercise of force would strengthen this prospect, not deter it. In the event of a Soviet-American war, Japanese officials fear that a "Europe first" mentality in Washington will result in inadequate protection of the vital sea routes on which the Japanese economy must rely. But this is a World War III scenario and does not pertain to a regional conflict limited to Northeast Asia. In this regard, the policy elite is in accord with public opinion and the mass media: there is no consensus that Soviet military power presents a clear and present danger to the security of Japan.

Issues and Interests

Aside from the unlikely prospect of war, Japanese-Soviet relations are complicated by issues over which conflicting interests can challenge foreign policy through the dynamics of domestic politics.[39] The most salient of such issues concerns the "northern territories." Officially, Tokyo demands the return of three islands (Kunashiri, Etorofu, and Shikotan) and a small archipelago (the Habomais), comprising an area of less than 5,000 square kilometers (2,000 square miles).[40] No Japanese have settled there since World War II. Those who did live there have since died or resettled successfully, mainly in Hokkaido. The is-

124 THE JAPAN CONNECTION

lands have little economic value except for fishing, and even there they are of interest to a relatively small group.

Yet the "northern territories" question arises repeatedly in public opinion polls, mass media, and domestic politics with sufficient force to block conclusion of a Soviet-Japanese peace treaty. An August 1979 survey found that this was the first explanation offered by those who held that relations with the USSR "are not good," 68 percent citing this issue.[41] Interviews with policy elites reveal a uniform sensitivity to the question, which is felt to preclude formal acceptance of the Soviet occupation, despite the passage of more than 35 years since World War II.

The issue is not seen identically by all groups. The government officially holds the three islands and one archipelago to be "inalienable," but the opposition parties insist that the entire Kuril Islands chain must eventually be recovered, although they differ on the tactics for pursuing this goal. Parochial fishing interests in the northern port of Nemuro are concerned only with Shikotan and the Habomais, while other fishing groups on Hokkaido focus on Kunashiri and Etorofu.[42]

For its part, Moscow has vacillated on the possibility of a compromise solution. In the 1956 Soviet-Japanese Joint Declaration, it promised "to transfer to Japan the Habomai islands and the island of Shikotan . . . after the conclusion of a peace treaty."[43] In 1960 Foreign Minister Gromyko declared that these islands would be returned only after all American forces had left Japan. Subsequently, Soviet officials hinted at a possible future compromise, but their remarks came under circumstances that obscured their meaning and invited misinterpretation by Japanese audiences.[44] More recently the Soviet media and officials have been adamant in declaring that there is no territorial question to discuss and no basis for Japanese interference "in a domestic matter," the issue having been settled in the Potsdam and Yalta agreements and the San Francisco Peace Treaty. A deputy foreign minister refused to accept a Diet resolution on the matter from the Japanese ambassador in March 1979, and in October the Soviet ambassador in Tokyo rejected another protest from a Japanese vice–foreign minister.[45]

THE JAPAN CONNECTION 125

The conflicting historical and legal claims are argued inconclusively by both sides.[46] Realistically, however, there is no prospect of the USSR giving back either the main Kuril chain or Kunashiri and Etorofu. Moreover, the previously stated willingness to return Shikotan and the Habomais is unlikely ever to be reaffirmed. Just as domestic politics within the Liberal Democratic Party and the Diet seem to block any abandonment of Tokyo's claim, so may bureaucratic politics limit Moscow's freedom to maneuver. Security interests often prevail over diplomatic considerations, and the growth of the Soviet Pacific Fleet probably increases the navy's influence in policy councils.

In this regard, a shift occurred in private Soviet discussion of the issue between 1975 and 1978. On the former occasion, the explanation for a rigid stance was primarily political and historical, with emphasis on the likely demands "other claimants to Soviet territory" (i.e. Chinese) would make if a concession were offered to Japan. However, in 1978 a high foreign affairs official dramatically slapped his hand over a map showing the Sea of Okhotsk and declared that "for strategic reasons" the islands could "never" be given up.[47] He claimed that during World War II eighteen Soviet ships were sunk by Japan before Moscow denounced the neutrality pact in April 1945, and that this proved the need to control all access routes to the Pacific.

The facts surrounding this charge are somewhat unclear. Soviet sources differ on the exact number of ships allegedly sunk, but they agree on the general complaint.[48] According to specialists in the Japanese foreign ministry, an unspecified number of Soviet protests were registered at the time but were rejected on the basis that no Japanese submarines were in the specified areas.[49] It was therefore suggested that whatever happened must have resulted from mistaken British or American attacks. Bizarre as this may sound, at least one such instance was subsequently revealed in an authoritative Soviet history; the survivors landed on Etorofu and were taken to Hokkaido, whence they were repatriated via Vladivostok.[50]

Whatever the facts, the Soviet perception of strategic significance is neither new nor wholly misplaced. Postwar references to the entire Kuril chain as a "screen of steel" and a "1,000-kilometer cossack sabre" echo Stalin's declaration in 1945 that the islands were both a gateway to the Pacific and a wall protecting the Soviet Far East.[51] Kunashiri and Etorofu are no less valuable in this regard, since they sit astride the southernmost entrance to the Sea of Okhotsk and the passage to the Soya Strait, which enters the Sea of Japan, home waters for ships based at Vladivostok.

With these two islands securely in Soviet control, however, Shikotan and the Habomais have relatively little military importance. This probably explains why Moscow has at times held out the prospect of returning them, albeit subject to improbable preconditions. They could provide useful radar sites to monitor air and sea traffic, but other means of surveillance are available to the U.S.–Japan alliance. Moreover, they are easily dominated by bases on Kunashiri were they to end up in hostile hands.

In view of Moscow's competition with Beijing for favor in Tokyo, it puzzled Japanese observers why the 1956 offer was not renewed after China's success in further cementing relations with Japan and the United States in 1978. However, although such a move cannot be wholly ruled out in the future, it does not seem likely. As a leading Soviet specialist on Japan, an apparent advocate of compromise, remarked, "Governments do not give something away for nothing. My colleagues ask me, what would we get in return? What difference would it make in Japanese policy toward us?"[52]

His point is well taken. In the first place, it is not clear that Tokyo would settle for Shikotan and the Habomais. In August 1955 Moscow responded favorably to a Japanese memorandum stating that "the return of the islands would be considered satisfactory grounds for a treaty," only to find that "at this point the Japanese government abruptly revised its position and extended the minimum territorial claim to include the southern Kuriles."[53] When Foreign Minister Shigemitsu Mamoru subsequently agreed in Moscow to accept the compromise settlement, he was overruled by the cabinet three days later.[54]

The circumstances surrounding the first reversal of policy have been variously interpreted. One American historian explained it wholly in terms of Japanese internal politics, specifically as a concession by the then Democratic Party leaders to win a merger agreement from the Liberal Party.[55] A Soviet historian, however, implied that it resulted from intervention by Secretary of State John Foster Dulles to block a Soviet-Japanese rapprochement.[56] In any event, the subsequent permutations of official statements from Tokyo left almost as much ambiguity surrounding the question as did those from Moscow.[57] A former Soviet diplomat to Japan specifically alluded to this concern in privately explaining the hardened Soviet position in 1969.[58]

As to the prospects for change in Japanese attitudes and policy in the event of a Soviet concession, Moscow's skepticism may be well placed. For example, fishing groups are not willing to compromise their interests in order to recover territory. On the contrary, the minister of agriculture and fishing reportedly claimed his hometown neighbors in Nemuro wanted Tokyo to "swap the islands for more fishing," even though Nemuro is usually seen as inflexible on the recovery of Shikotan and the Habomais.[59] Nor will Moscow's main concern over an emerging Beijing-Tokyo axis be relieved by a compromise settlement on the "northern territories." The economic interests and cultural factors that incline Japan toward China as compared with the USSR will not be reversed on this account alone. Finally, as already indicated, irredentist groups vary widely in their demands. Regardless of other real considerations, they may reject any compromise. This could cause intensified anti-Soviet feeling through the dynamics of Diet debate and leave the issue wholly in abeyance.

Reference to fishing raises another issue area that complicates Soviet-Japanese relations. This is a long-standing problem of considerable practical, as well as political, importance in both countries, but particularly in Japan. Traditionally, fishing communities are wholly dependent on the sea for their livelihood; any curtailment of the catch or the area of operation jeopardizes employment and income. This in turn makes fishing lobbies adamant in opposing international agreements that reduce national fishing rights. The question is especially sensitive in view of Japan's dependency on fish as a dietary mainstay and its postwar development of one of the world's most advanced and aggressive fishing fleets.

The loss of Sakhalin and the Kurils denied extensive fishing areas to the Japanese, except through specific permission of the Soviet Union. Difficult negotiations were made still more complicated because of the "northern territories" question. Tokyo sought to avoid any agreement that might implicitly recognize Soviet sovereignty, and Moscow fought any challenge to its legitimate rule over the islands.[60] In the mid-1970's the growing adoption by coastal states of the 200-mile economic zone put increased pressure on both sides to reach agreement, since they faced the loss of their previous freedom in offshore and high-seas fishing. But first Moscow and then Tokyo followed in declaring 200-mile economic zones, thereby further exacerbating their bilateral problem because of overlapping jurisdiction as well as increased national control.

In addition to the politics of the fishing lobby, press play given to Soviet harassment of Japanese boats provides a dramatic human dimension in an otherwise highly technical subject. The seizure of boats, the detention of fishermen, and the confiscation of catch reinforce popular images of superior Soviet power being exercised to the disadvantage of a weaker Japan. Surprisingly, a newspaper editor in Sapporo blamed the mass media for exaggerating the problem, noting that in his private view Soviet behavior was neither as bad as portrayed nor wholly unjustified.[61]

Informed sources in Sapporo and Tokyo privately confirm that blame rests on both sides. Aggressive fishermen violate the agreed limitation of catch, and they also poach in forbidden waters. Venal Soviet authorities encourage such activity by taking bribes. Intelligence activities further complicate the question of cause and effect.[62] The informal rules thus operate in contravention of official agreements and are subject to change, depending on the personality and influence of local groups on both sides. This makes the situation inherently unstable. Moreover, neither side will encourage an open and objective accounting of incidents. Too many conflicting interests are at stake, not the least of which is the threat of pressure and the use of public opinion as bargaining counters in the annual fishing negotiations. Finally, as we have indicated, the fishing problem cannot be wholly separated from the territorial issue.

This presents a constant, if low-grade, irritant in overall relations, and impedes development of a more favorable public image of the USSR. Given the traditional independence of fishermen, the uncertainty of identification and location in fog-enshrouded waters, and the inconsistent behavior of Soviet patrols, incidents are likely to continue regardless of the policy in Moscow and Tokyo. This helps to explain why, in contradiction to the facts, those who were polled in August 1979 as perceiving Soviet-Japanese relations to be "not good" included nearly two-thirds who alleged that "the Soviet Union has been unwilling to make concessions to Japan on fishery problems."[63] This was a number only slightly smaller than those who also identified the "northern territories dispute" as contributing to relations that were "not good."[64]

Yet after a period of tension and acrimony, fishing relations have improved at a higher level in recent years.[65] Japanese government and business sources complain of prolonged and tough bargaining on the part of Moscow's representatives, but they claim that this ultimately results in compromise agreements that seem fair and reasonable. Moreover, the outcome is scrupulously observed insofar as activity can be controlled from the center.[66] Agreement on the respective economic zones proved more readily obtainable than had been anticipated. Specific aspects, such as the salmon catch, appeared disadvantageous to Tokyo when published, but according to one of the interested companies, it affected too small a proportion of the total take to justify the attention given it in the press.[67] A principal negotiator also noted that anticipated changes in the international regulations controlling salmon fishing forecast a cut of nearly one-half in the Japanese share, thereby removing any potential Soviet leverage.[68]

Soviet perceptions of Japanese attitudes are derived largely from study of the mass media, and Soviet specialists on Japan express dismay over their failure to win favorable press treatment in Japan on fishing matters when accommodation has been reached through conventional negotiating methods.[69] They suspect that the media respond to government direction in a deliberate anti-Soviet campaign, a situation that is not helped by the tendency of Japanese negotiators to give background interviews that stress their country's weakness and vulnerability, thereby implying that concessions are invariably one-sided.

The China Factor

To make matters worse from Moscow's standpoint, Chinese propaganda aimed at worldwide audiences as well as audiences in Japan exploits the interlocking complex of issues associated with Soviet military violations of Japanese sea and air space, fishing, and the northern territories. Moscow closely monitors Beijing's exaggerated assertions of "Japanese public opinion," which are often based on obscure newspaper articles or miniscule protest groups representing ultra-Right sentiments. There is even fear among some Soviet observers that this propaganda influences Japanese policy. Others suspect acquiescence if not actual connivance by Tokyo.[70]

Chinese exploitation of these issues is especially galling to Moscow because the similar problems that exist in Sino-Japanese relations do not arouse the same degree of public attention and political sensitivity. The two countries disagree over ownership of the Senkaku Islands, presently held by Japan, and China regularly protests South Korean–Japanese exploration for offshore oil in the continental shelf as violating Chinese territorial sovereignty. Fishing is an issue negotiated annually between Tokyo and Beijing. Although some of these matters, such as access to the continental shelf or the final disposition of the Senkakus, may become more active in the future, through most of the 1970's they remained on the periphery of public consciousness in Japan. This was manifest in the August 1979 poll that showed 71 percent recording "friendly feelings" toward China compared with only 20 percent with "no friendly feelings," the remainder being "don't know."[71]

Moscow's inability to compete with Beijing, whether in image or on issues, is the subject of considerable comment in Tokyo. Government and business circles involved in negotiations unanimously agree that Soviet specialists are well informed, and that

THE JAPAN CONNECTION 131

they understand the Japanese scene quite well, but they feel that top Soviet officials, particularly at the Politburo level, lack this understanding and act independently of the experts. This situation is not unique to Moscow; most large bureaucracies suffer from a similar problem. However, Soviet leadership is at a disadvantage compared to the Chinese because of the absence of cultural and personal ties that facilitate formal as well as informal interaction in Tokyo. Many senior Chinese governmental and academic personages lived in Japan, often as students, in their early years. Others have had personal contact with Japanese political and business delegations during the past three decades. In addition to the obvious cultural overlap that contrasts with the gulf that separates Soviet and Japanese society, this background of personal familiarity offers a better basis for policy planning and implementation in Beijing than it does in the Kremlin.

Another factor that handicaps Moscow in its rivalry with Beijing is its vastly greater distance from Tokyo, in addition to which Moscow's primary orientation is toward Europe, while Beijing's is toward Asia. For example, according to an informed Japanese source, the Soviet fishing quota is nominally allocated on a global basis, but in actuality the ministry does not transfer the unused portion of its North Atlantic share to the Pacific fleet, in effect leaving the two regional headquarters to subsist as independent entities.[72] This reduces flexibility in adjusting local agreements.

Problems of distance are compounded by styles of decision making. Japanese businessmen complain that nothing agreed upon verbally can be considered as final when dealing with Soviet officials. Only after it has been communicated to Moscow and cleared through the bureaucracy will the deal be closed in writing. In one case Japanese firms responded favorably to a joint venture proposed by the Soviet fishing ministry. Tokyo officially approved it, only to find the formal agreement stalled in Moscow for a month while it was reviewed by the ministries of finance and foreign trade.[73] In contrast, agreement with Chinese officials, regardless of their rank, is considered final if given by telephone, and prompt action follows on both sides.

A third point of comparison is the differing intensity of bureaucratic interests involved in policy toward Japan. On the one hand, one-fourth of Chinese foreign trade is with Japan, compared with less than 5 percent for the USSR, and it is the cornerstone of China's economic modernization. On the other hand, it is safe to surmise that in particular bureaucratic terms, the salience of issues affecting relations with Japan is far higher for the Soviet navy, for instance, than for its counterpart in China. Similarly, though Soviet fishing fleets compete vigorously with Japan both locally and globally, no such situation exists for China. As one Tokyo specialist put it, "There is no time constraint on negotiating with the Chinese in order to get agreement so that we can begin our fishing as soon as possible."[74] These considerations permit greater freedom of maneuver on such issues for Beijing than for Moscow.

Soviet officials show awareness of their handicaps and failures. As a safeguard against inadvertent statements that might unnecessarily arouse adverse reactions, no major articles on Japan can be published without special review in the Soviet foreign ministry, except by *Pravda*, *Izvestiia*, and Tass.[75] The three exceptions are necessitated by the pressure of daily reporting, but even here special commentaries are cleared at a high level.

Yet this procedure does not protect Moscow from its own mishandling of Japanese sensitivities. Three such instances arose during the first half of 1980, as Tokyo attempted to maintain at least minimum compliance with Washington's pressures for an embargo on credits and technology following the Soviet invasion of Afghanistan. In mid-February an authoritative *Izvestia* commentary accused "the Japanese government, to the detriment of its relations with the Soviet Union and the independence of its foreign policy," of "openly conniving at the American 'positions of strength' policy."[76] Tokyo's contemplated sanctions were reported to be worrying Japanese firms because this could "deprive them of a number of lucrative commercial deals with the Soviet Union, including the delivery of raw materials critically needed by the Japanese economy." This thinly veiled threat was followed by reference to "marine products [that] hold a leading place in the Japanese diet," noting that "the Soviet Union has permitted Japanese fishermen . . . to fish for

THE JAPAN CONNECTION 133

all salmon in the northwestern Pacific Ocean, where the USSR, as the country in whose rivers these fish spawn, has the right of ownership over salmon schools." Once again the writer referred to alleged Japanese concerns that "the application of 'sanctions' against the USSR could be a two-edged weapon."

This transparent attempt to threaten retaliatory moves affecting Siberian resources and fishing was seriously misguided. Moscow, not Tokyo, has consistently been the initiator of proposals for joint effort and the supplicant searching for badly needed credits and technology. Any cutoff of trade would hurt the Soviet economy more than the Japanese. In addition, the public image of a greedy bear scooping up fish around the northern islands that rightfully belong to Japan, or sharing its illegal catch in a niggardly fashion, already impeded relations. Further irritation on this issue could deal a serious blow to what little good will Moscow may have hoped to gain by the 1977 compromise agreement. Neither threat materialized. Nevertheless, the abortive bluff rankled in influential business circles that resented the crude tactic.

In early April the same writer again accused Tokyo of bowing to another government's "anti-Soviet orientation," this time by allegedly responding to pressure from Beijing instead of Washington. Pegged to the first Sino-Japanese foreign minister's conference since conclusion of the 1978 Treaty of Peace and Friendship, the commentary reviewed the earlier exchanges of military delegations and implied a Japanese willingness to meet a "secret" Chinese request of 1975 for "missiles, tanks of various types, firing control systems, troop control systems, and similar items."[77] The commentary claimed this was shortsighted because it disregarded "the fact that Beijing has long been elaborating military strategic plans in pursuing its own hegemonistic aims both on a global scale and in the Far East region." In conclusion, the writer warned that Tokyo's "support for the Chinese foreign policy course can only cause serious harm not only to peace in the Far East but also to the security of Japan itself."

The closing words constituted only a veiled threat compared with the more pointed language of the February article. However, in Japanese eyes the words added insult to injury because the accusation of an interest in selling arms to China completely ignored Tokyo's absolute prohibition against any arms sales abroad. Moscow's refusal to acknowledge Japanese policies that in fact enhance Japan's avowed independence and also conform with Soviet interests puzzles and angers observers in Tokyo. This was particularly true when the joint communiqué concluding Premier Hua Guofeng's visit to Prime Minister Ohira in May failed to make any reference to "hegemony," Beijing's standard codeword for Soviet expansionism.[78] This was the first omission of the term in any high-level Sino-Japanese statement since its appearance in the communiqué on Prime Minister Tanaka's 1972 mission to Beijing to establish full diplomatic relations. Yet the omission passed without comment from Moscow.

Soviet specialists on East Asia privately manifest a sense of frustration at always losing out to Chinese competition for favor in Japan—and a latent fear of being confronted with a hostile racial coalition. On occasion, the racial concern breaks through to the surface, as when a Soviet diplomat in Tokyo remarked to an American, "One day it will be them [China and Japan] against us [the United States and the Soviet Union]!"[79] Objectively these concerns should heighten Soviet efforts to resolve issues and to placate interests in Japan, but subjectively they can induce impatience and rigidity, thereby exacerbating the situation. A dramatic instance occurred in July 1980 when Prime Minister Ohira's funeral brought Premier Hua and President Carter to Tokyo and Secretary Brezhnev was conspicuous by his absence. The Soviet leader's attendance at Tito's funeral less than two months earlier underscored this snub, while Hua's visit was the Chinese leader's second in six weeks.

Siberian Development and Japan: The Past Record

The overall framework of images, issues, and interests suggests a fundamental incompatibility in Soviet-Japanese relations, especially when compared with contemporary Sino-Japanese relations. Indeed, this is the conclusion of most western analysts.[80] Against this negative background there would seem little reason for the Japanese to become involved in the development of East Asian Siberia and good reason for Tokyo to oppose strengthening Moscow's hand in this area. American specialists who focus on the costs and difficulty of EAS projects voice considerable skepticism concerning their practical utility in general and their value to Japan in particular.[81] Neither politics nor economics is held to offer a firm foundation for Soviet-Japanese cooperation.

As might be expected, a contrary view is argued by Soviet writers. They maintain that a natural economic complementarity of Soviet-Japanese trade provides the logical basis for joint effort in developing East Asian Siberian resources.[82] Furthermore, they hint that better political relations can eventuate between the two countries as economic cooperation advances common interests.

The Japanese experience in Siberian development is more than ten years old and has involved more than $3 billion in loans and credits.[83] It has extended over a wide area, from Sakhalin to Yakutia, and has involved a wide range of activities, including port construction, offshore oil exploration, and coal mining. In contrast to these joint efforts, some Soviet proposals failed to win Japanese agreement, notably the shipment of oil from West Siberia via pipeline and railroad to Japan. Protests from Beijing and limited cooperation from Washington constrained Tokyo's participation. Basically, however, the overall pattern has been one of steadily increasing cooperation. This has barely scratched the surface of EAS development as envisaged in the more grandiose Soviet programs, most of which must await the completion of BAM. Nonetheless, the first decade provides a useful record for appraisal. It also gives Japanese views an informed perspective.

After considerable publicity, somewhat overblown and premature on both sides, the Soviet-Japanese Economic Committee was formed in 1966 to plan economic cooperation in the Soviet Far East. Seven major projects were initiated between 1968 and 1978. They included the construction of a major port and the exploitation and production of timber, wood chips, coal, oil, and gas.[84]

Port. In December 1970 agreement was reached to develop a new port facility to handle shipments of timber, wood chips, and coal; and to include the largest coal-loading pier in the world and a comprehensive freight-loading facility to handle both wood chips and containers. It is located at Wrangel (Votstochny), across the bay from the port of Nakhodka, itself 80 kilometers (50 miles) east of Vladivostok. Japan furnished $80 million in equipment and materials on a seven-year deferred-payment basis (12 percent down at 6 percent interest).

Timber. Two agreements were reached in July 1968 and July 1974. The first inaugurated Soviet-Japanese collaboration. Japan provided $133 million on a five-year deferred-payment basis (20 percent down, 5.8 percent interest) for technical assistance and machinery, plus $30 million for consumer goods. In return, the USSR provided 7.6 million cubic meters of timber and pulp at a fixed price between 1969 and 1973, and 320,000 cubic meters of lumber between 1971 and 1973. The second agreement was considerably larger. Japan furnished $550 million in loans, of which $435 million were for facilities for the exploitation of timber resources, $65 million for ships, and $50 million for local costs. In return, the USSR supplied 18.4 million cubic meters of timber and lumber from 1975 through 1979 at annually adjusted prices.

Wood chips. In December 1971 agreement was reached whereby Japan provided $45 million in wood-chip and wood-pulp equipment, together with special ships for hauling, on a six-year deferred-payment basis (12 percent down at 6 percent interest, excluding the ships), plus $5 million in cash for consumer goods to meet local needs. In return, the Soviet Union supplied 3.65 million cubic meters of chip timber and 2.7 million cubic meters of pulp timber between 1972 and 1977. From 1978 to 1981 another 4.4 million cubic meters of chip timber and 2 million cubic meters of pulp timber would be shipped, with payment to be calculated on quantity, not on value.

Coal. In June 1974 collaboration began on coking coal development. Japan agreed to provide $390 million for machinery and $60 million for consumer goods to exploit the Neryungri deposits in southern Yakutia. The loan was scheduled for delivery over the period 1975–82 with repayment in 1983–90 (interest at 6.375 percent plus consumer goods at 7.25 percent). This was

THE JAPAN CONNECTION 137

arranged separately from the schedule for coal shipments, which will total 104.4 million tons between 1979 and 1998, beginning at 1 million and reaching 5.5 million tons annually after 1985. Although the timing and value involved are not identical for the loan repayment and coal shipment, the agreement is virtually one of payment in kind.[85] Subsequently, rising costs prompted Japan to pledge an additional $90 million loan.

Sakhalin offshore oil and gas. In January and July 1975 agreements were arranged for $100 million in Japanese credits to cover exploration ships and ocean-bed drilling equipment, $22.5 million for machinery, instruments, and computers for ships, and $30 million for consumer goods, a total of $152.5 million scheduled to be paid over five years. In return, Japan will receive 50 percent of the oil and an amount of gas to be agreed upon later, to be supplied during the period of loan and interest repayment plus ten years. An American company, Gulf Oil, shares a 3.5 percent interest in the Japanese side.

Yakutian natural gas. In agreements of December 1974 and March 1976, the first trilateral Soviet-Japanese-American project began to explore for natural gas in the Yakut ASSR. A $50 million loan (half from the Japan Export-Import Bank, half from the Bank of America) was to support the exploration phase. Upon proving 1 trillion cubic meters of reserves, negotiations for the second phase would take place in 1980-81. If these evolved satisfactorily, the total estimated Japanese-American contribution of $4 billion to cover extraction, pipe, and liquefaction plant (but not the ships) would be paid back in the form of 10 billion cubic meters of natural gas annually to each country for 25 years. El Paso Natural Gas and Occidental Petroleum are the American participants.

The foregoing commitments, together with $1.4 billion in Japanese Export-Import Bank loans extended since 1975 for whole plant sales to the USSR, brought Tokyo's official credits for Soviet economic development to nearly $4 billion by 1979.[86] Although some of this amount is not involved in EAS projects, it nonetheless must be taken into account in evaluating governmental relations between the two countries.

None of these agreements came easily or progressed smoothly in their implementation, judging from Japanese comments. Nevertheless, the cooperative ventures were viewed as sufficiently worthwhile to justify the effort and expense involved. The comments represented only a preliminary assessment for projects that still awaited fulfillment, such as Yakutian coal and Sakhalin oil, but they covered the major portion of the timber, wood chips, and port agreements.

One consistent complaint focused on the complications of working with the Soviet bureaucracy. Problems arising in Sakhalin, for example, can be solved on an informal basis locally, but the solutions must await review in Moscow and communication back through the Soviet embassy in Tokyo before being applied on the spot. In one case, rivalry over jurisdiction between two ministries in Moscow over control of offshore drilling rigs blocked exploration for months until an agreement could be reached.[87]

Another criticism concerned the tendency of Moscow to change proposals, plans, and data without clear justification, and apparently without regard for Japanese planning and procedures. For instance, in the early stage of discussion on Sakhalin, a Soviet offer of 2.4 billion cubic meters of gas to be shipped annually to Hokkaido via a 1,100-kilometer (682-mile) pipeline was allegedly based on an estimated reserve of 70 billion cubic meters.[88] However, Premier Kosygin, a regular participant in the talks, subsequently declared that the reserve was only 15 billion cubic meters, and that at the previously agreed rate, it would be exhausted in six years. He therefore urged the Japanese to invest in remote Yakutia, where an estimated 1 trillion cubic meters reportedly had been discovered. As one Japanese participant later explained, "He was very strong on this, and I did not argue. He was the prime minister, so we went along."

In the more celebrated Tyumen oil project, Moscow made major revisions in its proposal, changes that were consistently to Japan's disadvantage, without explaining or making compensating offers.[89] In the beginning Japanese capital of somewhat more than $1 billion was to fund construction of a 4,440-kilometer (2,775-mile) pipeline from Irkutsk to Nakhodka to transport oil from the West Siberian field at Tyumen to Japan, annual shipments to range between 25 and 40 million tons. This proposal made in February 1972, was suddenly scaled down to 25 million tons maximum the following September, and costs were increased, allegedly because of inflation and currency exchange movements. The following March, Moscow informed Tokyo that, in addition to the pipeline, the Japanese would have to help in constructing BAM as a supplementary means of transporting the oil; Soviet negotiators also raised the total cost estimate to $3 billion, three times the original amount.

Speculation focused on three possible explanations for the Soviet changes: assumptions of increased Japanese need, competing Soviet bureaucratic pressures, and conflicting priorities in the demand for Tyumen oil from Soviet and East European sources.[90] As a further complication, the changes coincided with Chinese expressions of concern, voiced privately to Japanese groups, over the strategic implications of an improved supply of oil to the Soviet Far East.[91] According to an informed Japanese official, Beijing's protest prompted Tokyo to reject the proposal "at the highest level," although Moscow's revisions provided a sufficient rationale, and were so accepted both in Moscow and Japan.[92]

Although the consequences were far less serious, similarly peremptory behavior marred negotiations for Yakutian gas.[93] Initially Moscow proposed that it be shipped by pipe to Olga, a distance of more than 3,200 kilometers (1,984 miles) but only two and one-half days by sea from Tokyo. Then, in March 1978, high Soviet officials personally persuaded the Japanese to accept Magadan as a terminal port. This would shorten the pipeline by 1,400 kilometers (870 miles) but require longer shipping through the Sea of Okhotsk, where icebound conditions during the winter caused unease in Tokyo. But that same October, much to the consternation of the Japanese, Moscow reverted back to Olga as the preferred outlet, again without explanation.[94]

These changes arouse considerable frustration because Soviet secrecy and bureaucratic behavior obstruct efforts to understand the basis of different decisions. Hiroshi Anzai, chairman of Tokyo Gas and prime mover behind Japan's participation in the Yakutia project, responded bluntly to the question, Does the

USSR provide data that the Japanese desire? "No," he said. "They are very bureaucratic; they only *show* things to us. For example, when we asked for a map, they told us to copy it since they had only one."[95] He continued, "According to the Soviet map, the distance of the pipeline from Yakutsk to the port of Olga is 3,523 kilometers, while that of Japan, based on photographs taken by a U.S. man-made satellite, show it to be 3,200 kilometers. ... When we asked how the distance was measured, they replied [that it was done] by aircraft and motor vehicle. We presented them with a satellite photo since they said they had none."

Continued Soviet haggling after an agreement has been formalized occasionally becomes irritating to the Japanese. In the case of Sakhalin, an initial understanding that Tokyo's $100 million contribution would be used for specific equipment was subsequently reopened by a Soviet request that it be used to fund additional rigs. This would have reduced the number of exploratory wells that could be drilled, or alternatively would have required more Japanese funding—in effect, the provision of extra rigs on a virtual grant basis.[96] Tokyo's rejection of the request did not impair relations, but the incident typifies a recurring problem.

One presumed advantage for Japan in Siberian development is the lower transportation cost compared with more distant sources. However, considerable skepticism exists in Tokyo over Soviet pricing practices. Moscow's refusal to break down shipping costs or to justify transportation charges, for instance, makes it impossible to verify this portion of coal prices. As one informant remarked, "Proximity may or may not make a difference."[97]

In addition, Moscow's insistence on carrying cargo in Soviet ships denies reciprocal earnings to Japanese lines. Originally this practice stemmed from the traditional Bolshevik fear of espionage. More recently it has been reinforced by Moscow's desire to maximize its maritime fleet capability, since the Soviet Union is a latecomer to the world shipping scene. Regardless of the rationale, the result is an economic loss for Japan that remains a sore point, particularly in Diet debate.

Despite these difficulties, the net judgment on the desirability of continued economic cooperation is uniformly positive. The degree of enthusiasm varies from one source to another and among different projects. However, none of the individuals or groups involved expressed regret at the undertaking or advised against further joint efforts.

Although acknowledging slippage in construction and delivery schedules, Japanese officials and businessmen also speak warmly of Soviet sincerity in attempting to abide by agreements and to fulfill commitments. Impersonal criticism of the bureaucracy is countered by personal praise for individuals at various levels, whether it be a vice-minister in Moscow or an engineering foreman on Sakhalin. Soviet secrecy is seen as endemic and not as deliberately designed to deceive foreigners, although that may be one consequence.

This attitude occasionally includes giving Moscow the benefit of the doubt. The best example came in justifying construction of an 80,000-ton dry dock capable of servicing the *Minsk*, a *Kiev*-class aircraft carrier. A responsible official said, "They told us it would be for merchant ships, and we know they have ships this large. Therefore we had to trust their word, or we would have appeared hostile."[98] Defense Agency comment has privately questioned the wisdom of this venture.[99]

Sometimes vested interest is felt to compel a more favorable posture toward the USSR than might otherwise be taken. For instance, fishing groups on Hokkaido calculate that flattery may be repaid with favors. Whereas Tokyo officials steadfastly reject Moscow's proposals for a friendship treaty in lieu of a peace pact, thereby finessing the territorial issue, an assemblyman from northern Hokkaido publicly endorsed the idea in the hope of getting more generous fishing terms.[100] Hokkaido ports, underutilized since World War II, should profit from the increased trade that presumably would follow from Siberian development. This leads to support for economic cooperation that contrasts with local loudspeaker campaigns on the "northern territories" and with the private expression of latent concern over Soviet military activity in the area.

Vested interests aside, however, the political rationale for construction of the dry dock reflects a widespread attitude among academic, business, and government specialists; it is mainly the Defense Agency that is an exception. Concern over Soviet suspicion of Japanese collusion with China and a belief that Japan can contribute to defusing Soviet-American tensions produce added justification for projects that, despite their being economically profitable, might be open to criticism as facilitating the expansion of Soviet power in the region. In July 1978 a major business figure argued that "if we get a treaty with China, we will need closer relations with the Soviet Union."[101] He also noted that although United States–Soviet relations are very sensitive to such questions as human rights and SALT, Japan has no such problems and should take the lead in economic cooperation with the Soviet Union.

A foreign office specialist on Soviet affairs differentiated Japan's role from that of the United States in like manner. In his view, Washington confronts Moscow globally and therefore must react to daily developments everywhere, but Tokyo can act as "a stabilizer in the region." Whereas others have the responsibility of coping with the USSR strategically where it is necessary, whether in Africa, the Middle East, or Europe, Japan's long-term relationship is economic and is focused on East Asia.[102]

This approach was amplified privately by Takuya Kubo, who was then (1976–78), director-general of the National Defense Council after having previously served as vice-minister of defense. His remarks incorporated most of the themes encountered in other interviews and so deserve examination at length.[103] Kubo noted at the outset that most persons concerned with Japan's defense do not favor Siberian development because they oppose any increase in Soviet power. He nevertheless stated his own contrary position. He believes that a larger Self-Defense Force is required in order to cope with a possible Soviet threat but, at the same time, that policy should try to reduce the likelihood of a threat developing.

One approach for such a policy, in Kubo's opinion, lies in the possible linkage between interdependence and security. The greater the economic interaction and mutual benefit, the less

THE JAPAN CONNECTION 143

likely is a misperception of hostility to arise. This calls specifically for a policy of "balanced diplomacy" instead of "equidistance." Kubo pointed out that there could not be "equality" in Japan's handling of China and the Soviet Union. Japan and China have a long history of contact between the two peoples and the two economies. Since Russia's historic orientation has always been toward Europe, and no close contact has ever existed with Japan, he says, "We cannot have the same relationship with both countries."

However, Kubo adds that precisely because closer economic relations come naturally with China, Japan "must work on the Soviet relationship to make it better." Summing up this approach with respect to his specific responsibility, the former defense official continues, "There are two aspects to security: negative and positive. Negative security is military strength against attack. Positive security is economic cooperation to reduce perceptions of hostility that arouse tension and threat. We must pursue both aspects. We cannot have one without the other."

This dual approach is not without "a certain degree of danger, risk, and cost," but "to avoid the risk and reduce the cost, we should go ahead on such projects as Yakutian gas if United States cooperation is possible." One danger is the possible cessation of payment in mineral exports to Japan. American participation reduces this possibility. Moreover, Soviet self-interest cautions against any cutoff because of the long-run damage to its international credibility. There is also the risk of Siberian development strengthening Soviet military power in East Asia, but other factors contribute more directly to this problem, and decisions on Siberia should not be unduly influenced by it.

Kubo warned that nonparticipation holds risks that must be weighed against those of cooperation. For example, if Soviet energy resources are not made available because of insufficient foreign credits and technology, a shortage could develop in the next ten years that might prompt Moscow to increase its pressure on the Middle East and the Persian Gulf. Alternatively, Moscow might reduce its energy exports to East Europe. Either move would destabilize the international situation.

Kubo commented on the linkage between Soviet-American detente and joint Japanese-American participation in Siberian development: "In most of the world the search for resources leads to conflict. Here, however, it can decrease the potential for conflict." Acknowledging that the Chinese may not agree, he claimed that this is another reason for American involvement, since presumably Washington's participation would reassure Beijing. Kubo cautioned, "The Chinese should not have the power of veto, but we should persuade them that Siberian development will help the international economy." Possible Chinese disagreement cannot be decisive because "we have concluded the treaty with China against Soviet opposition, and we should cooperate with the Soviet Union despite Chinese opposition."

From this point of view, the danger or risk in Siberian development is not so much military as economic and political, both of which are aspects that can be offset to a certain extent by American participation. In this regard Kubo sounded a widely shared opinion that, without the United States, Japan can only cooperate on small-scale projects. The economic investment is too great to shoulder alone, the problem of payment is too large to confront in isolation, and the political reaction in Beijing may be too much for Tokyo to handle if Washington does not take part.

Sensitivity to the Chinese reaction results from the abortive Tyumen project, the only known case of the historic triangle of tension directly affecting a joint project. Although Chinese concern over the joint pipeline-railroad scheme for transporting oil was expressed in strategic terms to the Japanese, Chinese objections were tempered by the hint that American participation might alleviate this concern.[104] Precisely how this condition was conceived is unclear, particularly since Sino-American relations were not yet fully established and the Beijing-Washington line had remained relatively inactive for some time. The apparent Chinese willingness to acquiesce in the project if the United States were to participate may have been based on a naive notion of the degree of leverage that could be exercised on Soviet behavior if the project were trilateral instead of bilateral. Alter-

THE JAPAN CONNECTION 145

natively, the Chinese position may have represented a compromise of factional differences over how strong a stand could be taken to block Japan's growing economic and possible political rapprochement with the Soviet Union.

Against this background, it is interesting to note the total absence of subsequent Chinese objections to Japanese participation in Siberian development. None of the sources interviewed could identify a single instance of protest from Beijing over particular projects or the overall amount of Soviet-Japanese economic cooperation. On the contrary, Beijing invited the same company that was already exploring for Sakhalin offshore oil and gas to participate in the offshore oil program in Bohai Gulf.[105] The post-Mao regime did not abate its public attacks on "social imperialism," and it successfully persisted in the effort to win Tokyo's signature to the treaty condemning "hegemony." However, it remained quiet on Japanese participation in the timber, coal, and port projects, despite the absence of American involvement.

We will discuss the Chinese further when we examine the view from Beijing and the Sino-Soviet relationship. Although China continues to figure in Japanese thinking about involvement in Siberia, it is far less important than during the Tyumen negotiations. China is heavily dependent on Japan for its economic modernization. Japan's loans and investments in China far outweigh those in the USSR. This reduces the likelihood of Beijing applying pressure on Tokyo to reduce its part in Siberian development. Should Sino-Soviet relations deteriorate to the point of possible conflict, this issue might arise. In the meantime, however, Chinese opposition is not seen as a serious constraint.

EAS Energy Exports: Sakhalin and Yakutia

Officially the Tyumen project remained on the agenda for possible revival, but practically it was a dead issue after 1974. Widespread doubt over the ability of West Siberia to maintain sufficient productivity to meet the needs of West Europe, East Europe, and Soviet domestic consumption leaves little chance that a significant surplus will be available for Japan once 3AM is completed.[106] Instead, Tokyo's interest in energy resources from Siberia turns primarily on Sakhalin and Yakutia, where oil, gas, and coal offer good prospects. By examining each of these in some detail, we can add an understanding of the economic calculations that underlie Japanese policy to the political factors already discussed.

Sakhalin has long been the USSR's only source of oil and gas in the Far East, except for the small output of Yakutia. In 1978 approximately forty onshore fields produced 2.25 million tons of crude oil and 800 million metric tons of gas.[107] In 1975 Soviet estimates of offshore deposits were sufficient to win Japanese agreement to a program of joint exploration and exploitation. By 1978 the continental shelf structures in the northeastern and the southwestern areas appeared to be the most promising. Four oil reservoirs were subsequently confirmed, with expectation of productive fields over an area of 300 square kilometers. More test wells are scheduled to confirm preliminary estimates, and initial production is anticipated by 1984–85.

Ice presents a major obstacle to the rapid development of Sakhalin's offshore resources.[108] In the northeastern area normal operations are possible only 107 days a year, from July 1 through October 15. Ice between 100 and 120 centimeters thick extends one kilometer from the coast in March. In the southwestern area, above 47° 30' north latitude, work can proceed for 261 days, from March 15 to November 30, but all personnel and equipment must be removed by December 15. Below this line there are 291 days available for operations, from March 15 to December 31, and personnel and machinery must be out by January 15. Such extreme conditions constrain the pace of exploration and development.

In addition to oil, Soviet reports of sizeable gas reserves further stimulated interest in joint exploitation of Sakhalin's energy resources. Cape Soya, at the northern tip of Hokkaido, is only 46 kilometers (28.5 miles) from Cape Krilov at the southern tip of Sakhalin; the intervening passage is sufficiently shallow to permit use of a pipeline, which prompted a Soviet proposal to supply Hokkaido with offshore production. But the first high

THE JAPAN CONNECTION 147

enthusiasm for the project has faded on both sides. A 1973 survey in Sapporo revealed widespread reservations despite a consensus in support of the proposal.[109] Some respondents recalled Moscow's sudden renunciation of the neutrality pact and surprise attack of 1945. Others criticized Stalin's extension of his Kurils claim to include the northern islands. Resettled refugees from the islands spoke bitterly of their treatment by the Red Army. The continued seizure of fishing boats and crews angered some respondents, and some were worried frankly that the gas supply might suddenly be shut off.

These underlying doubts seemed to be confirmed when Moscow subsequently reduced its estimate of Sakhalin gas reserves and urged the Japanese to shift their attention to Yakutia. Further frustration arose over the slow pace of negotiations, which required that Soviet decisions be processed through Sakhalin to Moscow and back through the embassy in Tokyo. Minor resentment resulted from irritation that, although the project was a joint venture, "The Soviets never let you forget who is number one."[110] As a final point, informants in Sapporo who identified gas as their major interest felt that officials in Tokyo placed primary emphasis on oil. Tokyo informants confirmed their suspicions, citing existing data and the estimate that the most likely gas reserves were in northeastern Sakhalin, where ice imposed the shortest season on exploratory drilling.[111]

As a further impediment, Soviet interest in the Sakhalin offshore operations waned in 1978–79, as was reflected in negotiations over financial matters, where prolonged discussion repeatedly foundered on lack of money.[112] One participant called this a situation that is normal when a five-year plan is drawing to a close and anticipated more activity in a year or two, but another blamed it on bureaucratic politics in Moscow. The actual argument concerned how to define the Japanese capital investment, whether as risk money repayable through a proportion of the eventual output or as a loan with a fixed return and interest. After considerable haggling a compromise was reached, but meanwhile time was lost and operations suffered accordingly.

Whatever the explanation of the slackening in Soviet interest, the consensus in Tokyo expects little from Sakhalin before the mid-1980's, or perhaps later. Nor does either the Soviet or the Japanese side depict the ultimate return in particularly generous terms. Instead, private comment portrays the project as a "model" or "test" case in Soviet-Japanese cooperation. From this limited perspective the verdict in Tokyo was cautiously favorable, at least down to 1980.

American participation is minor but worth noting. Gulf Oil was at first interested as a major partner, but disagreement arose over control of the special survey ships, Moscow insisting on Soviet crews and Gulf worrying about Soviet access to technological information under such an arrangement.[113] This resulted in Gulf reducing its share in service development and production to 3.5 percent. Another American contribution is a computer center in southern Sakhalin contracted for by the Sakhalin Oil Development Cooperation Company (Sodeko) and supplied by the Control Data Corporation. With these exceptions, foreign participation is wholly Japanese.

The coking-coal project in southern Yakutia has fewer uncertainties. It is not Japan's first experience with Soviet coal. In 1961 a long-term contract was concluded for the annual supply of 2 to 3 million tons of high quality coking coal from Kuznetsk. The initial term of three to four years was renewable. However, the more than 6,000-kilometer (3,720-mile) distance caused short-term instability in supply.[114] Development of the southern Yakutian fields, with their estimated potential of 40–45 billion tons, offered a promising alternative that resulted in the 1974 agreement. The quality is similar to that of the United States, if somewhat below that of Australia, both of which are major sources for Japan. But compared with 6,790 kilometers (4,245 miles) to Seattle, the distance from Tokyo to Wrangel is only 1,656 kilometers (1,035 miles).

Problems at the Neryungri site have forced slippage in the production schedule. Soviet officials complain that American-designed excavators, built under license in Japan, proved useless under the rigors of the Siberian winter. According to one report, "Teeth on the gigantic 36-ton scoops broke like plastic even before the temperature plunged to 58 degrees below zero Fahrenheit in December. Metal wheels on the huge 180-ton dump trucks became brittle in the cold and cracked as they bounced over the rugged roads."[115] The chief Soviet construction engineer admitted being a year behind schedule: "These machines have to remove 240 million cubic meters of overburden and steam coal to get down to the coking coal. This year . . . we can remove only 15 million, less than half the plan." 1983 was set as the time to begin the shipments, which are to total 83 million tons at an annual rate of 5 million tons with completion by 1999. However, these delays will probably postpone deliveries a year or two. Meanwhile, completion of the coal-loading facilities at Wrangel permits the size of ships serving Japan to be increased from 15,000 to 100,000 tons and provides piers capable of handling 5 million tons per year.

By far the biggest energy project in term of cost, return, and risk is Yakutian natural gas. As noted earlier, a minimum of $4 billion in Japanese and American capital, matched by a comparable Soviet investment, is required for a 3,200-kilometer (1,984-mile) pipeline and a liquefaction plant to provide 10 billion cubic meters of gas (7.5 million tons of LNG) annually to both Japan and the United States for 25 years. This investment estimate does not include the special LNG ships, local Soviet costs, or terminal facilities in Japan and the United States.

The final funding and financial terms were to be determined after a minimum reserve of 1 trillion cubic meters of gas had been confirmed.[116] By May 1978 Moscow claimed to have verified 825 billion cubic meters, but American specialists expressed skepticism. To show its good faith, the USSR thereupon reversed its long-standing opposition to foreign inspection and invited a joint survey team to visit the Yakutian fields that fall. The Japanese admitted to insufficient expertise, so their team simply accepted the Soviet figure. The Americans questioned the accuracy of the Soviet estimate but privately expressed confidence that the necessary trillion cubic meters would eventually be established.[117]

Other problems remained to be negotiated. Soviet practice is to determine price mainly by the cost of investment, while the Japanese and American practice is to price according to world market conditions. This explains Moscow's short-lived preference for Magadan, where the shorter pipeline would have saved an estimated $570 million in construction costs, although Japanese shipping costs would have increased by more than one-fourth.[118] However, Moscow's bargaining position is weak because, as one Tokyo authority noted, "Natural gas is a buyer's, not a seller's, market. We have plenty of alternative sources, including Indonesia and Australia."[119] As a further complication, the Soviet demand for a 50 percent share in the LNG ships faced adamant resistance. Not only would this provide the USSR with the most modern technology, but it would result in considerable profit from shipping charges, perhaps more than from the gas itself.

In addition to price, environmental problems complicate LNG delivery in the Tokyo Bay area and are even more severe in the United States. By 1980 LNG depots were entirely excluded from the West Coast, there was only a small island in the Gulf of Mexico near Texas to offload in that area, and growing East Coast opposition left questionable the entire future of LNG imports in the United States. Finally, even should delivery of Yakutian LNG prove feasible, it would supply only one-sixtieth of the anticipated American consumption of natural gas in 1990, compared with one-fifth for Japan.

Without American participation the Yakutia gas project probably is not viable. Although its share of the U.S. market is miniscule, no alternative market may be available, and the Japanese share of production cannot be increased, because it is universally felt in Tokyo that a greater dependence on Yakutia presents an unacceptable level of risk. The reasoning behind the Japanese consensus is varied. A small minority warns against the danger of providing Moscow with leverage on Japan's supply of energy resources, claiming that the threat of cutoff is critical beyond a certain point, although there is disagreement on precisely where that point lies.[120]

The majority of specialists on the subject reject this warning. They point to the projection that 26 percent and 24 percent of the total consumption of natural gas in West Germany and Italy, respectively, will come from West Siberia in the 1980's, and that this does not deter NATO countries, who stand in far more direct

THE JAPAN CONNECTION 151

military confrontation with Moscow.[121] Instead, government and business sources argue that financial and technical risks require Japan to limit its dependency on Yakutian gas. The size of the total investment, uncertain monetary and market conditions, and the cost of ships justify seeking fiscal protection through American participation. In addition, the risk of interruption in the flow of gas could be serious. Whereas the West Siberian pipeline system provides an extensive network of alternate routes in case of a leak or break, Yakutia will have only a single outlet. This calls for sharing the hazard of lost returns with others.

As a further consideration, some officials question the Soviet ability to manage a complicated project of this magnitude. Tokyo intends to limit its dependency on Yakutian gas to one-fifth or less of total gas consumption, which in turn will supply only 10 percent of total energy needs. Nevertheless, reliable performance and productivity remain important. This is thought by the Japanese to be assured by the participation of better-trained and more experienced Americans, who also command the latest technology. From the inception of the project to the final production cycle the Japanese believe that results will be more reliable and more cost-effective if Americans take part.

Less frequently mentioned, but nonetheless important in the opinion of some, is the possible Chinese reaction. This concern prompted one government official to insist that without Washington's involvement through the U.S. Export-Import Bank, Japan could not go it alone. The head of Tokyo Gas dismissed the argument, noting that "natural gas is not military material; it cannot be used to fly aircraft or to move warships. China is not concerned at all about a natural gas pipeline."[122]

As with Sakhalin offshore development, a frank and full appraisal of the various problems leaves the advocates of Yakutian gas convinced that the potential gain still outweighs the risks, provided that the United States takes part. The 1973 OPEC oil embargo was critical in prompting the placement of a high priority on diversifying dependency on energy resources. The greater the proliferation of supply points and commodity utilization, the less vulnerable Japan will be to developments in any single country or any single resource. So far as its major communist neighbors are concerned, the prospect of acquiring natural gas from the Soviet Union, oil from China, and coal from both meets this economic requirement and also serves the politics of "balanced diplomacy."

Beyond this combination of national interests, a recurrent theme in business and government discussions is the larger regional and global interest to be served by cooperating in the development of Siberian energy resources. As one government official put it, "I think it is in the interest of the Free World to encourage the development in the Soviet Union of all energy resources—coal, oil, and natural gas. This will give Moscow foreign currency reserves, it will enlarge trade relations, and it will increase interdependence. Moreover, we must remember that there is no guarantee that the Soviet Union will always remain open to such interdependence and that it will remain willing to share Siberian resources. If we do not cooperate now, it may become resource nationalistic and keep everything at home."[123]

His closing remarks reflect the ambivalence of Japanese views concerning the USSR. Their sense of transience in the opportunity increases the willingness to take limited risks so as to keep open the possibility of greater gains. In addition to natural gas, Yakutia may have oil. Soviet geologists have not held out any promise in this regard, but the lack of adequate surveys together with the calculations of American specialists raises the prospect of additional discoveries of oil as well as gas.[124]

Unless foreign participation is guaranteed, Japanese analysts see little likelihood of unilateral Soviet development of such resources, in contrast to the decision to build BAM following Tokyo's refusal to take part. Moscow lacks not only the technological resources but also the incentive. The hydroelectric power and coal in East Asian Siberia far exceed present and prospective local needs. Unless foreign exchange earned through export can justify the costly investment and long delay in returns, Soviet planners will probably not be willing to undertake expensive and difficult projects. But such earnings will be highly uncertain unless tied to compensatory payments for foreign capital and technology. It is this interdependence that encour-

THE JAPAN CONNECTION 153

ages Japanese officials to minimize the strategic risk of reliance on Yakutian gas while acknowledging the financial and technical risks that require American participation.

The Wider Perspective and Future Prospects

The degree of interdependence in Soviet-Japanese relations depends on much more than development of Siberian energy resources. Timber must be considered, as well as ferrous and nonferrous minerals. The completion of BAM will expand the "land-bridge" capacity for container shipping between the Pacific Ocean and Europe. Continued negotiation and cooperation will be necessary to manage ocean resources, particularly fishing. Industries that require large amounts of energy might be transferred from Japan to Siberia on a joint basis. Against these potential areas for positive interaction must be weighed the negative implications of continued growth in the Soviet Pacific Fleet and Moscow's attitude toward Tokyo's ties with Washington and Beijing.

These matters cannot be explored exhaustively here, nor can their future evolution and ramifications be determined at this time. However, they deserve at least summary review if the implications of Siberian development from the Japanese perspective are to be properly appreciated.

As for timber, the Japanese interest, although substantial, is not critical. However, the market is important to the USSR. The Soviet share of Japanese imports of wood products is between 17 and 20 percent, which constitutes approximately 40 percent of Japan's total purchases from the Soviet Union.[125] Moreover, Soviet softwood has no alternate market in Asia at present. Korea and China may become importers in the future, but specialists in Tokyo doubt that Southeast Asia is a possibility because of termite problems.[126]

In short, the bargaining advantage lies on the Japanese side, and the advantage is enhanced by the availability in North America of first-grade softwood and in Southeast Asia of first-grade hardwood. Not only is the Soviet product markedly inferior in both cases, but it is further diluted in quality by the requirement that purchase be of an entire stand and not of selected or graded trees. Yet timber constitutes a major item of trade for both Moscow and Tokyo. Whether it will increase in volume depends on several factors, including Japanese demand and non-Soviet sources of supply.[127] For the USSR, expanded production faces the same obstacles that plague all Siberian development, i.e., the shortage of labor and the difficulty of resource extraction. North Korea has been an important source of labor for logging in Siberia since the early 1960's, but the Koreans cannot be counted upon indefinitely.[128] Soviet incentive schemes provide a weak lure for the internal recruitment of workers because the impact of harsh climatic conditions is particularly severe in timber operations. Another impediment is the adverse location of desirable reserves, which are remote from both road and railroad. River floating is risky for larch, the dominant variety of tree in much of EAS, because of its propensity to sink.[129] Despite these obstacles, pulp and chips are likely to remain important as Soviet productivity expands, provided that Japanese demand grows accordingly. Because of this prospect, new pulp mills have been discussed for joint construction in Sakhalin, Khabarovsk, and Amursk, and one of the main loading piers at Wrangel will handle wood chips.

Iron ore may enter Soviet-Japanese trade after BAM becomes fully operational. The reserves in southern Yakutia are high grade and are believed sufficient to support a modest annual production of perhaps 12 million tons for several hundred years. Whether they are eventually available for export depends upon the degree of local utilization. Soviet plans remain uncertain both as concerns the desirability of a regional steel industry and its exact location. An impasse among competing interests and pollution problems have combined to prevent a decision down to 1981.

Discussion of a joint venture to exploit Aldan iron ore in conjunction with Neryungri-Chulman coal foundered in the Soviet-Japan Economic Committee in 1979 because Moscow proposed to repay Tokyo in finished steel. With the Japanese steel industry already suffering from a severe recession and fearing future competition from South Korean exports, there was no

THE JAPAN CONNECTION 155

basis for agreement.[130] However, this does not preclude renewed interest in the project at some later time.

Proposals for exploiting Udokan copper also failed for lack of systematic Soviet study and insufficient Japanese interest, but this situation too may change in the future. Udokan has been described by both Soviet and foreign sources in grandiose terms, one official estimate claiming reserves of two billion tons.[131] However, the cost of development has been put at between one and two billion dollars. With the world market price dropping in the late 1970's and plenty of ready suppliers with easy access, Japan had no reason to consider an expensive and difficult Siberian venture prior to 1980.

Future circumstances may prompt Tokyo to reexamine the Udokan project. The world market conditions for copper are extremely volatile. Civil turmoil in Zambia and Zaire, for example, could make delivery by some suppliers unreliable. Since five to six years are required before full production can be achieved in a new mine, increases in short-term demand cannot be easily met, and the Japanese development of Udokan could safeguard against unforeseen contingencies.[132] Countering these considerations is the reluctance to commit such a large sum long in advance and with little certainty of what the actual market conditions may be at the time production is finally possible.

There is no need to examine here each of the additional mineral resources whose exploitation in nearby Siberia may eventually interest Japan. Possibilities exist for modest amounts of tin, nickel, lead, zinc, mica, molybdenum, and asbestos.[133] None is in short supply elsewhere, but the advantage of diversified dependency and proximate location may induce participation in their development or in their purchase after Moscow has brought them into production. In purely economic terms, the individual ferrous and nonferrous resources are unlikely to match energy resources and timber in value or importance. Nevertheless, in the aggregate they may add a further sense of interdependence.

Transportation provides another area of cooperative interaction. In 1975 the Soviet Far Eastern Shipping Company agreed to allow Japanese shipping companies to share in the "land-bridge" container traffic over the Trans-Siberian Railway, with a fifty-fifty split envisaged by 1980.[134] The total container flow grew from 2,314 twenty-foot containers handling 50,000 tons of freight in 1971 to some 80,000 containers handling approximately 150,000 tons in 1976.[135] One estimate forecasts 1 million tons of container traffic in the near future.[136]

Up to 15 percent of all containerized traffic between Europe and the Far East was already traversing the "land-bridge" route by 1979, so Japan's interest is certain to grow.[137] Wrangel, which has a capacity of 140,000 units per year with Japanese assistance, surpasses Nakhodka.[138] BAM will provide an important addition to the overworked Trans-Siberian Railroad. A container factory in Abakan can produce 40,000 units annually, together with 5,000 flatcars. The certain mutuality of interdependence in the "land bridge" lies in its provision of foreign exchange for Moscow, estimated at $140 million in 1975, and its nearly 50 percent reduction in the time required for Japanese shipments to West Europe.[139] Lesser levels of cooperation in transport activity include the reopening of passenger and freight service between Siberia and the western coast of Japan and new air routes for Japan Air Lines and Aeroflot, both of which service the Niigata-Khabarovsk route.[140]

These various interactions represent a modest thickening of ties that contribute to and are strengthened by joint effort in Siberian development. Their significance is easily overlooked. Statistics on Soviet-Japanese trade only show the commodity exchange. The actual trade between the two countries is small, and it will probably remain a miniscule proportion of their total foreign commerce, not exceeding 5 percent on each side. Taken in isolation, this figure understates the economic interaction manifest in other activity.

Looking further into the future, Soviet specialists privately speculate about the possibility of Japanese cooperation in the joint development of industries with high energy input that can exploit the abundant hydroelectric and thermal power in East Asian Siberia and utilize both indigenous and imported raw materials.[141] American analysts have also suggested this possibility, specifically citing mineral fertilizers, copper, and alu-

THE JAPAN CONNECTION 157

minum as "energy-embodied products" that provide points of convergence in Soviet-Japanese interest.[142] Japanese aluminum interests see a steady decline in domestic production because of high fuel costs that require investment abroad in joint ventures, as in Australia and Canada.[143]

Against these prospects of closer economic relations must be weighed the political problems that impede greater cooperation. The impasse over the northern territories is likely to obstruct a formal Soviet-Japanese peace treaty throughout the 1980's. Public opinion and opposition party tactics will keep the issue alive, despite the impossibility of forcing Soviet withdrawal from the islands. Media attention to Moscow's military forces there, if stimulated by periodic Defense Agency briefings, may raise the level of concern above that in the past.

The steady expansion of Soviet naval activity in Southeast Asia and the West Pacific is certain to make Japan's security needs an increasing subject of discussion and debate, in marked contrast to previous decades. Already in 1980 the question won attention in the election campaign for the Diet, although it was not yet a major issue, as it was in the United States. This concern may be either alleviated or exacerbated by Soviet diplomatic behavior, depending on whether Moscow learns a more subtle style or persists in its heavy-handed treatment of Tokyo. Persistent railing against "Japanese militarism" and "collusion with China in an anti-Soviet front" will only worsen the Soviet position without changing Japanese behavior.[144]

Finally, Soviet behavior elsewhere in the world can raise the level of confrontation with the United States, thereby constraining Japan's economic cooperation and perhaps halting the further expansion of involvement in Siberian development. This prospect became serious after the invasion of Afghanistan, although in May 1980 Washington approved the sale of an oil rig through an American company for use in joint exploration off Sakhalin.[145] Further expansion of Soviet influence in the Middle East or South Asia could arouse doubt in Japan over the wisdom of extending assistance to Moscow in any form, especially if it might strengthen the Soviet hand in Asia. The Japanese penchant for consensual decision making does not preclude the

158 THE JAPAN CONNECTION

possibility of sharply conflicting views or of circumstances wherein the Defense Agency might attempt to assert its interests vigorously enough to block Soviet-Japanese agreement on pending projects. In short, economic interaction can become hostage to political and military relations, depending on external events and domestic politics.

Should these negative trends not eventuate, however, economic interaction may affect political relations positively. The record to date is mixed. Joint projects such as Sakhalin and Wrangel offset the impasse over Tyumen oil. Despite the Soviet invasion of Afghanistan, and Washington's initial reaction, Tokyo persisted in the regularly scheduled Soviet-Japanese discussions on Siberian development in 1980 and signaled its willingness to continue delivery on existing commitments without interruption.[146] Yet so far as the long-run future is concerned, the determining factor will be global Soviet-American relations and the degree to which these emerge as a zero-sum confrontation or as a mixture of political confrontation and economic cooperation.

In the final analysis, most Japanese agree that their only potential enemy is the Soviet Union and their only ally, the United States. Beyond this simple proposition, however, both governmental and public opinion are opposed to any major changes in defense spending or foreign policy in the aftermath of Afghanistan and the attendant deterioration in Soviet-American relations. In particular, popular resistance to an anti-Soviet coalition of China, Japan, and the United States counters Chinese pressure to promote such an alignment.

The moderate, middle-ground view has been well expressed by Kiichi Saeki in his assessment of the Soviet threat and the preferred response. On the one hand he noted that "the military power balance between America and the Soviet Union has further destabilized. Not only has the U.S. lost its military superiority, but there is every possibility that the balance will shift in favor of the Soviet Union if recent trends continue. . . . The Soviet Union has been accelerating its military build-up in the Asia-Pacific area. Although the primary purpose of the build-up might be to catch up with American military power and to guard

THE JAPAN CONNECTION 159

against China, we cannot deny that such a move increases the potential threat to the security of Japan."[147] But on the other hand Saeki warned, "The use of a united-front military strategy among the U.S., Europe, China, and Japan, or any action which suggests the development of such a strategy as a response to the Soviet threat to the security of the free world, must be carefully avoided. We must not behave in a manner which will induce the Soviet Union to overreact due to phobia that it is besieged."

As long as this attitude prevails among Japanese intellectual, business, and political elites, the possibility of an expanded involvement in Siberia remains a serious option. It is not precluded by a "tilt" toward China because these elites do not see an exclusive orientation as either necessary or wise. By 1981 Takuya Kubo's hope for a "balanced diplomacy" had virtually faded away; Tokyo had persistently refused to negotiate a treaty of peace and friendship with Moscow, had publicly criticized the Afghanistan invasion, and had held cabinet-level discussions with the Chinese that included the two states' foreign ministers.[148] But at the same time prospects for Sino-Japanese economic interaction had sharply decreased as a result of Beijing's cancellation of major contracts like the $900 million steel plant installation near Shanghai. That and the Japanese inhibition against joining China's all-out attack on Soviet foreign policy left Tokyo considerable incentive and flexibility in its handling of Soviet proposals for Siberian projects.

6 The China Factor

Analytical Problems

A different mode of analysis is required to assess China's role in future Siberian development as it is viewed from Beijing. Unfortunately, there is little direct evidence to draw on compared with Japan. No public opinion polls record popular attitudes on foreign policy, their intensity, and their potential for change. The Chinese mass media provide powerful images of Soviet perfidy in world affairs and reams of material detailing Moscow's military growth, its expansionism, and its alleged design for world domination. The Chinese media are centrally directed and usually can be presumed to reflect official policy, despite a small proportion of material that reflects bureaucratic and factional output.[1] The meager predictive value of these images for long-run developments can be best illustrated by the regime's record to date. Beginning in 1950 there was a decade of "learning from the Soviet Union," during which the media lectured Chinese audiences interminably on the virtues and benefits of Sino-Soviet friendship. But in 1960 Mao Zedong launched his ideological offensive against Khrushchev's "revisionism," triggering the sudden withdrawal of all Soviet aid and advisers.[2] The Sino-Soviet dispute became an open split that by 1969 verged on war.

Similarly, for more than twenty years Beijing's propaganda attacks against "U.S. imperialism" depicted Washington as the worst threat to China and the world at large. In May 1970 Mao Zedong's call for the people of the world to "unite and defeat the U.S. aggressors and all their running dogs" reportedly mobilized 400 million in mass demonstrations throughout the country.[3] Then, less than two years later, the Chairman personally received President Nixon and shook his hand while American aircraft and artillery were still pounding communist forces in South Vietnam.

These instances of policy reversal caution against basing predictions solely on the product of the Chinese media. It is true that clues can be discerned.[4] The potential for change may be inferred from silence on presumably significant matters, and shifts in emphasis and nuance may anticipate changes in posture, but it is hazardous to project future policy from the images and themes that appear in Chinese propaganda at any given time.

Another analytical problem lies in the relative uniformity of informal interviews with Chinese officials on foreign policy in general and Soviet relations in particular. Whereas a wide range of views on domestic issues was reported by scholars and visitors after the death of Mao, far less variation emerged in conversations on foreign affairs.[5] The duration, intensity, and sensitivity of the Sino-Soviet dispute inhibits Chinese from expressing anything but the public line to foreigners. In 1980 the editor of a regional academic journal lost his job for publishing the contents of a scholarly debate because a majority spoke in the affirmative on whether the Soviet Union could be termed a socialist society.[6] High officials hastened to reassure foreign visitors that the article did not signal any lessening of Beijing's hostility toward Moscow.[7]

This general ambience impedes the separation of Siberian development from the overall Sino-Soviet relationship so it can be examined as a separate phenomenon. As long as Moscow and Beijing continue to regard one another as potential enemies in a zero-sum confrontation, no aspect of Soviet society is likely to be viewed positively in China; Soviet economic developments will be weighed solely for their relevance to China's security. But should the two states settle their border dispute and reduce their military forces in the area, altered conditions could open up the possibility of mutual economic benefit in East Asian Siberia, including joint projects.

This suggests that it may be useful to project alternative future Sino-Soviet relationships and calculate their probability so as to provide different frameworks within which to analyze the relevance of China to our central inquiry. Such projections are subject to several constraints, however. Changes will occur in the individuals and interests that dominate the policy process in Beijing and Moscow over the coming decade. This can affect how the two future regimes will interact in their disputes. In addition, third parties, particularly the United States and Japan, can influence the bilateral relationship through their interaction with each side. This opens up an agenda of issues and possibilities that goes far beyond the span of this study.

These considerations compel us to make a somewhat truncated and tentative assessment of China's relevance for Siberian development. It will be recalled that our analysis of the likely strategic consequences of that development revealed relatively little negative impact on China's security, aside from the precombat logistical advantages offered by BAM. Similarly, our examination of economic aspects showed Japan to be pivotal as a source of capital and technology and as a market for natural resources; China is of only peripheral importance by comparison. We will review these findings in more detail from Beijing's perspective, but first we must weigh alternative future contexts for the overall Sino-Soviet relationship within which Siberian development will occur.

No War – No Peace

During the 1960's the Sino-Soviet dispute grew from a polemic over policy to armed clashes along a disputed border with overtones of possible war. In the 1970's this escalation stopped as both sides entered a prolonged siege marked by mutual recrimination and competition for influence in third countries.

THE CHINA FACTOR 163

Chapter 3 offered a brief prognosis for the 1980's of a "no war, no peace" relationship that will neither lead to major conflict nor be resolved harmoniously. The evidence and logic for this prognosis deserves fuller treatment at this point, and a comparison with the alternative possibilities of total conflict and total cooperation.

Ten years after the fighting at Damansky Island, the posture and behavior of Moscow and Beijing gave no evidence of imminent war being anticipated in either capital. According to U.S. intelligence estimates, between 675,000 and 725,000 troops, or slightly more than 15 percent of the Soviet armed forces, manned the China front in 1978, an increase of 70 percent over 1968.[8] This accounted for between 10 and 15 percent of Moscow's military budget.[9] Of the approximately 43 ground divisions deployed opposite China, roughly half were at one-third strength or less.[10] Only one-fourth of the Red Army faced China; three-fourths faced NATO.[11] In short, the Kremlin's allocation of money and manpower suggested a continuing defensive concern but no anxiety over a sudden Chinese attack.

Similarly, Chinese behavior, as distinct from public pronouncements, belied any serious apprehension over the prospects of a Soviet attack. After Lin Biao's downfall in late 1971 following his alleged plot to assassinate Mao Zedong, expenditures for the People's Liberation Army fell and did not recover their previous peak during the remainder of the decade.[12] In 1978–79 Chinese military missions traveled throughout West Europe examining air and ground weapons systems, but they failed to make any major purchases.[13] The war alarms that had resounded had long since disappeared. Thus Beijing's postures implied a relaxed if cautious calculation of the likelihood of major combat.

This view has considerable logic behind it, mutual recriminations notwithstanding. As one high Chinese official remarked privately in 1975, "The Soviet Union won't attack us until after they have defeated NATO."[14] A prolonged war with China would expose Moscow's position in East Europe to internal and external attack. Anti-Soviet or anticommunist dissidence would be encouraged. The memory of East Germany (1953), Poland (1956), Hungary (1957), and Czechoslovakia (1968) is a strong deterrent against inviting another such instance by engaging China's massive army in lengthy fighting. Nor could NATO be counted upon to stand passively by as it did in these past crises of Soviet control.

The chances of a quick and successful "surgical strike" against China's nuclear production facilities have decreased with each passing year as Beijing's nuclear retaliatory capability improves. U.S. military estimates credit Chinese missiles with "guaranteed survivability" because they are dispersed in narrow mountain valleys that are difficult to locate, and emplaced in solid rock.[15] In addition, Moscow must take into account Washington's experience in Vietnam and the cost of underestimating how much a determined enemy will endure without surrender. China's dogged resistance against the Japanese invasion from 1937 to 1945 proved that vast nation's ability to survive despite marked military inferiority. Thus their superiority in nuclear and conventional weapons does not offer Soviet planners a sufficiently promising advantage to make a deliberate attack on China likely.

There is even less reason to expect the Chinese to initiate a war with the USSR. Beijing's gross inferiority in strategic weapons invites the wholesale devastation of urban industrial areas. Should Moscow wish to maximize fallout from ground-burst nuclear weapons in conjunction with favorable prevailing winds, the resulting radioactivity could lay waste to much of China's agricultural base for years to come. These are catastrophic costs, regardless of Mao's alleged observation that if half the population were destroyed, half would still survive to leave China the largest country in the world.[16]

Should nuclear weapons not be used, a contingency that cannot be counted on in Beijing, China's huge population would nonetheless be of little use in an invasion of the Soviet Union. Except in the northeast, the PLA is logistically very weak throughout the border areas adjoining Soviet territory. Once initial deployments outran their prepositioned stocks, reinforcement and resupply would be severely constrained by the absence of an adequate transportation network. Nor could a ground attack go very far without air cover, the capability for which will remain beyond Beijing's air force for the foreseeable future.[17] The even-

THE CHINA FACTOR 165

tual modernization of the PLA air force will in all probability still leave it vulnerable to superior Soviet ground and air defense systems.

On rational grounds, a Sino-Soviet war that is planned in advance by either side seems inconceivable. An unplanned conflict that inadvertently escalates from border clashes is only slightly more plausible. These incidents have occurred at various points over more than a decade without serious consequences. Moscow and Beijing appear fully capable of containing them within manageable limits, and their ability to do so is enhanced by the relative isolation of border confrontations from population centers where casualties and damage could become serious. Furthermore, except for the area near the Trans-Siberian Railroad, no strategic point is involved that would warrant the increased investment of force that would be needed to capture or to protect it. Finally, the remoteness of these clashes from public awareness in either country and in the world at large permits them to be handled secretly should both sides so desire, thereby reducing or eliminating considerations of prestige and national honor.[18] These conditions offer considerable assurance against a Sino-Soviet war arising from the dynamics of uncontrollable escalation initiated by border incidents.

In addition to purely bilateral hostilities, third parties could trigger major Sino-Soviet fighting, although such scenarios are highly problematic. Another Chinese invasion of Vietnam might prompt Moscow to make good its 1978 treaty commitment to Hanoi by attacking remote border points. Because three sides would be involved instead of two, the possibility of unanticipated escalation would be somewhat greater. Moreover, news of a Sino-Vietnamese war would become known abroad, thus narrowing the options available to the leadership in Moscow, Beijing, and Hanoi. This would be especially true were the conflict to occur over disputed islands in the South China Sea, rather than along the Indochina border as in 1980. The incentive for Soviet support of Vietnam in this case could include promise of a permanent naval base in Cam Ranh Bay, as opposed to the brief periodic use of facilities there that resulted from the 1979 war.

A still more complicated scenario posits warfare between

Vietnam and Thailand prolonged enough to induce Beijing to help Bangkok by a diversionary attack in Laos or Vietnam. This in turn would probably force Hanoi to call on Moscow for compensatory action against China. Much would depend on the command and control of the respective armies and the nature of the fighting in each instance. This sequence of events might be wholly confined to peripheral areas with carefully limited levels of combat, but it conceivably could get out of hand and result in a Sino-Soviet war.

This does not exhaust the circumstances that can be hypothesized as potentially leading to conflict between the two largest communist nations. Further elaboration of scenarios, however, is unnecessary. The improbability of a chain reaction involving Moscow and Beijing in a war they otherwise would avoid is sufficient to argue against making serious policy projections dependent on such remote contingencies. Down to 1981 the behavior of both sides in situations of genuinely high risk has consistently been rational and prudent.[19] There is no reason to expect this pattern to change.

If the prospects for war are slight, so is the likelihood that the confrontation will be resolved in the near future. More than two decades of bitter dispute have produced hostile interaction in United Nations debates, public media exchanges, and crises elsewhere that invite outside intervention. The initial hostility has been reinforced by this patterned behavior. In addition, bureaucratic inertia and domestic politics tend to perpetuate the dispute. Both societies are highly authoritarian, a situation that inhibits any innovative analysis and policy prescription that might challenge the status quo. Career advancement is more certain for the individual if argument is avoided. Similarly, bureaucratic interests, military and civilian, become locked into existing policy and resist any change that threatens those interests.

Moreover, indirect benefits have accrued to both sides from the confrontation. Moscow strengthened its position in Mongolia and in Indochina as a direct result of its dispute with Beijing, as did the Chinese vis-à-vis the Soviets in Romania, in Albania for many years, and in Yugoslavia more recently. Among noncommunist Third World countries, the gains were less clear, less constant, and less certainly a consequence of the dispute. However, China's position in Egypt and Moscow's influence in India stem in large part from Sino-Soviet competition and confrontation.[20]

As for direct benefits, Moscow won economic concessions from Washington during the 1960's mainly because it appeared to be more moderate than Beijing in its support for world revolution and its handling of relations between the superpowers. The situation was reversed in the 1980's when China's winning diplomatic recognition and economic assistance from the United States and Japan came about in large degree because of its avowed opposition to expansionistic Soviet activity.

These circumstances, together with genuine issues of difference between the two regimes, contribute to the seeming permanence of the dispute. But history demonstrates the diplomatic axiom that there are no permanent enemies in world politics. This is amply revealed by Beijing's behavior over the past three decades. The People's Republic of China allied itself with the Soviet Union against the United States during the 1950's, opposed both superpowers in the 1960's, and sided with the United States against the Soviet Union in the latter 1970's. Another change in the 1980's, although not strictly predictable from the recent past, certainly cannot be ruled out.

Not all relationships need be wholly dichotomized, as if between friends and enemies, nor would so radical a reversal of the Sino-Soviet relationship be likely if Beijing were to change its posture toward Moscow. Neither side is likely once again to entrust its military security to an alliance with the other, given developments since 1960. Any significant Soviet assistance to Chinese military modernization is inconceivable, in contrast with the early period when Moscow provided Beijing with an entire jet air force, the productive capacity to duplicate Soviet tanks and artillery, and the nucleus of a coastal navy, including diesel submarines.[21] Such Soviet largesse and such Chinese dependency will not recur.

Nor can the economic relationship of the 1950's be restored. At that time the People's Republic faced an American embargo that extended into third countries, a condition of extreme Chinese isolation that effectively left only the Soviet Union to provide it with credits and technology. Now the advanced industrial nations of the world compete to provide the essentials for the modernization of China's science, industry, and agriculture. Moreover, the Soviet Union not only is unable to offer comparable aid but in fact needs credits and technology from the same sources for its own economy. This is particularly evident with respect to Japan, where both Moscow and Beijing offer coal, oil, and natural gas in exchange for financial and technical assistance in the development of mines and port facilities.

Last but not least, the political relationship is complex and in some respects contradictory, yet it basically precludes reconstruction of the "monolithic unity" that was ritualistically avowed during the heyday of the Sino-Soviet alliance. Even at that time the assertion of unity proved untenable as Moscow and Beijing vied for influence in what was then known as the Afro-Asian world. Their rivalry did not reach the point of mutual denunciation until after the open break in the early 1960's, but even in the mid-1950's Zhou Enlai competed with Khrushchev and Bulganin in the capitals of South Asia and the Middle East while each sought to outdo the other in economic assistance programs for less developed countries.[22]

Since that time the rivalry has intensified. Each side has increased its capability to act abroad and in the process has acquired client states that seek to manipulate and perpetuate Sino-Soviet competition to their own advantage. For example, Moscow, its East European allies, and Cuba help South Yemen with economic and military assistance; Beijing plays a similar role, albeit on a smaller scale, in North Yemen. Soviet and Cuban support for Angola confronted Chinese involvement in Zaire. Each side backed rival guerrilla factions in Zimbabwe, as they had in Angola. This pattern will not be reversed even should a reduction in bilateral tensions succeed in producing a border settlement and a drawdown of the forces in confrontation.

The competition has important implications for Chinese security where it involves neighboring regimes. Beijing's tacit alliance with Islamabad, founded in the 1950's, matches in word if

THE CHINA FACTOR 169

not in deed Moscow's more formal arrangement with New Delhi. This interlocks the Pakistani-Indian with the Sino-Soviet dispute. We have already referred to the informal Beijing-Bangkok tie, which offsets the Moscow-Hanoi treaty link. Mongolia has remained an exclusive Soviet protectorate since 1960. Only North Korea has managed to maneuver successfully between its two aspiring patrons so as to avoid a total commitment to either rival.[23]

These struggles for influence in countries bordering China present Beijing with a potentially serious challenge wherever they threaten territorial integrity through disputed borders or raise the prospect of subverting minority peoples. The Tibetans and the Mongols have long been anti-Chinese, and their antipathy has occasionally flared into open revolt. Under certain circumstances, Soviet attempts to exacerbate such tensions by overt and covert means can provide a worse threat to Chinese security than that posed by Moscow's military buildup. Provocative publications, directly and indirectly attributable to the Kremlin, heightened Beijing's sensitivity to this threat in the late 1970's.[24]

Against these negative trends, which impede resolution of Sino-Soviet differences, a major ideological development has muted much of the original polemic while minor improvements in state relations have been occurring after the death of Mao. To take the more significant factor first, in 1978 Beijing virtually abandoned its charges of heresy—the castigation of Moscow as "revisionist." This charge had first appeared in surrogate attacks against "Yugoslav revisionism" in the late 1950's. Its international manifestation came in the following decade, when the Chinese Communists sponsored radical splinter groups in Europe and elsewhere as "true Marxist-Leninists" and rejected all association with the established Communist parties of such countries as France and Italy. On the thirtieth anniversary of the People's Republic in 1979, however, China's senior Long March veteran, Ye Jianying, declared that "revisionism" had been "incorrectly defined" at the start of the Cultural Revolution.[25] In 1980 the Chinese Communist Party ostentatiously hosted the Italian Communist Party leadership.[26] Mao's ideological indictment faded away, although no improvement in Sino-Soviet party relations followed.

Instead of attacking Moscow as having betrayed Marxism-Leninism, Beijing concentrated its fire on Soviet "social imperialism" and "hegemonism." The shift of emphasis to foreign policy transformed the dispute into a traditional "Great Power" struggle: national interest, not ideology, became its basis.[27] This removed the incompatible dichotomy of moral good versus heretical evil that made compromise inconceivable. China's confining the dispute to world politics removes an obstacle to negotiation that ostensibly leaves only the requirement of a change in Soviet external policy, not a radical shift in domestic policy as well.

Tokens of a Chinese willingness to improve relations have emerged from time to time. In February 1973 local branches of the Sino-Soviet Friendship Association in northeastern China laid wreaths at tombs and monuments to honor Soviet troops who died there in World War II.[28] The practice continues on Soviet Army Day. In November 1977 the national Sino-Soviet Friendship Association gave a film reception to honor the sixtieth anniversary of the October Revolution.[29] The first exchange of delegations brought a Moscow counterpart group to Beijing on February 17, 1979. Unfortunately, this proved to be the first day of Beijing's "counterattack" against Vietnam, and the Soviet delegation returned to Moscow the next day.[30]

At a higher level, two developments in the fall of 1977 strengthened these signals. Considerable foreign speculation accompanied the visit of Foreign Minister Huang Hua to the Soviet embassy on the anniversary of the Bolshevik revolution, since he was the highest Chinese official to have been there in eleven years.[31] The visit gained significance when it was learned subsequently that in September the two sides had quietly arrived at a settlement of their longstanding differences over navigation at the juncture of the Amur and Ussuri rivers opposite Khabarovsk.[32] Beijing agreed to inform Soviet authorities of any intended passage of its ships through the eastern channel adjoining the city, although it insisted that this did not prejudice its claim that the channel is the legitimate boundary between the

THE CHINA FACTOR 171

two countries. Moscow for its part did not relinquish its claim that the western channel at the opposite end of Bear Island is the official line, but it freed passage through the Amur-Ussuri confluence in response to Beijing's symbolic concession of authority. Although technically the issue was not resolved, the agreement represented the first instance in ten years of progress toward resolving the border dispute.

China's invasion of Vietnam seemed to close the door to any further amelioration of the dispute. In April 1979 Beijing announced it would not renew the Sino-Soviet Treaty of Friendship and Mutual Assistance at its formal point of termination one year later.[33] However, China also said it was prepared to discuss Sino-Soviet relations without preconditions, a reversal of the stance it had adopted over previous years. In September talks began between deputy foreign ministers in Moscow.[34] No agreement was reached on the agenda, so the meetings were adjourned, supposedly to resume in Beijing at an unspecified date, but then the Soviet invasion of Afghanistan prompted China to declare the exchanges indefinitely suspended, presumably until Moscow withdrew its forces.[35] Meanwhile, propaganda attacks against "Soviet expansionism and hegemony" reached new levels of intensity as the Beijing leadership proclaimed to one and all that Afghanistan proved that Moscow's global strategy aimed at strangling the West and Japan by seizing control of vital Middle East oil supplies.

All things considered, the political prospects for an end to the Sino-Soviet dispute appear dim for the next several years. The disappearance of ideology as a point of controversy could facilitate compromise, but the emergence of powerful national security concerns as an overriding issue makes such compromise exceedingly difficult. The Chinese demand for a withdrawal of Soviet forces from Mongolia and Afghanistan, while perhaps intended as tactical bargaining points, goes well beyond the initial insistence that Soviet troops evacuate all border territory allegedly in dispute.[36] Moscow's intransigence on the border withdrawal is certain to be matched in the case of Mongolia as well, although the Afghan situation might change in time. The asymmetry of power relieves Moscow, the dominant party, from any compulsion to make concessions and inhibits Beijing, the weaker side, from backtracking on its position. Moreover, the Soviet position in Vietnam, though not an explicit item in the Chinese agenda, further hardens the impasse. As a final consideration, leadership transition, whether recent or imminent, may also limit flexibility by narrowing the range of debate in each capital on so sensitive and volatile an issue.

Yet it is worth noting that Beijing initiated the dispute and has pressed it to the present, whereas Moscow has persisted in intermittent attempts to patch up the quarrel, although without success. This suggests that if a major breakthrough is to occur, it will come on the Chinese side. One development that might bring this about could be a loss of confidence in the utility of siding with the United States against the Soviet Union. This calculation could result from several factors. The relative power of the USSR and the respective record of expansion and contraction of influence of the superpowers might gradually shift so decisively to Moscow's advantage as to persuade Beijing that a limited accommodation was wiser than total confrontation, Soviet terms permitting. Or developments on Taiwan could take an alarming turn from Beijing's perspective, for instance, if the island should move toward independence when the present Nationalist leadership leaves the scene. Regaining Taiwan, by force if necessary, could take priority over placating Washington. Under these circumstances, the PLA would logically want to reduce the need to safeguard the long Soviet frontier against attack and might seek a settlement with Moscow toward that end.

The latter half of this decade may thus find a marked reduction in direct Sino-Soviet confrontation with competition continuing mainly in third countries. Lowered tension in bilateral relations will not lead to an alliance, but it could permit limited cooperation in areas of mutual interest. This level of Sino-Soviet detente is not impossible in the 1980's, any more than was detente between Beijing and Washington during the 1970's. In the latter instance, China had suffered 300,000 casualties fighting the United States in Korea. It had faced a total American embargo on trade for twenty years with spillover effects in its trade with many other countries. It had been excluded from its rightful seat in the United Nations down to 1971 as Washington maneuvered to maintain Taiwan as the representative of China. Worse, Washington's formal defense of Taiwan had frustrated certain communist victory in the prolonged Chinese civil war and had separated the island from mainland rule.[37]

Moreover, Soviet proposals for collective security arrangements in Asia found few takers throughout the 1970's, largely because of their implied anti-Chinese goal, but United States' military bases and allies confronted China with a semicircle of hostile power extending from Korea and Japan to Thailand during the 1950's and 1960's. Nor was this power alignment passively confined to "containment." Clandestine operations for espionage and sabotage mounted from Taiwan and the offshore islands combined with U-2 reconnaissance overflights as constant reminders of the efforts of the "U.S. imperialist–Chiang Kai-shek clique" to undermine Chinese Communist rule. In Tibet this effort succeeded in making a bad situation worse.[38] By comparison, only in Xinjiang was Soviet subversion charged explicitly with attempting to "separate" the region from Chinese control.[39] Moscow's maneuvers otherwise failed to elicit accusations comparable to those directed against Washington.

The Nazi-Soviet pact in 1939 revealed the power of realpolitik to overcome deep-seated patterns of hostile behavior reinforced by strong ideological antipathy. On a more positive note, the Nixon-Mao handshake in 1972 symbolized the ability of strong-willed leaderships to reverse course when circumstances demand it. The latter event was particularly striking because it occurred while American forces were still locked in combat with Vietnamese troops and the world was anticipating a Nixon-Brezhnev summit in Moscow. Yet notwithstanding the personal ideological commitments of Mao to an anti-American policy and of Nixon to anti-communism, Beijing and Washington succeeded in defusing more than twenty years of armed confrontation in a mere seven months of secret negotiations.

A Sino-Soviet detente is not likely to produce the dire consequences of 1939 or the human drama of 1972. It can, however, have far-reaching implications should it bring the two sides to explore the possibilities for joint economic effort in northeastern Asia. This circumstance would drastically alter Beijing's perspective on East Asian Siberia compared with the existing bitter Sino-Soviet confrontation. The prospects for such a detente are both dim and distant. Nevertheless, they are considerably more probable than the extremes either of major war or of harmonious alliance. And they are sufficiently plausible to warrant examination of how EAS projects may benefit China as well as the Soviet Union.

A Symbiotic Relationship?

As indicated at the outset of this chapter, evidence on Chinese attitudes toward Siberian development is scarce, particularly for recent years. The 1974–75 protests against possible Japanese participation in the combined pipeline-railroad proposal to ship West Siberian oil to the Pacific have no subsequent counterpart. On the contrary, Chinese contracts with Japanese firms engaged in Sakhalin offshore oil exploration and the construction of BAM imply a willingness to accept Tokyo's posture of "balanced diplomacy."

In addition to the relative inattention of the Chinese media to Siberian development compared with that given to other indicators of Soviet strength in Northeast Asia, especially as pertinent to Japan, several points deserve mention. First, the implications of the development are frequently discussed in terms of the threat to Europe rather than to Asia. Second, when the threat to Asia is identified, it is expressed in general terms or with specific reference to Japan, rarely to China. Third, the assertion of threat is often attributed to Japanese sources and is defined generally. Only infrequently is it offered as original Chinese comment, and rarely is it substantiated by identification of projects with potential strategic significance such as BAM.[40]

Thus, in October 1977 a Chinese scholar based in Heilongjiang posited a wide range of goals behind "exploitation of the eastern region" of the USSR: (1) the export of natural resources to earn foreign exchange, (2) the development of industry to improve the distribution of economic activity, (3) the provision of

THE CHINA FACTOR 175

Tyumen oil for "its mammoth armed forces and naval fleets in the Far East," (4) the separation of Japan from the United States through "cooperation" that would result in economic control over Japan, and (5) the firming of control over East Europe by supplying energy and raw materials from the eastern region.[41] The author alleged that Moscow had "spared no efforts in establishing strategic communication routes and in building and expanding military airfields, harbors, fuel and ammunition depots, and large clandestine granaries in its eastern region." Yet he summarized these steps as aimed at serving "the strategic counterrevolutionary Soviet scheme of seeking European and world hegemony." His omission of Asia from this formulation and his broad list of the goals being pursued by Siberian development drastically diluted the sense of threat to China's security and stated the threat to Japan in nonmilitary terms.

An anonymous commentary broadcast in early 1978 stated flatly, "The purpose of the Soviet leading clique's development of Siberia and the Far East at all costs is to support its major contention in Europe and its ultimate aim of exercising hegemony over the whole world."[42] The lengthy piece made only one reference to Japan (it mainly described the territorial expanse of Siberia), and none to China. The emphasis throughout was on the West, as in the assertion, "The Kremlin . . . thinking is that, once war begins, it can make the east the rear of its western front." Almost as an afterthought, the writer noted in addition that "by developing the Tyumen oilfield in the east, the Kremlin can also insure a sufficient fuel supply for its mammoth army and fleets in the east." But with the growing recognition that the Tyumen fields might prove inadequate for western deliveries to Soviet and East European markets, allusions to their eastern potential disappeared from Chinese commentaries, and no other project replaced Tyumen as evidence of the strategic threat to China inherent in Siberian development.

Perhaps in deference to Japanese sensitivities in the wake of the Sino-Japanese friendship treaty, down to 1981 Chinese media dealt with Soviet-Japanese discussions of joint Siberian efforts in a muted and truncated manner. Before and after the semiannual meetings, Beijing's articles on Soviet-Japanese relations either omitted any reference to Siberian matters or dismissed them in brief commentaries.[43] An exceptionally long *People's Daily* analysis following the September 1979 meeting relied on an unidentified "Japanese commentator" for the bulk of its harsher attacks, which it deleted from the version broadcast abroad in English.[44] No mention was made of BAM or Wrangel as facilitating future Soviet military activity.

In fact, BAM's absence from Chinese propaganda assertions of growing Soviet military power in Asia is particularly striking. A rare mention in August 1980 recounted a USSR Council of Ministers decision "on setting up the Baikal-Amur Railway office" that was initially relayed by Tass.[45] It reported that one-fourth of the line would be open to traffic by early 1981 with complete operation "expected in 1984." The Beijing account noted, "The world press has pointed out that the USSR is constructing this second railway line in eastern Siberia not only out of its economic need to develop its eastern region but also out of its strategic need to strengthen its military deployment in the Far East." This isolated reference, low-key in its presentation and indirect in its attribution, suggests the lack of significance accorded to BAM by Chinese analysts.

Although negative Chinese attention to East Asian Siberia is relatively slight and unfocused, no positive articles appear at all, quite understandably. Reliance on evidence from the 1950's before the Sino-Soviet dispute erupted is necessary to infer what possible economic benefits China may derive from EAS development in the 1990's. Admittedly, conditions have changed drastically in the interim. Whereas China formerly depended on trade with the Soviet bloc for industrial imports, which were paid for with exports of food, raw materials, and light industry, neither aspect is important at the present time.[46] In addition, both sides then saw their mutual interests as served by their contiguity as a basis for joint efforts in transportation, irrigation, and other developmental projects. Now the frontier is in dispute, and large armies stand in confrontation.

Despite these fundamental differences between the distant past and the future, suggestive precedent exists for a symbiotic relationship between the local economies of East Asian Siberia and northeastern China. EAS, a food deficit region, has traditionally relied on supplies from across the border. Soybeans, vegetable oil, grain, and fruit comprised a major part of regional trade during the early 1950's.[47] Salt lakes in the Liaotung Peninsula offered another important resource, with at least 100,000 tons available yearly to meet Siberian needs.[48] In EAS the only source of salt, essential for the Far East fishing industry, is one site in remote Yakutia.

As previously noted, the BAM zone must import two-thirds of its required foodstuffs. Transportation from distant points of production in the USSR is costly and places an added burden on an already overloaded rail system. Use of Chinese sources could facilitate Siberian development by providing a reliable nearby supply. The actual availability of Chinese foodstuffs may be reduced by the demands of a much larger population in northeastern China with increased purchasing power. However, Beijing retains considerable freedom to direct the flow of produce abroad if the utility value of imports justifies it.

This, in turn, raises the question of what EAS has to offer in exchange. The Udokan copper deposits could provide a valuable supplement to China's reserves, which have yet to become available in sufficient amounts to meet the vast need that will grow as economic modernization moves ahead.[49] Proven deposits, while large, are poorly located and of low grade. In addition, China is extremely deficient in timber and wood products. Siberian reserves are virtually inexhaustible; new processing plants for pulp and other items will require foreign markets to absorb their output and to justify their cost. As an added dimension of mutual interest, Moscow has considerable difficulty recruiting workers for timber felling, while Beijing faces a serious unemployment problem in the years ahead.[50]

According to Khrushchev's memoirs, in 1954 he proposed that "a million or more Chinese workers be sent to Siberia to help us take advantage of the vast timber resources there."[51] Mao demurred in the first instance, calling the proposal "embarrassing" because it implied that China "represented a good source of cheap labor," an image he attributed to "the capitalist West." Later, however, Mao agreed, and 200,000 Chinese workers went to Siberia. Khrushchev claims that Moscow resisted Beijing's pressure to send a second contingent when the first contract expired because "they wanted to occupy Siberia without war, . . . to make Siberia Chinese rather than Russian."

In subsequent years North Korea supplied workers for Siberia's forests.[52] Then in 1979 China began to contract for labor to serve in projects in the Middle East and elsewhere.[53] The completion of BAM will open up an extensive amount of virgin timber, with the shortage of manpower an important obstacle to the plan to increase roundwood exports severalfold. Should the Sino-Soviet border dispute be resolved, this could be a mutually attractive area for joint effort.

A more far-reaching and complex undertaking envisaged in the mid-1950's concerns the joint development of river resources linking Siberia and northeastern China. In 1956 the two governments agreed to research the possibility of an economic complex on the Argun River and the upper course of the Amur, together with projects in the Amur basin. Three years later S. V. Klopov, the Soviet leader of the joint survey expedition, published the results in a book, *Amur—reka druzhbi* (Amur—river of friendship).[54] His focus encompassed problems that demanded solution as well as a vision of the potential to be exploited through joint effort. Addressing the former aspect, Klopov declared, "The problem of the Amur—one of the greatest economic problems of international significance. It includes a broad complex of questions connected with the development of the national economies of the Soviet Far East and Transbaikalia and also the northeast provinces of China, . . . first of all, measures to combat floods that at present inflict heavy sacrifices on the population and economy of Primoria."[55]

Noting that "catastrophic floods occur every seven to eight years," Klopov argued that recent disasters on the Zeya and Amur rivers in the USSR and the Sungari River in the PRC demonstrate the need for a comprehensive joint plan. This in turn would lead to hydroelectric plants to support "industry, agriculture, the electrification of transportation, cities, and villages. Distribution on the frontier could equally serve energy to Soviet and Chinese territory and tie into the energy networks of the

Soviet Far East and Northeast China." Coal and iron deposits in the Amur basin could make possible use of this supply of energy to support a metallurgical industry on both sides, in addition to the possibility of producing chemical and forest products in Primoria. The roughly equal division of the basin's 1.95 million square kilometers (760,500 square miles) between the two countries—except for the 1.5 percent that lies in Mongolia—seemed to Klopov to provide a good basis for cooperation.

At the start, this cooperation made significant progress: "Their [the Chinese] participation gave us the possibility to determine the damage by flooding on the Chinese shore of the Amur, to systematically study both banks of the river and complete all the work necessary for the research stations, and to choose the areas for putting up dams, determining the regulatory possibilities of reservoirs and the capacity of hydroelectric stations, and calculating the costs of their construction."[56] Parenthetically Klopov paid tribute to "many of our Chinese comrades [who] understand Russian; to our shame, they master it faster and better than we do Chinese. Several know English, German, and French."

The Soviet side proposed a five-year plan for joint expeditions to "develop and confirm a single program with a common methodology," including detailed topographic, hydrographic, and geological surveys preparatory to planning hydroelectric stations on the upper Amur. However, aside from two meetings of the United Study Council, one in Moscow in 1957 and one in Beijing in 1958, apparently no further activity took place. The worsening of Sino-Soviet relations as a result of the Great Leap Forward and foreign policy differences overshadowed the nascent economic relationship. In this context, Klopov's reference to developments in 1958 had negative as well as positive connotations: "In the past year there has been a remarkable change on the Chinese shore. New houses have sprung up in Moche, Xuma, and other towns and villages in the border regions. Tens of thousands of new settlers have arrived from the central provinces of China to the Amur. They began to develop virgin land. They are organizing cooperative agriculture."[57]

Sent to press in February 1959, Klopov's book was soon an

anachronism. The Amur ceased to be a "river of friendship" but instead became the focus of incidents that eventually triggered armed clashes in 1969. Nevertheless, the earlier joint survey revealed the basis for a wide range of cooperation and potential interdependency between East Asian Siberia and northeastern China should the overall political situation come to permit it. At a minimum, flood control programs on the Zeya, Sungari, and Amur rivers would benefit both countries by eliminating extensive damage to crops, transportation, and population centers. At a maximum, the harnessing of hydroelectric power would facilitate industrialization based on locally available resources.

China enjoys alternate energy resources, yet they are not without problems over the long run. The Daqing oil field near Harbin has reached its maximum level of production and will diminish in the future. Coal exists in abundance but poses serious pollution problems. Hydroelectric power, by comparison, is virtually inexhaustible and clean. The ability of northeastern China to support a considerable expansion of population lies in industrialization, for which an increased energy supply is necessary.

Whether Moscow would welcome this development depends, of course, on the prospects for Sino-Soviet relations. The climatic conditions of East Asian Siberia and the costs of building an infrastructure preclude a population expansion comparable to what would occur across the border. The fear of more than one billion Chinese overrunning relatively vacant neighboring land is not likely to disappear quickly in the aftermath of a border settlement and a reduction of military forces in the region. In the meantime, unilateral steps, such as the Zeya hydroelectric project and BAM, will reduce the Soviet incentive to reopen the joint Amur River scheme.

In sum, the degree of cooperation that eventually may emerge in Sino-Soviet economic relations cannot be forecast at this point, but neither can such cooperation be wholly foreclosed as a possible consequence of detente. If it occurs, the results will probably be peripheral for each country—in economic value as well as location. Yet the fact remains that Siberian development has potentially positive implications for China.

This finding is important, not only for Beijing but also for Tokyo and Washington. The China factor will remain relevant to their separate and joint deliberations over the consequences of involvement in projects proposed by Moscow. Seen in this perspective, Yakutian natural gas, for instance, might be examined with a view to making part of it available to serve northeastern Chinese as well as Soviet, Japanese, and American consumers. The route to Olga would run sufficiently close to the border to permit provision of a branch pipeline with no difficulty and little cost. Conversely, Beijing's cooperation in allowing use of the Chinese Eastern Railway across Heilongjiang province could enhance the usefulness of Wrangel, especially for Japanese purposes. The result could be an appreciable saving of time and cost in transporting freight across the USSR as compared to both the more circuitous Trans-Siberian line along the Amur and BAM farther north.

Any trend toward Sino-Soviet cooperation would be welcome in Japan, since it would relieve Tokyo of the sensitive problem of having to pursue "balanced diplomacy" through economic assistance to both sides in the present Sino-Soviet dispute, and it would validate Tokyo's basic hope that the traditional triangle of confrontation can evolve into one of cooperation. In this sense, Siberian development is a means to an end rather than an end in itself. Yet, as is acknowledged throughout this chapter, the possibility of benign relationships depends on how Moscow and Beijing handle their larger bilateral concerns.

7 Soviet Decision Making, Development, and External Influence

Introduction

At various points we have suggested that among the factors to be considered in understanding the implications of Siberian development, one that can prove important over time is the Soviet decision-making process. The dynamic interaction between development and decisions is an ongoing process in which different outcomes depend on different inputs. On the domestic side, these inputs include changes in the decision makers, feedback from the field registering success or failure, competitive demands from other regions for capital investment, and the economic calculus of Siberian resources. To illustrate the possible negative inputs more specifically, Brezhnev's successor may reorder economic priorities to the detriment of East Asian Siberia, BAM may encounter greater costs and problems than anticipated, the exploitation of West Siberia could preempt investment funds, or an inability to induce necessary migration without inordinate incentives and service costs may prompt planners to look elsewhere for resources. Any of these considerations, alone or in combination, can radically reshape the final outcome.

On the foreign side, the political environment may change,

the degree of foreign participation may fall short of expectation, or the international market may prove inadequate to justify the effort. For example, the threat of war with China may appear too serious to warrant the risk of further large-scale Soviet investments in EAS, where the return cannot be realized for many years. Japanese capital may find more promising ventures elsewhere or be dissuaded from continuing by an American refusal to take part in Siberian development. Competitive suppliers in the Pacific basin or a prolonged slowdown in economic growth abroad may shrink the demand for Siberian resources below the point of profitability for high-cost exploration and extraction projects. These external phenomena would affect the pace and content of the Soviet effort.

Some of these factors have elements of uncertainty in common with similar situations elsewhere and should not be viewed as unique to either Siberian development or Soviet decision making. They illustrate why the money advanced for such ventures is appropriately termed "risk" capital. Whether the area to be developed is in Siberia or the Amazon basin, the mixture of political and economic considerations that cannot be forecast with confidence more than a few years ahead makes investors cautious lest they find themselves involved beyond the point of prudence.

Not all of these factors are subject to systematic analysis, much less to forecasting their future evolution. Soviet leadership changes are unpredictable, as are world market conditions. However, at this point we want to focus on one aspect that is particularly elusive but nonetheless germane to our inquiry, namely, how Siberian development might affect Soviet decisions. In this context, the role of foreign investment and technology can be examined for its impact on the interaction between development and decision making.

First, of course, we must grapple with the antecedent question of how Soviet decisions are arrived at, implemented, and changed. Unfortunately, scholarship has so far been unable to describe this process on the basis of empirical research. It has, however, evolved two conceptual models with differing assumptions and implications.[1] The traditional model depicts a monolithic system with a wholly directed society that functions under the authoritarian rule of a single dictator (Stalin) or a small elite (the Politburo). A more recent model draws by analogy on the studies of Max Weber and on western behavior to present a more complex system where bureaucratic pressures and vested interests are balanced or brokered by a Party that itself has parochial points of division. The earlier approach presented the political pinnacle in Moscow as the prime point of leverage over events. It was conventionally referred to as the totalitarian model. The newer approach probes bureaucratic, vested, and regional or local interests to discern the dynamic interactions that determine the main direction of developments, on the assumption that relatively narrow choices remain to the top officials. Since the entire Soviet Union is in effect one bureaucracy, we term this the bureaucratic model.

One of the foremost exponents of the bureaucratic model pointed out that "not less than 560 institutes and agencies were engaged in shaping and providing the details of the Five Year Plan (1971–76); under this condition conflict, compromise, and cooperation must necessarily arise."[2] Another analyst noted that the general plan for development and location of industry up to 1980 had involved more than 20,000 scholars and specialists.[3] Former participants in Soviet society testify to the multiplicity of interests that affect the planning and implementation of decisions.[4] The sheer scope of the economy, whether measured in geographic, demographic, or output terms, argues for the bureaucratic and against the totalitarian model.

Yet it must be conceded at the outset that much of what is written about Soviet decision making is based on *a priori* assumptions that cannot be tested against reality because the leadership has succeeded in maintaining sufficient secrecy to veil most, if not all, of its deliberations from foreign observation. The one informed defector to describe the inner political process was Leon Trotsky, but his highly polemical account applied essentially to the period before Stalin's ascendancy, the years down to the mid-1920's.[5] The supposed memoirs of Nikita Khrushchev are of uncertain reliability and in any case throw little light on subsequent years; they overdraw Stalin's personal rule and omit the details of Khrushchev's own leadership patterns and procedures.[6]

Therefore, the analysis that follows is necessarily a compound of surmise and speculation sprinkled with such scholarly investigation as has been possible. Its lack of analytic rigor does not wholly vitiate its value. To the extent that foreign firms and governments can be sensitive to the possible role of outside influences in Soviet decisions, they may consciously help to shape the course of Siberian development so as to reduce the sense of threat and tension that has dominated relations in northeastern Asia for most of its modern history. Because so little is known of the Soviet decision-making process, it would be wrong to make this factor the determining one with respect to foreign involvement, but it would be equally mistaken to ignore it altogether on the assumption that the system is completely closed and impervious to external influence. To understand the Soviet system's points of potential susceptibility, we first must step back from our focus on Siberia and examine the Soviet political system as a whole.

Levels of Decision Making

Whereas the totalitarian model focuses exclusively on the Politburo, the bureaucratic model treats the Politburo as the highest but not the only level of importance in the political system. In addition to its obvious role as the locus of ultimate power, the Politburo is comprised partly of individuals who presumably reflect bureaucratic interests because of their lifetime associations and career patterns.[7] For example, the April 1973 naming of the ministers of defense and foreign affairs and the head of the Committee on State Security (KGB) to the top Party body raised the possibility of these groups having their interests articulated and defended at the highest level.

This is, of course, pure inference. Nothing definite is known about how the Politburo functions or what views these three individuals may have expressed at such meetings. Yet their expertise and command of information give them an advantage over their colleagues in discussing matters related to their governmental responsibilities. It is difficult to believe that they could divest themselves so completely of the organizational values and interests that are the main concern of their daily duties as to act in a wholly disinterested fashion within the Politburo.

The Politburo was involved in decisions on Siberian development, at least in the initiatory phase and at certain benchmarks thereafter. Presumably decisions as far-reaching as BAM, the involvement of Japan and the United States in development of Yakutian gas, and the Tyumen pipeline received Politburo consideration before being finally approved. Such matters involve a major commitment of investment funds and affect foreign as well as domestic policy. Everything that relates to the China question requires high-level discussion. The Politburo may also resolve major differences within EAS, for instance, as between alternative routes for a pipeline or the development of competing port facilities. Finally, stocktaking and renewing commitments in the preparation of each five-year plan probably involve the group in an overall review of Siberian development.

But interesting as it is to speculate on how this elite body operates, its relevance for most of what occurs across the wide expanse of Siberia over the course of several decades is largely peripheral. The group is too small and its responsibilities too great for it to exercise the detailed supervision necessary to keep cognizance of the many decisions that cumulatively determine Siberian development. For this we must turn to the overall political structure.

Four hierarchical levels affect the economic decision-making process, namely, the all-Union, republic, regional and city, and enterprise levels.[8] The first consists of the Supreme Soviet; the Supreme Council for the National Economy; the Council of Ministers and the individual ministries that govern virtually all important industrial, agricultural, and service activities; Gosplan and its affiliates; national and investment banks; and the Academy of Sciences. The second level is comprised of subsidiaries of these organizations. The third is similar but includes local agencies as well. The fourth covers the individual factories and mines—and the combinations, trusts, or associations, as the various larger production and service complexes have been termed.

Like any large system, the top layer is literally supported by those below, which provide information, propose projects, and implement decisions. Information is necessarily selective and filtered as it passes up the line. Project proposals structure decisions by narrowing the perceived range of choice. Implementation may be supportive or subversive, depending upon the lower levels' reaction to decisions from above. As a high Soviet official once remarked, "This is not a strictly peaceful process. Each struggles for his particular plans and plant—inside the all-Union Gosplan and the Gosplans of the Union Republics—until a decision is reached. Most issues can be smoothed out by argument and figures, but sometimes the government must make the decision."[9]

According to one scholar, "New projects which cost over 1 million rubles, use complex imported equipment, or constitute 'especially important projects' are examined by Gosplan and Gosstroi."[10] Prior to this point, however, the projects must receive technical evaluation, after which they become investment projects that qualify for feasibility studies by Gosplan or the appropriate ministry. Approval leads to eligibility for inclusion in a subsequent annual investment plan.

This central capitalization accounts for the overwhelming proportion of Soviet investment. Aggregate allocations are made among major industrial branches and regions, with short- and medium-term decisions consistently favoring certain interests: industry over agriculture, heavy industry over light, producer goods over consumer and service goods, sector or vertical interests over regional-local considerations, and major industrial enterprises over city and district government agencies.[11]

Although in theory it might be expected that Gosplan would exercise close control over regional development, particularly in such a vast and virginal area as Siberia, in fact the main levers lie largely in the hands of central ministries and their subordinate levels. Their span of control is wide-ranging, from schools and hospitals to hydroelectric dams and railroads. Once they have received the funds on a national or republic basis, the ministries in large degree determine the pace of economic activity in various regions by the manner in which they dispense the money, assure delivery of materials, supervise the quantity and quality of production, and coordinate with other ministries as may be necessary for particular projects or production processes. The single most common complaint at lower levels is against ministerial default on some or all of these responsibilities. A constant cry resounds through the media for greater coordination at the top and better performance at the bottom.

But it would be wrong to assume that all the influence is exerted at the center. In order to understand the process more fully, it is necessary to descend to a more mundane level of authority, the Party secretaries who head oblast, krai, and autonomous region.[12] These three administrative divisions are roughly equal in importance, since they constitute the first step below the fifteen nationality republics. They differ in that the oblast is a purely administrative division with no connotations of nationality, the autonomous region is based on a particular nationality, and the krai combines features of both, having broad territorial powers but including a smaller administrative unit based on nationality.

The geographic span of responsibility at this level can be fairly extensive. Thus, in EAS Magadan Oblast covers nearly 1.2 million square kilometers (480,000 square miles), Khabarovsk Krai contains 825,000 square kilometers (330,000 square miles), and the Yakut ASSR has 3.1 million square kilometers (1.24 million square miles).[13] Within these areas, of course, lower administration levels exist, autonomous oblasts in some, autonomous okrugs in others, and raions in all; raions are similar to the American rural county and urban ward or borough. For the sake of convenience we will refer to the heads of the three large administrative divisions as provincial secretaries and to those of the lowest level as city secretaries.

The administrative and supervisory roles of provincial and city secretaries are complex and contradictory.[14] On the one hand, as representatives of the Party, they are expected to be above the bureaucratic battle, seeing to it that the Central Committee's directives are carried out on all fronts, whether economic, social, or political. On the other hand, they represent provincial and local interests to higher levels. In their first capacity the secretaries are the arbiters of short-run, immediate conflicts among local enterprises and institutions. In their second capacity they are the spokesmen for these enterprises and institutions in the search for outside funds.

The question of which role is dominant is relevant to determining which of the two models of analysis, the totalitarian or the bureaucratic, is valid. The evidence is insufficient to answer this question, but the very existence of the second role is sufficient to our need, and can be demonstrated empirically. For example, in speeches at the Party Congress provincial secretaries appeal for specific projects and programs in their separate areas, whether it be auto works in one, river diversion for irrigation in another, or expansion of coal and rice production in a third.[15] Press articles, interviews, and internal memoranda to central ministries provide additional channels for lobbying on behalf of local constituencies. This process proliferates competing demands, and the consequent jockeying for funds among provincial secretaries tends to dilute their sense of common interest in carrying out Central Committee directives and to increase their separation and identification with local interests.

One factor that contributes to this behavior is the career pattern and professional expertise of regional and city secretaries. Statistical analysis shows a high correlation between the dominant economic activity of a province and the special knowledge of its party secretary, according to whether the area is mainly industrial or mainly agricultural.[16] Specialization is further enhanced by staff support; subordinates are assigned to those responsibilities for which the secretary has less background. This develops separate cores of cadres familiar with specific areas—cultural-educational, industrial, and agricultural—through years of intimate association.

Of course, the socialization process need not have the same effect in all instances, nor are all provincial secretaries narrowly conditioned by an unbroken career in a single field of endeavor. Their broader perspective will necessarily somewhat modify the views of the factory branch managers or the hospital superintendents with whom they have associated most closely in the past. However, it is reasonable to assume that the party secretary normally is inclined to support the local interest because of his or her familiarity with its main line of economic activity.

Three additional factors contribute to the tendency toward local loyalty.[17] First, the party secretary knows that his or her region always will have more demanded of it next year than this. What has been called the "ratchet principle" in planning compels the party secretary to keep pressing for more funds to invest in more productivity.

Second, the lack of information on the comparative economic advantage of investment in other provinces deprives the party secretary of the objective data needed to question proposals and demands from rival secretaries. Without such knowledge, he has no rational basis for giving up what might come to his own area for the sake of developing another province.

Third, if the party secretary does not look out for his province, it very well may be overlooked at higher levels. At the top, Gosplan is badly understaffed in its territorial planning department.[18] It focuses primarily on branch-industry lines and seeks to balance the national output of different products. Nor do the planning commissions of the large economic regions have sufficiently defined functions and authority to redress the situation. This leaves it to the provincial and city secretaries to ensure that the local community has at least a competitive chance at capital appropriations.

The importance of this lobbying or leverage lies in the fact that funds are allocated through central ministries and departments with no local leeway for discrimination. Once the battle of the budget is resolved at the provincial center, or in Moscow if it is an all-Union enterprise, these headquarters offices determine specifically where the funds will flow. This permits provincial and city secretaries to lobby for separate bureaucratic interests within their geographic zone of responsibility so as to serve all constituents without having to make choices that might cause local cleavages.

The situation was summed up in a complaint by the Ministry of Machinery Industry of local bias in communications from provincial party and economic organizations: "Analysis shows that they are chiefly demanding money for supplementary capital construction or are asking us to assign them material and equipment. . . . It is difficult to recall even one case of a refusal of capital construction because of a better utilization of the capacity of the enterprises."[19] No distinction was drawn between party officials and industrial administrators in this regard.

A former Soviet free-lance political writer has provided a lively eyewitness account of how a Soviet factory manager manipulates his telephone contacts to secure necessary supplies.[20] Success in this venture depends on his proximity to the provincial committee and his ability to arrange deals with other first secretaries if the local head cannot help. "The first secretary of the provincial committee exercises supreme control over the local economic empire," according to this émigré, who defines the Plan as a function of "vertical arbitrariness" by central ministries plus "horizontal intervention" by provincial secretaries.[21]

In one crucial area the totalitarian model clearly applies. According to the Party Rules, the secretaries are confirmed by higher levels, and the evidence indicates they are removed by the same process.[22] This is an important check on the power of provincial and local interests, although the decision to dismiss, if not to promote, probably is often influenced by local views.

It is difficult to assess the degree to which excessive "localism" results in replacement of party secretaries. The cause for dismissal is usually masked in vague language. Thus, in December 1978 the first secretary of Magadan province was fired for "unsatisfactory leadership."[23] The next month announcement was made of the dismissal of the head of the agricultural department of the party committee of the Maritime province, the first secretary of a district party committee there, and the director of the Far East Chemical Industry.[24] Whether any of these individuals were actually responsible for shortfalls in productivity, were scapegoated for circumstances beyond their control, were guilty of malfeasance and corruption, or simply had failed to ap-

192   SOVIET DECISION MAKING

pease influential interests above or below is impossible to say. The fact remains that the party secretaries at middle levels are vulnerable to pressures from all sides, but the decisive pressure for their career comes from higher up.

Provincial Interests and Siberian Development

East Asian Siberia provides scattered evidence of competitive lobbying. For example, in 1957 the first secretary of Krasnoyarsk province wrote in *Pravda* on the advantages of the local hydroelectric station compared with others, including the Bratsk plant in Irkutsk province, and called for accelerated construction of the Krasnoyarsk dam.[25] This brought a strong rejoinder from the Irkutsk secretary and supporting specialists, who specifically noted that the Bratsk project was two years ahead of Krasnoyarsk and insisted that the rates of construction not be altered.

Twenty years later the competitive instincts of regional spokesmen sparked a debate over the location of an iron and steel complex in the BAM zone. The occasion was an all-Union conference in September 1977 on the problems of opening up the BAM area.[26] In a lengthy defense of his area's advantages, the first deputy chairman of the Yakut ASSR Council of Ministers declared:

> In the opinion of the planning organs, of the scientific and project organs, and in our opinion, ferrous metallurgy must become the second core branch of the South Yakutia TPC [territorial production complex]. The already-surveyed reserves of the Yuzhno-Aldan region can become the reliable raw material base for a metallurgical factory with a capacity of 9 million tons of pig iron per year. Geological searches of the last years gave us the new Charo-Tokin iron ore region, widening the perspectives for the further growth of the reserves of the Aldanskoi iron ore region.
>
> Many scientific and project organizations have fully argued and expressed themselves in favor of the construction in the east of the country of a metallurgical factory with a capacity of 11-12 million tons of steel per year. The exact address of this factory remains an undecided question. We are deeply convinced of the preference for the Chul'man variant: the successful territorial combination of reserves of the basic and auxiliary raw materials, the presence of iron ore, coking coal, natu-

ral gas, the BAM-Tynda-Berkakit railroad (with future continuation to Aldan and Tommota) and energy perspectives—all these create excellent economic prerequisites for deciding the question in favor of Chul'man.[27]

Not to be outdone, the Amur secretary countered with specific figures purporting to show the advantage of his area, without, however, explicitly attacking Yakutia's qualifications:

Taking into account the presence of the fuel-energy base, the arrival of the transport magistral' [BAM], and the possibilities for the construction industry, we consider that one of the main directions of economic development in Primoria must be the development of ferrous metallurgy. According to the studies of Sibgipromix and Gosplan RSFSR, the address of the new metallurgical factory in the Far East must be the city of Svobodnyy. By comparison with others, this variant is winning out according to economic exponents (indices)—lower cost by 12 to 15 percent in capital investment, and lower cost per ton of rolled metal by 3 rubles.[28]

The spokesmen for Yakutia and Amur argued over the new complex, but the Khabarovsk province secretary chose to remind the audience that his area already had an operating facility that should be expanded while a final decision was still pending: "The factory Amurstal (Komsomolsk-on-Amur) is the single ferrous metallurgy enterprise in the Far East. The factory provides only a small share of the consumption of rolled ferrous metal for the region east of Baikal. And as long as there is a delay in the solution of the problem of creating in the Far East its own metallurgical base, [we must be] engaged in the expansion of Amurstal—in increasing its capacity and in significantly improving its assortment of metal products."[29]

The competition for a new iron-steel complex was intense because only one would be built. However, the limits on other industrial investments were not so severe. This permitted somewhat less intensive lobbying, such as that over the development of wood-processing complexes. Nevertheless, even though lower keyed, the positions enunciated ran true to form. The Khabarovsk province secretary noted:

In the territory adjoining the magistral', the capacity of the functioning timber enterprises provides for an annual volume of cut timber of 7 million cubic meters. With the coming of the railroad, there will be a reconstruction of old and a building of new enterprises to allow for an increase of cut timber capacity by another 6 million cubic meters. Simultaneously with the development of timber cutting, it is necessary to organize [production for] the chemical and mechanized processing of wood and for the construction of enterprises for the cellulose paper and microbiological industries.[30]

His remarks came in response to the Irkutsk secretary, who had recalled that at the first such conference two years earlier he had proposed "establishing in this region three forest-industry complexes with extensive mechanical and chemical processing of wood materials." He claimed that "exploitable reserves of over 1.2 billion cubic meters allow for the future processing of 12 to 13 million cubic meters of wood materials." But he had warned that this would not be possible if the better quality and better located wood was taken "for the other Union republics and oblasts of the RSFSR. Unfortunately, in the last few years this 'laying aside' for one's own stores has not diminished—on the contrary, it has increased like mushrooms. In fact, more than 4 million cubic meters of wood a year has been set aside for assignment."[31]

On this point the Irkutsk secretary struck a note of appeal common to his Siberian colleagues. So long as the region exports its resources to other parts of the Soviet Union, it has little chance of developing local industry and stimulating the economic growth necessary to sustain higher living standards and to attract a larger permanent population. Under such circumstances, East Asian Siberia will remain backward, being exploited for raw materials like a colony to benefit the metropolitan centers.

Moscow's alleged neglect of Siberian development is a frequent complaint of provincial spokesmen. At the 1977 conference, the Chita secretary touted the prospects for Udokan copper but frankly declared that "the Ministry of Industrial Construction by different pretexts has declined all its planned responsibilities for Udokan. . . . And the Ministry of Non-Ferrous Metals truly did not display the necessary persistence in working out the problems of the beginning of experimental en-

SOVIET DECISION MAKING 195

terprises."[32] Instead the ministry was engaged in research "for the transporting from Udokan to Moscow of 2,000 tons of copper ore." He warned that if work on the design of a mining-processing complex were not accelerated, "the country will not receive any Udokan copper until many years after the completion of the mainline." In like fashion, the secretary underscored the need for cement, currently in regional shortage, and charged that despite a decision to build a factory "on the huge deposits of Ust-Borzinskii limestone and Urtuiskii clay, . . . neither the Ministry of Industrial Construction nor Gosplan has done anything practical for its realization."[33]

Even when a major project has been started, the perceived lack of priority for remote areas arouses criticism. In December 1978 the secretary for Magadan province expressed alarm when he learned that no hydroelectric units or transformers were scheduled for the Kolyma River dam in 1979.[34] He claimed that because financing had not been fully ensured, equipment deliveries were delayed. Since Magadan province had limited reserves, the situation required greater attention at the all-Union level, specifically by the ministries of Power and Electrification, Power Machinery, and Electrical Equipment Industry, as well as by Gosplan.

Whether Siberia actually suffers more from ministerial neglect than do other regions nearer to Moscow cannot be determined without a comprehensive comparison covering the whole USSR. In part, the provincial secretaries may merely be practicing a typical middle-level bureaucratic tactic intended to deflect criticism upward and to keep pressure on higher levels to increase funds. In part, their complaints may result from justified ministerial reluctance to invest resources in their regions because of higher costs and slower returns. Whatever the cause, the fact remains that the provincial secretaries are more than submissive links in a chain of authority from the top down. They are also active agents for articulating demand from the bottom up.

Although these lobbying efforts are readily identifiable in speeches and articles, their effect is less easily established. As long as central decision making remains closed to outside observation, it is difficult to establish a specific linkage between the words of provincial secretaries and the actions of central ministries. Without a demonstrated linkage we can show correlation but not causation, which limits analysis to hypothesis and inference.

Within this limit, however, interviews provide suggestive evidence concerning the function of provincial secretaries as influential lobbyists on behalf of local interests. Their lobbying appears to have played a part in the decision to have Yakutian gas flow by pipeline to Olga instead of Magadan. As explained by a highly placed official responsible for Siberian planning, the Magadan route offered the shortest and cheapest line to Japanese and American markets, an important consideration if the two countries were to share in the venture and be paid back in liquefied natural gas. This explains why, although no less a figure than Baibakov, the head of Gosplan, vigorously promoted Magadan in discussions with the Japanese in early 1978,[35] only six months later an informed official from Vladivostok forcefully rejected the Magadan route in private conversation.[36] An impassioned spokesman for local interests, he insisted that Yakutian gas was needed for the economic development of the Khabarovsk-Maritime region. A few weeks later, an authoritative source admitted that Magadan was no longer the preferred route, although it had been his own choice.[37] Apparently the growing uncertainty of foreign markets for Siberian products in general, and for gas in particular, made it increasingly important that the project recover some of its cost through local consumption. The decision to build the Kolyma hydroelectric station had eliminated the market for any additional energy source in Magadan province, so the longer southern route to Olga became the only viable alternative. At his next meeting with the Japanese, the change was duly communicated by Baibakov without explanation.[38]

Two bureaucratic positions had converged through coincidence. Local interests in the Khabarovsk and Maritime provinces wanted more energy for industrial development, and pollution-free gas was preferable to coal or oil. Central planning, concerned about the foreign financial return on the Yakutian investment, wanted maximum local usage. This example highlights the need for provincial secretaries to find parallel interests at the center in order to win a sympathetic hearing. Otherwise, the asymmetry of power leaves middle and lower levels with too little leverage to move Moscow on their own simply by direct assault or appeal.

The spillover effects of the Yakutia pipeline decision could cause a similar situation to arise with respect to the iron-steel complex. According to one official, the Ministry of Ferrous Industry was opposed to the South Yakutian location because of excessive costs and preferred to ship the ore elsewhere for processing.[39] He felt, however, that vigorous local lobbying could overcome this obstacle. An advocate of the Yakutia gas project, faced with the pipeline's diversion to Olga instead of Magadan, proposed to link it to the iron-steel complex as an economically feasible way to solve the pollution problem in southern Yakutia and to increase the local use of gas, but he admitted that contention remained strong among competing provinces and that the final decision was still uncertain.[40] In fact, it was still possible that in the end no complex would be built in the region.

These two cases illustrate the fluidity of decision making on Siberian development. The process is dynamic, and the participants and the pressures can vary over time, so differing outcomes are possible. As development progresses, the economic and political influence of provincial and lower levels increases, both collectively in the region and differentially in separate provinces according to their respective growth rates.

Territorial Production Complexes

An additional locus of domestic political influence on Siberian development may eventually be the territorial production complex. This concept is widely used in Soviet writings, but not always with the same meaning.[41] In its loosest form, a TPC is simply a designated area of development keyed to a dominant economic activity around which subsidiary activities turn. In its most rigorous conception, the TPC becomes a comprehensive planning and administrative structure that designs, coordinates, and integrates all economic, demographic, and natural elements within its designated territory.[42] Reality varies as widely as theory, depending upon whether the complex has been grafted to an existing industrialized area or is being designed for a wholly undeveloped region.[43] The TPC also is an evolving concept that changes according to the experience acquired through its application at successive points in time.

We will consider the TPC as an ideal type rather than attempt a detailed examination of its actual operations. The latter effort is not central to our need. If the concept is eventually successful in winning support, its success will result from proselytizing at the planning level; it is this that justifies our focusing on what its theoretical advocates envision rather than on past experiments. Its interest to us lies in the potential for TPCs to become another point of pressure to assert local interests. However, it is precisely because of this potential that its adoption is likely to meet with resistance among provincial secretaries and in the central ministries, both of whom probably view it as a threat to their present power.

To paraphrase the words of its foremost exponent, a TPC is an aggregate created to interrelate and proportionately develop units of the national economy. It is set up to allow joint resolution of one or several problems, is concentrated in a relatively limited area, has resources sufficient to facilitate participation in solving large-scale national problems, will allow efficient use of local and imported resources, will insure protection of the environment and renewal of natural resources, and, finally, will be served by a common infrastructure.[44] This holistic approach to economic development must, according to its advocates, begin at the earliest planning stage: "Creation of the TPCs should not be spontaneous or emerge on the basis of territorial concentration of units as a result of uncoordinated sectoral designs. . . . Creation of particular elements of each complex must be strictly proportional in terms not only of composition but also of time and space."[45]

Ideal as the theory may be, in practice this stricture imposes still another bureaucratic burden on a planning system that is already complicated by a proliferation of levels (Union, republic,

SOVIET DECISION MAKING 199

economic region, and province) and time-frames (ten years, five years, and one year). Critics of the TPC claim that the speed and the scope of Siberian development preclude such thorough preplanning.[46] They see the problems of new cities as overwhelming this effort because of the need for simultaneous solutions to sudden unforeseeable crises.

TPC proponents deny that the situation need become so desperate, provided that two conditions are met: "The area in question should have adequate economic or natural potentialities, [and] the authorities at the corresponding level should be able to control the processes of TPC creation."[47] The element of control is critical, not only because of the need to coordinate subunits of different ministries, as is true for any administrative unit, but also because the large-scale TPCs rarely cover the same area as conventional administrative units.[48] They may overlap adjoining provinces, as with the Irkutsk-Cheremkhovo and Middle Angara TPCs in Irkutsk province. But because the TPCs "are not recognized as autonomous subjects of long-term territorial planning, development of particular . . . elements of the complex is planned separately," which leads to failures in coordination.

In addition, there is the problem of adjudicating between TPCs. "Since some TPCs of a region may participate in solving the same problems [that are] to be solved by the region as a whole, they begin to compete with each other in terms of location of the same productive activities, allocation of the production program, scarce resources, [and] output. . . . All TPCs are competitors as far as [they are concerned in the] choice of variants of . . . a joint energy system, development and location of aluminum mills and . . . energy-consuming productive activities of the chemical industry, [and] determination of the schedule of distribution of electric power."[49]

At present such decisions remain in the hands of central ministries, with parochial bureaucratic interests determining the outcome. However, while it might be cheaper, for instance, to install and operate a plant further north because of resource location, the infrastructure necessary to support the labor force might cost four times as much as a more southerly site.[50] Without some higher level of TPC jurisdiction, the advantage of this administrative concept would be lost.

The optimization of resource allocation considered in the total context of environmental, demographic, and productive factors is the TPC's basic rationale, as is argued by a leading specialist:

> For the TPCs of Siberia this condition is of especially great importance, since labor is here one of the most expensive resources. Demand for manpower can be reduced in Siberia not only by using modern techniques, advanced technologies, and engineering, but also by creating a higher standard of living as compared to that in the old regions of the country. . . . [This] will pay from the national economic viewpoint as a result of a total saving in aggregate working time stemming from a decrease in migration intensity, increase in the stabilization rate, a cut-off in expenditure on providing people with services needed, training of personnel, and a number of other factors. Thus, the index of standard of living is connected with the requirement of the maximum utilization of local manpower resources and a reduction in expenditure on attracting people from the other regions of the country. This is relevant to the criterion of minimization of aggregate overall expenditure on creating and operating TPCs.[51]

He claims that the best means of planning toward this end is mathematical modeling, whereby productive facilities, infrastructure, population, and natural resources all can be calculated in terms of their interaction so as to realize an optimum level of operation.

Although the TPC nomenclature is widely applied, it nowhere approximates this ideal type. However, the TPC may eventually be recognized as an autonomous administrative unit with its own command and control over the manifold economic and social activities that comprise an integrated urban complex. If so, it would provide a new point of input for decision making. What is now primarily a loose geographic designation for developing areas with a few interrelated industries could become in aggregate a powerful bureaucratic bargaining entity competing for central resources.

The TPC is not a new phenomenon. Its antecedents can be traced back to the Dnieper River projects and Angarsk in the 1920's and 1930's.[52] Its subsequent permutations have spawned a voluminous literature; nearly a thousand major items were published between 1965 and 1969 alone.[53] The advent of computers and systems analysis has brought new dimensions of feasibility to a subject that previously had been purely theoretical in its conceptualization.

The opportunities for implementing theory are widespread in Siberia. In the BAM service area, five TPCs are envisaged: Chulman-Aldan or South Yakutia, Zeya-Shimanovsk, Svobodnyy-Fevralsk, Sovetskaya Gavan–Vanino-Kholmsk, and Komsomolsk. Only the last two are to be imposed on existing industrial areas; the rest are to start almost wholly from scratch.

Whether these evolve according to the ideal type may depend on the degree of resistance from party secretaries and central ministries. The pace and scope of Siberian development also may simply outrun and overwhelm the TPC's academic proponents. At this juncture we can only identify them as a potential avenue of administrative change and watch their progress.

Spatial Decision Making and the External Factor

What happens in East Asian Siberia and where it happens depends basically on investment decisions in Moscow. Soviet writings enumerate various criteria that theoretically guide those decisions; the most important specify that (1) the social costs, including transportation, in the production of national resources should be minimized; (2) manufacturing industries should be near either the resources or the consumer market, depending on transport cost; (3) regional industrialization should follow the principles of specialization and complex development, thus pursuing both division of labor and autarky; and (4) less developed regions should be raised to the most developed level through the "law of planned proportional development of the economy."[54] Others address rural-urban equalization, national minority regions, and the international division of labor among socialist states.

The question remains to what extent these vague and contradictory criteria provide a dominant guideline that is operational. If the equalization of industrial development and of standards of living between regions applies, then the economics of deciding where to invest may become secondary. But if minimizing the social and transportation costs of production is uppermost, the incentive to equalize is offset, if not nullified, for high-cost regions such as East Asian Siberia.

Despite protestations by the highest Soviet officials, including Leonid Brezhnev, that "equalizing the levels of economic development" dictates policy, western analysts find no support for this in the pattern of economic growth over recent years.[55] Some believe that spatial decisions are randomly justified according to one or another of these criteria, depending on the vagaries of the bureaucratic process.[56] Others argue that they are mainly determined by calculations of cost and the return on investment.[57] But they agree that regardless of the rationale, in practice politics as well as economics affect decisions.

As one Soviet specialist explained, the great distance from Moscow to East Asian Siberia makes it difficult for central ministries to "appreciate the potential gains from their investment."[58] Geographic remoteness reduces perceptual awareness. Moreover, unlike the United States, where only a single investment decision is needed, the absence of a supporting infrastructure in Siberia requires a whole set of decisions for any large project. This necessarily introduces political considerations because on strictly economic grounds the funds could go elsewhere in the USSR with quicker returns—unless, as in the case of energy resources, there is no real alternative to Siberian development.

In addition to the possibility of necessity forcing decisions advantageous to Siberia, the debate over alternative investment choices in terms of cost effectiveness may ultimately be resolved in Siberia's favor. In 1980 A. G. Granberg, deputy director of A. G. Aganbegyan's prestigious Institute on the Economics and Organization of Industrial Production, attacked extant practices of pricing and cost calculation as concealing the true value of return on Siberian investment. Whether his challenge eventually succeeds or not, it bears recapitulation as running counter to conventional assertions in the USSR and abroad concerning the utility of Siberian development compared with other regions in the Soviet Union.

Granberg summarizes the argument of "industrial executives and scholar-economists" who allege "a contradiction between the necessity of developing the eastern regions and the task of raising the efficiency of the national economy."[59] In an initial thrust he notes the omission of "rent valuation of scarce natural resources" in the calculation of expenditures and wholesale prices. He centers his criticism, however, on the demonstrable underpricing of extractive and agricultural products as against the overpricing of many manufactured items. This devalues Siberia's main output. On the basis of econometric models and the comparison of domestic and world prices, Granberg asserts that "the proportional weight of Siberia is artificially understated for indices of national income and gross social product of the country, thereby deteriorating the total indices of efficiency for its regional complexes."[60] He specifically cites "a substantial gap between world and domestic prices for petroleum, natural gas, many products of petroleum-refining, petrochemicals, ferrous metallurgy, and the forest and wood-processing industries."

According to Granberg's revised calculations, indices of Siberian labor productivity should be increased 20–30 percent while the region's proportional weight in the USSR gross product and national income should rise a minimum of 10–13 percent. Equally important for the debate over capital allocation, a colleague of Granberg, the economist R. I. Shniper, found that the use of world market prices gave Siberia an export surplus of 8–9 billion rubles, in contrast to the official 1975 estimate of an import deficit of 3 billion rubles.[61]

The relevance of this analysis to investment decisions is highlighted by Granberg's observation of a decline in the average annual rate of growth of capital investment in the USSR from 7.3 percent in 1966–75 to 4.4 percent in the Tenth Five-Year Plan. He warns that this seriously threatens the acceleration of production in Siberia—unless, of course, his own recalculations prompt a higher proportion of total investment in the region.

In this context, the availability of foreign capital can play an important role. This is particularly evident in the case of Yakutian gas. Without foreign investment, the project has little chance of being realized in this decade, perhaps in this century. Should it not be developed, Yakutia is likely to remain on the sidelines of Siberian development, except for the coal and iron ore in the south. The funds that would have been earmarked for Yakutian gas will go elsewhere in the region, if not to another part of the Soviet Union altogether. The exploration for Yakutian oil also will be delayed. Politically the Yakut ASSR would play a lesser role in determining the shape and content of Siberian development than if the gas product comes to fruition.

Beyond these domestic considerations, international relations, particularly with China, might be affected. From Beijing's vantage point, the more distant from its borders Siberian development is, the less threatening are the implications for China's security. For instance, should railroad construction push north to Yakutsk from Berkatit, the impact on regional development would be different than if the same resources were to be used for additional spur lines between BAM and the Trans-Siberian in the region east of the Berkatit line.

It is difficult to separate military from nonmilitary factors in Siberian development, particularly where railroads are concerned. The Japanese refusal to take part in the proposed linkage of an oil pipeline with the construction of BAM illustrates how external influences can affect projects that have military implications. By contrast, Japanese capital is available for Yakutian gas. Where the need for foreign investment and technology is critical, their availability can draw development in one direction rather than another. As a result, different projects will materialize and different bureaucratic, vested, and regional interests will aggregate, thereby feeding into subsequent development decisions outputs different from those that would have applied otherwise.

The penetration of domestic decision making by foreign influences, which creates a linkage between domestic and foreign policy, is a common phenomenon in the modern world. Transgovernmental and transnational interactions are more frequent, and possibly have greater effect, than strictly intergovernmental relations. The foremost exponents of interdependence theory have noted this:

Bureaucrats from different countries, . . . nongovernmental elites, . . . [and] multinational firms and banks . . . are important not only because of their activities in pursuit of their own interests, but also because they act as transmission belts, making government policies in various countries more sensitive to one another. . . . The availability of partners in political coalitions is not necessarily limited by national boundaries as traditional analysis assumes. The nearer a situation is to complex interdependence, the more we expect the outcomes of political bargaining to be affected by transnational relations.[62]

A former Soviet political analyst argues that "without the advanced Western technology, without Western engineering, organization, financial and scientific 'know-how,' real [Siberian] development within the foreseeable future is inconceivable."[63] He proceeds from this premise to call for large-scale foreign involvement comparable to the Marshall Plan after World War II; his purpose is to increase the political influence of those domestic groups in the USSR whose interest lies in detente. He points to a modernizing managerial class that is frustrated with the system, especially in its upper levels, and therefore is allegedly interested in orientation toward the West as a means of accelerating economic growth.

It is easier to identify the particular projects that might be included or excluded from Siberian development, depending upon foreign involvement, than it is the sectors of the political system that might be most susceptible to foreign influence and influential on domestic policy. Energy extraction will require highly advanced technology, particularly in the north. This can only be obtained abroad. Energy intensive industries in the south, such as pulp, aluminum, and electroplated steel may require foreign markets to justify investment. At a more general level, the lure of foreign exchange has a powerful pull on Soviet planners who must balance scarce capital and costly imports against the natural resources of East Asian Siberia.

It is more difficult to demonstrate where and how foreign influence is most likely to impact on the decision-making process. Some observers see bureaucratic battles being waged between military and civilian interests.[64] Others focus on alleged factional cleavages within the Politburo and Central Committee. These analyses attempt to forecast the prospects for arms control agreements and budgetary allocations, depending on how external events and actors might affect developments. Yet the results are disappointing to the skeptic because of insufficient evidence.

Our more modest approach assumes the plausibility of bureaucratic politics operating along interest lines; it attempts to infer what effect external influence might have if this model resembles reality. More systematic research is necessary to determine its validity, but in any calculation of the prospects and implications of Siberian development, the dynamics of domestic politics and their interaction with foreign inputs deserve careful consideration.

8 United States Policy Interests

Recent Policy Developments

The problem of overall American policy toward the USSR greatly transcends the specific focus of this study, but it must be considered as the determining framework for American interests in East Asian Siberia. At the most fundamental level, this question involves basic assumptions concerning Soviet policy goals. One school of analysis takes these goals to be nothing less than world domination by overt and covert means of expansion, including armed aggression if necessary.[1] This point of view is justified by reference to historic Russian expansionism, the tenets of Marxism-Leninism that support world revolution and inevitable conflict between capitalism and communism, and classic Great Power competitive behavior. The only realistic response to this challenge is held to be total confrontation of power with superior power to deter attack, and if necessary to defeat it. Any cooperation runs the risk of strengthening Soviet power and signaling weakness that can be exploited by Moscow at a time of its choosing.

A second school holds that Soviet policy is a less threatening mix of offensive and defensive goals.[2] This analysis calls attention to the repeated invasion of Russia by outside powers, its long-standing economic backwardness, and, until very recently, its military inferiority to the United States and sense of vulnerability to China's vastly larger population. In addition, although the factors cited by the first school are conceded to prompt expansionist goals, they are also seen to be in competition for resources and priority in an ongoing debate that is subject to influence by external forces. The appropriate response, according to this approach, is a mixture of sufficient power to deter aggression, but not enough to provoke fear of attack, and of economic cooperation to provide reassurance of peaceful intentions.

These policy prescriptions are mutually exclusive, and neither is susceptible to final proof until it is too late to remedy the situation should the policy be in error. If world domination is a single-minded Soviet objective, a mixed posture of confrontation and cooperation with a limited defense program will lead to U.S. submission or defeat at some future time. However, if Soviet goals are subject to debate between offensive and defensive concerns with civilian economic interests serving as a mediating factor, a U.S. posture of total confrontation and maximum military force risks triggering a permanent arms race and eventual war.

As is clear from the preceding pages, our approach is that of the second school. In this view, Soviet policy is a function of competing interests. The policy debate is basically determined by domestic factors but is nevertheless influenced by external factors as perceived internally. In addition to the points of reference already cited in support of this approach, analogy with other large bureaucratic systems argues that different organizational interests will attempt to enlarge their share of scarce resources in arguing from the risks or gains to national interests posed by foreign forces.[3]

But adoption of the second school of analysis does not end all argument. The approach includes divergent assumptions about the best way to influence debate within the Kremlin, and the argument turns around the concepts of linkage between Soviet behavior, domestic and foreign, and economic interaction with the world at large.[4] Proponents of linkage claim that the Soviet treatment of human rights manifested in Jewish emigration and the Soviet policy of expansion abroad shown in its intervention

UNITED STATES POLICY INTERESTS 209

in Angola, Ethiopia, and Afghanistan can be influenced by economic sanctions that offer punishment and reward chosen in consonance with American interests. Moscow's need for grain and its desire for advanced technology, especially computers and equipment for oil and natural gas exploitation, is considered to offer Washington leverage that can be applied negatively or positively, depending on the situation. Moscow's problem of payment for these imports adds further potential leverage in the form of credits and most-favored-nation treatment for its exports.

Opponents of linkage challenge its assumptions and its feasibility. They believe that overt attempts to manipulate Soviet behavior are counterproductive because they strengthen nationalistic forces that are resistant to compromise and insistent on self-assertion.[5] They further assert that an authoritarian regime can allocate priorities without reference to its citizens' interests, whether in political or economic matters, thereby denying leverage to outside powers in such areas as human rights and consumer needs. Last but not least, they point to the inability of Washington to control competitive suppliers of most items aside from military weaponry and technology of clear strategic sensitivity. Therefore, unless there is an absolute U.S. monopoly on the particular commodity, the loss of leverage through competition results in harm to the American, not the Soviet economy.

The legislative framework surrounding the debate first emerged with the Export Control Act of 1949.[6] Successively extended and amended through three decades, its latest embodiment is the Export Administration Act of 1979, which remains valid until 1983. The basic assumption of such legislation is that under U.S. law the freedom to export is a privilege, not a right, and therefore may be restricted by the President with the approval of the Congress. Exercised through the granting or withholding of export licenses for products and technologies on a list of controlled commodities, this power is authorized in pursuit of three specific goals: denying another country the capability to injure the national security of the United States, advancing U.S. foreign policy, and promoting U.S. foreign trade.

These goals vary considerably in their implementation as well as their intent. Determining an item's capacity to threaten national security is basically a technical judgment to be made by the Department of Defense. Advancing foreign policy, however, is so broad and loose a criterion as to provide the President with a wide range of discretion on highly subjective grounds. Finally, promoting exports inherently conflicts with the first two goals because it calls for a minimum of restrictions and a maximum of freedom for individual entrepreneurs.

The legislative record of export control reveals a persistent trend in support of the third objective through the narrowing of restrictions on foreign trade. Toward this end, a general license that permits the export of certain commodities and technical data without requiring the individual to make formal application or to obtain a license covers 90–95 percent of all U.S. exports. The remaining categories specified in the Commodity Control List issued by the Department of Commerce require a validated license. This list has shrunk steadily since the 1949 act, which was designed to deny as much as possible to communist countries. However, despite its reduction over the years, the list still leaves considerable opportunity for the President to embargo items not normally thought of as strategic or as pertinent to national security; he simply need act in the name of foreign policy. Moreover, new items can be added; in June 1978 oil drilling and processing equipment joined the list by federal decree. That summer President Carter withheld permission from Dresser Industries for the export of equipment to manufacture high-quality drill bits for oil exploration in the Soviet Union. His action followed Moscow's trial and sentencing of a noted dissident who was specifically accused of being a CIA agent. Again, in 1980, after the Soviet invasion of Afghanistan, new restrictions imposed a partial embargo on transfers of plant and technology already contracted for or under negotiation with the USSR.

In addition to the general export control system, the proponents of linkage and leverage succeeded in 1974 in winning passage of two key pieces of legislation connected with EAS development and the larger Soviet-American trade relationship.[7] The Stevenson amendment to the 1974 Export-Import Bank Act imposed a limit of $300 million on new loans and guarantees to the USSR. Further, a ceiling of $40 million was set for energy exploration and research, and no loans at all were to be available for energy production and transmission. Periodic congressional review was to test the continuing utility of these measures, and the President was authorized to lift the restrictions if he determined this to be in the national interest and if Congress agreed by concurrent resolution.

Overriding the Stevenson amendment, however, was the Jackson-Vanik amendment to the Trade Act of 1974. This prohibited the extension of any U.S. Government credits or investment guarantees, the signing of commercial treaties, and the granting of most-favored-nation status to any nonmarket nation that denied its citizens the right or opportunity to emigrate or obstructed emigration by abnormal fiscal measures such as fees and taxes. Communist countries that already enjoyed most-favored-nation benefits, such as Poland and Yugoslavia, were exempt from these provisions, but others could receive them only when the President certified that the stipulations were being met. He could waive the restrictions if he determined that this would substantially promote the objective of free emigration and if he had been assured that free emigration would eventually result. However, his waiver could be canceled within 90 days by a majority of either house in the Congress.

Within the limits of this study, we cannot address the merits and demerits of these general policies and the attendant debate. Evidence on the success of embargoes as an instrument of policy is inconclusive. The determination of precisely how specific commodities and technologies contribute to Soviet military power is an extremely complex and uncertain process. The weighing of short-run versus long-run effects on Soviet policy and Soviet-American relations is a necessary but complicated undertaking. Finally, the assessment of whether Soviet policy can be positively affected is highly conjectural, given the paucity of reliable information on decision making in the Kremlin.

But we can take up some of the particular aspects of U.S. policy that pertain to EAS development. Although we must remain mindful of the general conditions that have been established in recent years, the possibility of Presidential action, either through special waiver or through recommendations to repeal or amend existing legislation, justifies examining the implications for American interests of inhibiting foreign participation in EAS projects as opposed to encouraging it. Some have already been alluded to in our analysis of the strategic and economic factors, especially as they relate to Japan and China. However, these observations deserve recapitulation within the specific framework of U.S. policy. In addition, the broader conditions of regional and global access to natural resources warrant assessment of East Asian Siberia's potential importance in this regard. The weighing of these different factors, pro and con, provides the basis for our final policy recommendations.

Strategic Factors

Chapter 4 showed that the specific projects planned and anticipated for East Asian Siberia have little likelihood of adding significantly to Soviet strategic capabilities in Northeast Asia. The most important effort, BAM, will strengthen precombat logistical services and relieve the Trans-Siberian Railroad of the overload resulting from its steadily expanding use. It also provides a valuable alternate route for supplying East Asian Siberia and the Soviet Pacific Fleet in the event of traffic on the Trans-Siberian being interrupted through local fighting along the Sino-Soviet border. But BAM's reliability in peacetime is uncertain because of natural hazards, and its vulnerability to air attack in wartime lessens its strategic utility. BAM does not threaten to transform the power balance in Northeast Asia as did its predecessor at the turn of the century. Soviet judgments to this effect probably explain the lack of priority funding and servicing of BAM's construction.

The new port of Wrangel will improve the seaborne strength of the USSR by serving a greatly expanded merchant fleet that provides a potential auxiliary support force for the navy. The Soviet Pacific Fleet also will benefit from the additional oil available from Sakhalin's offshore fields, which together with expanded production from the island's onshore reserves will help to meet local needs that presently require sizeable shipments from West Siberia.[8] Paradoxically, both Wrangel's development and the exploration of Sakhalin offshore oil have been facilitated by Japanese investment and involvement, despite the apparent increased threat of Soviet military pressure made possible by their realization. Japanese judgments, however, hold the increased risk to be more apparent than real.

"Development" is a misleading term to the extent that it connotes a major expansion of population and industrialization in East Asian Siberia. The climatic conditions require too large an investment of capital and technology for Moscow to transform the vast wilderness into a major power center commensurate with other regions in the USSR, let alone one sufficient to threaten China. Instead, Soviet planners foresee a modest incremental growth in the population and the supporting infrastructure, but basically they want to exploit Siberia's natural resources, and the availability of foreign markets provides their main economic justification for the initial investment.

These markets will not be sufficiently large and dependent on the USSR to offer Moscow strategic advantage. Japanese imports of Siberian energy resources will not exceed 20 percent of total consumption in the case of oil and natural gas, even should exploitation of the Yakutian reserves occur. Moreover, these commodities can be supplied from other points in the Pacific region should the Soviet supply cease, given the prospective offshore production in Mexico and Southeast Asia. Coal imports may loom proportionately somewhat larger, but they can be readily replaced by shipments from China and, though at greater cost, from the United States.

Conversely, Moscow's need for the Japanese market should inhibit any threat to cut off energy supplies. Earnings in hard currency will be needed by the USSR to service existing debts and to pay for future imports of grain and technology. The USSR also faces the likelihood of an American counterembargo on these critical items, should it embargo energy exports to Japan. It will be dependent on grain imports throughout the foreseeable future because of Soviet agriculture's chronic vulnerability to bad climate and its inability to raise output.[9] It also will need advanced oil technology to exploit offshore resources in the Caspian Sea and the Arctic Ocean in order to compensate for the eventual depletion of West Siberian reserves.[10]

From the Japanese perspective, a modest level of interdependency with EAS will provide an increased diversification and nearby source of supply for important commodities. This will reduce reliance on the Middle East, a key consideration after the turbulent 1970's. It also lowers shipping charges, which have become increasingly costly as a result of rising petroleum prices. Finally, by providing capital and technology for the development of resources in both China and the Soviet Union, Japan can make credible its claim to "omnidirectional diplomacy" by being the friendly neighbor without antagonism toward either side in the Sino-Soviet dispute.

China's perspective understandably differs from that of Japan because of the extensive land frontier it shares with the Soviets—and the past twenty years of bitter confrontation. Yet so far as can be inferred from available evidence and from the logic of the situation, prospective EAS development does not arouse an acute sense of increased threat in Beijing. The earlier concern expressed to Tokyo over a joint pipeline-railroad project for shipping oil from West Siberia to the Pacific has had no recent counterpart. Japanese firms assisting Soviet projects such as Sakhalin oil, Wrangel, and BAM have won contracts in China. Furthermore, it is conceivable that the past tradition of a symbiotic economic relationship between EAS and northeastern China might be revived, should the two sides settle the border dispute and reduce their military force levels in the region. This could lead to an expanded exchange of goods in a virtual barter arrangement and possibly engage China and the Soviet Union in the joint Amur River project that was first surveyed during the halcyon years of alliance in the 1950's.

On balance, the strategic factor in EAS development works marginally against the interests of Japan and China only on "worst case" assumptions. Otherwise, it is essentially irrelevant to the security concerns of both countries. This minimizes its import for U.S. policy. Viewed positively, Tokyo hopes for an eventual improvement in Moscow's perception of the relationship as a result of Soviet-Japanese economic cooperation. If this should indeed occur, it would relax one side in the traditional triangle of tension that has historically dominated Northeast Asia. This would indirectly serve U.S. interests insofar as they are allied with Japanese interests.

Whereas Soviet-Japanese economic interaction in Siberia may improve political relations, the reverse is true for the Sino-Soviet side, where only an improvement in political relations will lead to increased economic interaction in EAS. Whether such an improvement is in the interest of the United States is somewhat more questionable than in the case of Japan. A border settlement and a reduction of forces in confrontation along the extensive Sino-Soviet frontier would permit Moscow and Beijing to deploy most of these forces elsewhere, possibly to the disadvantage of American allies and friends in Europe and Asia. China might feel more free to apply military pressure against Taiwan if it did not fear its Soviet neighbor. NATO's anxieties might increase if it perceived an increase in Soviet strategic and tactical flexibility. Neither front is likely to become active solely as a consequence of Sino-Soviet detente, but subjective perceptions can distort objective facts, both in Taiwan and in Western Europe. In either case, the United States' desire that hostile force not be brought to bear in local confrontations could pose fresh demands on American policy.

Against these negative prospects, the relaxation of tension in the Sino-Soviet side of the triangle could permit the two capitals to reach agreements favorable to U.S. strategic interests. Discussions among the three major powers of their commitments to defend either Seoul or Pyongyang might lead to a halt in the arms race between North and South Korea. This would at least relieve both regimes of an extremely costly burden, and they might be encouraged to agree on a formal resolution of the divided country's legal status. Although Moscow and Beijing might continue to jockey for influence in Pyongyang and Washington to maintain its responsibility as protector of Seoul, the likelihood of multilateral negotiations would be considerably increased by a Sino-Soviet detente.

Other matters like the exploitation of ocean resources have a less obvious security dimension but nonetheless can cause tension and might spark incidents with escalatory possibilities. Although fishing disputes are unavoidable in the area, establishment of 200-mile economic zones complicates the problem and adds a more volatile dimension in the potential it creates for dispute over offshore oil. Ownership of the continental shelf may be claimed either on the basis of its extension from the mainland to the depth of 200 meters or on the basis of a median line drawn between countries contiguous to the waters. Although China has not formally and finally defined its position, its official protests over Korean-Japanese exploration of the shelf between the two countries establishes a precedent that may be built upon at some future time.[11] The regional reduction of tension among all parties could provide an auspicious atmosphere for multilateral agreement on these issues, which otherwise must be approached on a unilateral basis.

None of these potential benefits of Siberian development are certain, least of all those associated with a Sino-Soviet detente, but similar uncertainty holds for the potential risks that are commonly stressed in conventional projections of the future. If "worst-case" analysis deserves attention, so does "best-case" analysis. The one can reveal threats that may require preventive measures. The other can pose new goals that may lead to beneficial revisions of policy. Under optimum conditions both situations can be addressed simultaneously so as to guard against the worst and work for the best. Short of that, a negative or pessimistic prognosis should be accompanied by a positive or optimistic forecast so as to disclose opportunities that may be missed in a single-minded concentration on defensive concerns.

This two-sided approach to the strategic factor takes on added importance because it parallels the view held in Tokyo. The security problems in northeastern Asia that result from growing Soviet power are primary for Japan, while for the United States they remain secondary by comparison with other points of possible confrontation with the Soviet Union. The previously quoted observation of a former Japanese national security official bears restatement in this context: "Negative security is military security against attack. Positive security is economic cooperation to reduce perceptions of hostility that arouse tension and threat. We cannot have one without the other."[12]

New differences between the United States and Japan emerged following the Soviet invasion of Afghanistan. After considerable pressure from Washington, Prime Minister Ohira announced limited compliance with President Carter's request for an embargo on credits and technology exports to the USSR.[13] Ohira's move was less a function of agreement with American policy over the Afghanistan issue than it was a calculation of what was necessary to reduce strains on the alliance that came from other differences. The long-standing trade imbalance in favor of Japan had come under fresh scrutiny with the sudden growth of Japanese automobile sales at the expense of American manufacturers. In addition, Tokyo had belatedly and reluctantly stopped oil imports from Iran in response to the seizure of Americans by Iranian militants demanding the return of the Shah.[14] Under the circumstances, some concession on the Afghanistan imbroglio seemed necessary.

Tokyo's position was carefully stated, however, so as to block only uncommitted contracts and credits without interrupting standing arrangements. Problems arose, nevertheless. Sakhalin offshore oil exploration faced suspension because American subcontractors could not take part in drilling activity.[15] A more serious threat concerned a major Japanese-American project to build the world's largest plant for manufacturing electrical steels, a complex that is to have an annual output of 480,000 tons and is to be built south of Moscow.[16] Nippon Steel had joined with Armco Incorporated, an Ohio-based industrial and steel manufacturer, to negotiate the $353 million contract with low interest on credits from Japan's Export-Import Bank. Armco's inability to validate the contract on the deadline of February 15 because of Washington's restrictions threatened Tokyo with a serious embarrassment, but Moscow agreed to a last-minute postponement of validation to await resolution of the United States position.[17]

Japanese business concern over the situation was accentuated by news that their West German competitors were continuing to press for Soviet contracts without regard for American policy.[18]

Japanese negotiations for the sale of large-diameter pipe to service West Europe with natural gas from West Siberia halted when Tokyo blocked all new Export-Import Bank credits for the USSR, but Bonn remained prepared to back its badly depressed steel pipe industry.[19] Finally, in April Tokyo announced that the Sakhalin offshore oil project would be exempted from the February embargo policy and that drilling would resume in mid-July.[20] In May Washington relented and approved sale of a $5 million rig through an American subsidiary for use in the project.[21] An interagency compromise ruled that licenses could be granted for oil-drilling equipment but that the technology for manufacture of the equipment would remain embargoed.

We have already highlighted the symbolic significance of Sakhalin and its substantive importance in supplying a strategic commodity that can serve Soviet military needs. Soviet-Japanese cooperation under these circumstances illustrates how the mix of political and economic factors must be weighed in U.S. policy toward Siberian development. If either set of factors is examined in isolation from the other, the project becomes marginal from the viewpoint of Moscow and Tokyo. Politically, Sakhalin—unlike the disputed northern islands—is not of sufficient importance to determine the overall coloration of Soviet-Japanese relations. Its anticipated oil output is too small to be decisive for either country. However, the combination of potential political and economic benefits outweighs the risks, at least as seen from Japan. Tokyo's calculus should suffice to win Washington's approval of American support, since other considerations are of lesser weight.

Siberian Development and Soviet Strategy:
The Broader Perspective

So far we have discussed strategic implications mainly in terms of capability, not intent. This is an appropriate approach where the uncertainties are many and the consequences of error can be great. Human behavior cannot be predicted with confidence for single instances, since contextual changes can prompt unanticipated reactions, but hypothetical scenarios can serve to

UNITED STATES POLICY INTERESTS 219

illuminate possibilities so that they may be allowed for in contingency planning.

The "what if" approach to contingency analysis has considerable elasticity, depending on the individual imagination. For example, one military specialist compiled a short list of possible future developments that would seriously change the strategic situation in East Asia.[22] This included the Japanese or Philippine cancellation of U.S. base privileges; the Soviet acquisition of base privileges in Japan, Korea, or Taiwan; a Sino-Soviet war arising out of a Chinese invasion of Vietnam; and a Sino-Soviet reconciliation that would free Soviet forces for action elsewhere. Such changes in context and capability could trigger changes in Soviet intention.

These hypothetical futures vary considerably in their plausibility. Unfortunately, the very nature of forecasting requires that it rely less on empirical evidence than on informed intuition and judgment. Yet a judicious balance is necessary in making policy decisions and in allocating limited resources to meet contingency preparations. This compels choosing from among a wide range of alternative projections those that most warrant serious consideration. The selection will differ among governments as well as among bureaucratic interests within governments. We probed some of these differences when we examined the strategic situation from the perspectives of Beijing and Tokyo. Insofar as evidence for the logic of Soviet military behavior is concerned, the following prognosis represents a consensus that is shared among informed observers of the East Asian scene.[23]

Three points of analysis sharply reduce the plausibility of deliberate Soviet aggression in Northeast Asia. First, a regional conflict with either China or Japan is highly unlikely to come through Soviet initiative. A war with China offers no visible chance of victory without the use of nuclear weapons. This in turn could raise uncontrollable risks of fallout threatening Soviet Central Asia and Siberia. China's population of more than one billion is roughly four times that of the USSR. Its demographic composition increases the advantage further, since China has a proportionately larger reserve of males in optimal age groups.[24] Moreover, it is relatively homogeneous in ethnic composition as compared with the USSR, where non-Russian peoples will soon predominate in the aggregate, many of them Asian and of uncertain reliability in a Sino-Soviet conflict.[25] As for war with Japan, as long as it remains allied with the United States the danger of underestimating Washington's reaction is certain to deter Moscow from attack.

Second, if a Sino-Soviet war does occur, it will more likely result from misperception and escalation than from design by either side. Siberian development could prove to be a restraint on Soviet crisis behavior. On the one hand, BAM's reduction of the consequences of a sudden interdiction of the Trans-Siberian Railroad should raise the threshold of Soviet tolerance for Chinese provocations along the border. On the other hand, Moscow's considerable investment in highly vulnerable projects scattered throughout the region should inhibit Soviet provocative activity. Prudent cost calculation does not always condition military and political action, but to the extent that this is a factor, the larger the effort expended on Siberian development, the less willing Moscow may be to risk its destruction in a local war.

Third, in a global conflict with the United States Soviet security would require strategic strikes against all points of potential nuclear attack, regardless of location. This could involve Japan, depending upon the disposition of American nuclear weapons. It could also involve China if Moscow fears that Beijing might take advantage of a Soviet-American nuclear exchange to open a second front. But basically Soviet strategy in Asia will seek protection against attack with the minimum necessary deterrent capability; the USSR will continue to concentrate its maximum effort against NATO and American strategic forces. Under these circumstances, East Asia could prove to be virtually irrelevant to the war, even though it may not remain wholly uninvolved.

In the highly unlikely event of a prolonged conventional Soviet-American conflict, the Soviet Union might seek to neutralize Japan by interdicting its supply lines and to deny the United States access to bases in Japan by threatening attack. The success of such efforts depends on the American capacity to respond. Siberian development will contribute only peripherally to Moscow's ability to bring pressure on Tokyo.

Given the past one hundred years of tension in the Northeast Asian triangle, this prognosis may seem unduly sanguine. If existing disputes are taken into consideration, even greater pessimism would appear to be called for. In addition to its heritage of historical enmities, the Soviet Union has territorial disputes with both Japan and China, the latter involving an undemarcated border over which bloody clashes have erupted in recent times.

Yet it would be wrong to assume an unbroken continuity from past wars in the present and future perceptions and calculations of these regimes as they apply to regional conflict. The reach and destructive force of modern weapons have raised even the costs of winning to the point where national survival must be profoundly threatened for a rational leadership to deliberately attack a country possessing retaliatory capability. This applies to all parties in Northeast Asia, whether in terms of indigenous forces or forces available through alliance.

Throughout this section we have discussed Siberian development in static terms as a given. However, it might also be a variable with differing strategic implications as concerns Soviet intent, the variable depending upon whether development is undertaken by the USSR alone or in concert with other countries, primarily Japan and the United States. In the first case, Moscow would have to stretch out its development plans for a much longer period of time, and certain projects may have to be abandoned as beyond its capability. In the second case, a broader effort could be set in motion and greater returns anticipated in a shorter time.

This raises a question: what difference might be anticipated in Soviet perceptions and intentions from a delayed and partial unilateral development of Siberia as compared with a quicker and fuller program achieved with foreign participation? Quite obviously this is only a small part of the total input to Soviet decision-making, which will be largely determined by the entire range of interactions with the United States and by other events elsewhere. Yet we can at least speculate as to whether Siberian development is likely to improve or worsen the relationship according to the way in which it occurs.

Our examination of Soviet decision making suggested that Moscow's being forced to go it alone would generate less relaxation in the Soviet view of the U.S.-Japan alliance than would trilateral participation. Denial and obstruction usually cause frustration and resentment. Agreement and cooperation do not necessarily result in satisfaction and harmony, but they make reduction of hostility more likely. In an exclusively Soviet program, a "worst-case" view of Japan is less susceptible to internal challenge than it is in joint projects that result in the successful exploitation of Siberia's resources.

The diversity of inputs to decisions may also be furthered by a multiplicity of economic and political interests. More such interests will result from an ambitious and complex EAS program involving foreign participation than from an exclusively Soviet effort. The choice of projects may differ under these two situations, as may their location. These choices can affect both actual capability and the bargaining ability of different economic sectors and geographic regions.

In short, Siberian development is not cast in concrete as a full-blown long-range plan. It is subject to the dynamics of Soviet decision making, which themselves are a function of internal and external inputs and influences. We will return to this phenomenon later. For the present it serves as an appropriate reminder that forecasting is a hazardous art, but one that can be useful to the extent that it takes account of all intervening variables.

Economic Factors

The economic aspects of Siberian development link with the larger Soviet economy, which in turn influences regional and global situations, particularly in energy resources. Whether it is viewed alone or in its actual and potential interdependence with the world economy, the size and nature of the Soviet energy system commands attention. By 1978 the USSR had become second in the world in the total production and consumption of energy while depleting its reserves less than any other industrial country.[26] Its energy consumption exceeds that of the entire European Economic Community, its oil output is first in the world, and its gas production will surpass all others very shortly.[27] Soviet hydrocarbon production has sufficient surplus to supply the bulk of Eastern European needs and an important share of Western European consumption, at least until the mid-1980's. It provides more than one-third of total Soviet export earnings and more than half of the hard currency the Soviets earn abroad.[28] This pays for the importation of advanced technology and grain as well as for the considerable amount of equipment that is needed to service the energy industries.

In 1974 a NATO study of Siberia's natural resources and their relationship to NATO interests concluded that "while large-scale deposits have not yet been confirmed in Eastern Siberia, in the Soviet Far East, in offshore Sakhalin and in the North Arctic offshore area, geological formations in all these areas favor the existence of such reserves."[29] It struck a cautiously optimistic note concerning the prospects and the problems of tapping these deposits for the benefit of Western Europe: "Looking so far ahead, one could only venture the prediction that in the 1980s, a successful development of oil and gas in Asiatic USSR (especially East Siberia) could bring about a further transformation in the COMECON [communist economic bloc] energy balance and a return to the export surplus conditions experienced in the 1960s and the first half of the 1970s. However the scale of the volumes required and the problems involved to achieve this look daunting."[30]

A debate identified negative and positive arguments for providing Moscow with western technology to explore and exploit these resources. Opposition stemmed from the fact that much capital would be required to develop complementary and alternative energy sources in the noncommunist countries outside the Middle East. Siberia was said to pose serious uncertainties in the volume of its reserves, the feasibility of extraction, the lack of supporting infrastructure, and the long distances and inhospitable terrain over which the output would have to be transported. In addition, the West would have little control over development procedures, pricing, and end use, and would have virtually no recourse should political conditions interrupt payment or suspend delivery of oil and gas. The long lead time necessary to realize delivery heightened this risk.

The argument in favor of cooperation, while much shorter, carried considerable weight in the immediate aftermath of the 1973 OPEC oil embargo. Proponents stressed the likelihood that a faster growth of Soviet oil production, especially in West Siberia, could help COMECON become self-sufficient and even supply an export surplus that would have a "stabilizing effect on world oil markets"; the lack of such growth might result in COMECON becoming a large-scale importer of oil. In summing up the majority viewpoint, one speaker identified two main conclusions: first, "Siberia has the world's largest fuel deposits and therefore is a potential major exporter of the various fossil fuels"; and second, "Siberian development, necessary for the Soviet Union, is in the final analysis desirable for the West."[31]

By 1980 Western Europe received between 7 and 8 percent of its oil from the Soviet Union and 10 percent of its natural gas.[32] For specific countries the proportions varied, the Soviet percentage of French energy imports standing at 4.7 percent for oil and 14 percent for gas, of Italian at 3.8 percent and 24 percent. That year West German negotiations for the largest East-West project to date aimed at a gas pipeline estimated at between $9 billion and $13 billion to transport 40 billion cubic meters over a 4,800-kilometer (3,000-mile) distance by the mid-1980's.[33] This would triple the total Soviet gas delivery of 21 billion cubic meters to Western Europe in 1979 and increase West Germany's proportion to an estimated 26 percent of its natural gas consumption. Bonn officials reportedly determined that national security placed a ceiling of 30 percent on the Soviet supply.[34] West German confidence in the new project stemmed from existing arrangements agreed to in the early 1970's that provide 12 billion cubic meters of natural gas annually until the year 2000 in payment for pipeline and associated equipment.

Thus, the NATO calculations proved valid, at least in the 1970's, on several counts. Although the 1973 OPEC oil embargo was not repeated, instability in the Middle East increased the

UNITED STATES POLICY INTERESTS 225

uncertainty of delivery from that region. In 1979 American pressure for an embargo against Iran followed seizure of the hostages in Teheran, and West German expectations of receiving 7 percent of its natural gas from Iran via a pipeline through the Soviet Union collapsed with the Iranian revolution and its subsequent economic dislocation. Finally, the pessimistic prognosis for Soviet oil output in the 1980's was more than offset by the discovery and exploitation of supergiant natural gas fields in West Siberia.

A study in 1977 undertaken by the Atlantic Council came to conclusions similar to those reached by the earlier NATO discussion, namely, that "given the interdependence of the world energy economy, the more energy supplies developed within the nonmarket economies (for either external or internal use) the less pressure will be placed on other energy supplies."[35] The study added that "any increased sale of fossil fuels could have an impact on the foreign exchange positions of the nonmarket economies. Hard currency indebtedness is a major impediment to the East's ability to import the goods it needs from the West." Its recommendations were that "authority be given to the President to permit Export-Import loans to East Europe and the Soviet Union in a nondiscriminatory way, i.e., [according to] standard criteria of creditworthiness," and that "the Export-Import Bank legislation and the 1975 Trade Act should be amended."[36]

The principles, observations, and experiences outlined above with respect to Western Europe are relevant for East Asian Siberia and Japan, although several important points of difference make EAS prospects somewhat less certain. Foremost is the remoteness of EAS from the European centers of Soviet industry and population, which sharply reduces the accessibility of its output to the domestic market; accessibility is needed to help justify the heavy capital investment necessary. Second, the EAS domestic market is already more than adequately supplied with energy from hydroelectric and thermal power available in virtually inexhaustible reserves throughout the area. Problems of transportation and pollution may eventually constrain the use of the lignite or brown coal that exists in abundance, but thermal springs along the BAM route offer a promising source of heating in place of conventional fuel, and they also can facilitate the greenhouse production of the vegetables that presently must be shipped from distant points at great expense and risk of spoilage.[37]

These considerations place primary emphasis on export markets if the energy resources of East Asian Siberia are to be tapped by the end of this century. Yet, to extend the contrast with Western Europe, where nine noncommunist countries are potential consumers, only Japan and the United States offer markets sufficient to justify the difficult and costly effort of unlocking the permafrost and offshore storehouses of oil and natural gas. As we have observed, Japan has a far greater interest in the Soviet supply than does America. Not only is the United States much less dependent on Middle Eastern oil, but it also has access to its own hydrocarbon resources, onshore and offshore, and other offshore reserves are still to be fully explored in waters adjacent to Alaska, the East Coast, and Florida. In addition, Canada and Mexico offer advantages over Siberia in proximity, facility, and political sensitivity.

In the final analysis, the determination of resource utility, of whether it is marginal or central, can be made by government fiat on the basis of gain compared with risk, and security considerations can be made the primary factor. Alternatively, it can be made by private entrepreneurs where calculations of economic profit and risk prevail. Finally, a combination of these two approaches can be used to arrive at a consensus. Japanese behavior basically results from the third pattern of decision making, and U.S. policy has increasingly tended toward the first, less by design than in outcome. The Atlantic Council study, however, concluded that "the decision to import is and should continue to be made by United States companies and regulatory agencies on a commercial basis."[38]

The specific implications for East Asian Siberia of following Western European and Japanese policy would affect the Yakutia natural gas project first. Assuming a continued interest over the coming decades by American firms deriving from the U.S. market for LNG, the freeing of Export-Import credit and the lifting of technological restrictions would enable this joint Soviet-Jap-

UNITED STATES POLICY INTERESTS 227

anese-American project to proceed immediately. It is possible that no further reserves will be found and that production will simply run its course as planned. It is more likely, however, that additional gas—and possibly oil—will be discovered for further joint efforts. Western technological developments will enhance capabilities for exploration and exploitation in the less accessible EAS areas both onshore and offshore.[39] The consequent Soviet allocation of capital and human resources can strengthen the leverage of EAS interests on central decision making as it affects infrastructure support. This, in turn, will facilitate the development of other natural resources for export to Japan and the larger Pacific basin.

We indicated earlier the impossibility of predicting the economic value of specific minerals at a remote point in time, because global supply and demand cannot be determined ten to twenty years ahead. Changing patterns of extraction and processing, consumption, and secondary recovery can quickly render forecasts of resource availability obsolete. In theory, the interaction of geology, technology, and economics precludes any danger of exhausting the world supply of resources necessary to an advanced industrial society for at least a half century or more.[40] Moreover, this time frame is highly elastic and is almost certain to be extended. The definition of reserves is conservatively predicated on that which is known to be exploitable with available technology and prevailing cost-profit calculations. But the components of this definition are subject to positive change. Most of the world has yet to be adequately surveyed; more deposits will be discovered for most minerals; advances in mining and processing can enhance the use of existing deposits, enlarging the exploitable reserves at acceptable cost; and higher market prices can provide profitable return for resources presently considered uneconomic. Economies of use and recycling can further stretch availability. Finally, many minerals have substitutes that can replace them, depending on technological and economic factors.

In 1910 Gifford Pinchot, a pioneering advocate of conservation, made a dire forecast: "We have anthracite coal for but fifty years and bituminous for less than two hundred. Our supplies of iron ore, mineral oil, and natural gas are being rapidly depleted."[41] But 50 years later anthracite no longer had any use. High-grade iron ore was less economical than lower trade taconite because of available technology and cheap energy.[42] Natural gas was more plentiful than ever because of new discoveries. Similarly, a strict calculation of production increase compared with known reserves as of 1977 predicted depletion by the year 2000 of asbestos, cadmium, cobalt, copper, diamonds, fluorspar, gold, lead, nickel, silver, sulfur, tin, tungsten, and zinc.[43] However, a projection of the 1977 reserves as a percentage of increase over what was known to be available in 1950 provides promise of ample supply in all these minerals except tungsten, and possibly nickel and antimony.

Two Siberian examples of how access, technology, and economics can expand known reserves in the distant future concern gas hydrate and the Arctic Sea shelf. Frozen solid-state gas trapped under the permafrost offers exceptionally high yields from small deposits, since concentrations exceed 200 cubic meters of gas to 1 cubic meter of water.[44] The depth of deposits, which are often at 2,500 meters (8,250 feet), complicates the requirements for special equipment to raise the hydrate to the surface or to transform it underground into a gaseous state that can then be extracted through a pipeline; but if these obstacles can be overcome, gas hydrate can significantly enlarge present calculations of Soviet energy reserves. Much greater promise, albeit accompanied by equally serious problems of production, is offered by the Soviet Arctic. The area contains the world's largest unexplored offshore shelf, into which extend at least two onshore petroleum-bearing basins, and its eastern extremity under the Chukchi Sea is geologically a part of the Alaskan North Slope.[45] It is only a matter of time before exploration and exploitation of this area is technologically feasible, but whether politics and economics will make it practicable ten years hence remains to be seen.

These are reassuring rejoinders to pose against expressions of concern over long-run resource availability. They do not, however, resolve all the real difficulties that confront governments and societies in the near term. A global inventory is irrelevant if

UNITED STATES POLICY INTERESTS 229

production or delivery is obstructed by deliberate action or accidental developments. Political change can reduce output by design or through disruptive violence. Inflation and recession can drastically alter production costs and market demand, thereby affecting the rate of investment in exploration and exploitation of resources. Cartelization can restrict supply to the detriment of consumers.

Advanced industrial countries are able to respond to these problems through advance stockpiling and reduced rates of growth. But less developed or poorer countries cannot cope as effectively with wide fluctuations in resource availability and cost. OPEC price increases for petroleum had far-reaching consequences throughout non-OPEC Third World economies, which are heavily dependent on oil for energy and petrochemicals for fertilizer. Nor can shortages resulting from rapid industrialization necessarily be overcome in time to avoid serious cyclical problems. For example, it may take five to seven years for a copper mine to come into full production, during which time serious bottlenecks can occur.

These considerations call for a long-range perspective on the potential contribution of East Asian Siberia to the raw material supply for Pacific basin economies. In this regard, a Soviet geographer has analyzed the economic promise for the USSR of its coastal orientation on the Pacific as compared with that on the Atlantic; he notes that Siberia enjoys good access to the ocean, whereas Soviet ports in Europe are far from the Atlantic and separated by a closed sea.[46] The Pacific coastline is three times longer than the Atlantic, and the ratio of coast to hinterland is nearly double. It offers continuous seaward frontage to facilitate intercoastal transit, and its north-south orientation offers a greater range of marine life, with the North Pacific continental shelf containing approximately one-third of the entire world catch.

Against these advantages stand environmental obstacles like fog and ice, and competitive suppliers in the Pacific basin who can supply many minerals at lower coast. Tin from Malaysia and copper from Chile and Peru are presently in ample supply to meet demand.[47] But technology can reduce environmental obstacles, if not eliminate them altogether; present reserves can be depleted; and demand can increase. These considerations justify examining the EAS potential for supplementing regional and global resources.

We have referred earlier to the copper fields of Udokan, where an estimated 1.2 billion tons of ore make up the largest deposit in the USSR, perhaps in the world.[48] Ideally suited for open-pit mining, the ore offers a valuable alternative to South American supplies, especially should China's anticipated increase in demand not be filled by domestic discoveries over the next decade. Although 40 percent of total world consumption is met by recovery from scrap, this will not suffice for newly developing industrial economies like China, which has relatively little copper already in use.[49] Its use in electrical and allied manufacturing, in shipbuilding and construction, and in strong alloys such as brass and bronze for general engineering and the motor industry, make copper a necessary ingredient for advanced economies.

China's large tungsten exports will also be affected by greater domestic needs. Tungsten is critical for high-speed machine tools, drill bits, and cutting instruments, and tungsten alloys are important for jet engines, rockets, and missiles. Beijing's professed goals of industrial and military modernization will give this mineral special value, but by the time that stage is reached, present Soviet imports of tungsten may have become unnecessary through the exploration and exploitation of EAS reserves, thereby relieving pressure on the world supply.

Less exotic minerals also play a major role in the modern world. For instance, zinc ranks fourth in production for global trade—behind iron, aluminum, and copper.[50] It is believed to be in abundant supply throughout the Trans-Baikal region, as is lead, considered the fifth most important metal for industrial economies. The USSR at present is surpassed only by the United States in lead production, so output from EAS deposits should far exceed domestic demand. The USSR is the fifth largest importer of tin in the world, and as EAS supplies increase, self-sufficiency should eventually become possible. Another mineral—antimony, which is normally found alloyed with lead—is an important EAS resource for use in semiconductors.

UNITED STATES POLICY INTERESTS 231

The Soviet production of asbestos is second to that of Canada but is likely to become first in the world when EAS reserves come in. It is principally used in cement products, but it is also important for water and sewer pipe, and the exceptionally high textile-grade quality of EAS asbestos lends additional value to the unusually large quantity. An anticipated decline in global reserves by the year 2000 may make these deposits essential to a stable supply.[51] Finally, among the minerals in which USSR output ranks third or better in the world, molybdenum is another EAS resource.[52] It provides an excellent substitute for tungsten in the manufacture of high-speed steels, where half the amount of molybdenum can achieve the same result.

An omnibus study, *The Global 2000 Report to the President*, collates available estimates of governmental and nongovernmental agencies and analysts in order to project the life expectancy of selected minerals based on 1976 world reserves utilized at two different rates of demand, no growth and modest growth.[53] It identifies six minerals available in EAS in the following order of probable world shortage by the year 2000: silver, zinc, lead, tungsten, tin, and copper. It also calculates the probable resource potential that could be exploited for needed minerals, and of those listed as available in EAS, the order of greatest world scarcity is silver, tungsten, tin, lead, copper, and zinc.[54]

A more focused and sophisticated analysis of the export potential of resources in the BAM service area and its contiguous zone projects a major impact among the Pacific Basin economies for timber and asbestos by 1990, and for phosphate and potash fertilizers thereafter.[55] A lesser but nonetheless substantial impact is projected during the 1980's for copper and iron ore, graphite, abrasives, crude phosphates, sulfur, and bituminous coal, with smelted and refined copper, pig iron and crude steel, and smelted zinc coming on stream after 1990. The possibility of crude phosphates, sulfur, natural gas, titanium, and nickel playing a role by the end of the century is raised, but without specific forecast because of market uncertainties or strategic complications such as influence the marketing of titanium and nickel. Finally, lignite, antimony, platinum, vanadium, and cobalt are held to have only minor potential for impact.

This provides a crude measure of the utility of these items,

232 UNITED STATES POLICY INTERESTS

although three earlier reservations deserve restatement. First, projections are not predictions. They cannot take into account all the intervening variables and manifold fluctuations that can affect developments over a twenty-year period. Second, we cannot determine the magnitude, quality, and accessibility of most EAS resources on the basis of available data. Less than 10 percent of the area has been adequately surveyed. A much larger allocation of specialized personnel and equipment will be necessary before firmer estimates of reserves can be made, and probably the completion of BAM is necessary to insure a full survey. Finally, there is no certainty that capital and technology, whether Soviet or foreign, can make these resources available at costs that will be competitive with alternative sources of supply. China, for example, has yet to realize its full potential for mineral production.

With these caveats in mind, however, this preliminary survey and informed projection of potential mineral needs and availability serve to widen the conventional focus on EAS energy and timber resources. This permits a broader perspective on the area's eventual contribution to regional and global needs. Soviet geologists express confidence that the future mineral wealth of Siberia will justify the great investment in BAM in terms of both domestic utility and export earnings.[56] Their confidence is a compound of professional expertise and patriotic sentiment that only time and effort can validate.

The Larger Policy Framework: Autarky, Dependence, and Leverage

Chapter 4 linked strategic and economic factors in examining the potential for exercising economic and political leverage through trade where credits, technology, and raw materials are exchanged, as between the USSR and Japan. Viewed narrowly within the confines of the bilateral relationship, the degree of leverage varies in time and nature; it favors Tokyo at the outset and is shared mutually in a mixed gain-risk situation during the production-payback period. Seen more broadly, however, Soviet dependence on imports of grain and technology makes

UNITED STATES POLICY INTERESTS 233

Moscow vulnerable to an embargo by other suppliers, especially the United States, thereby sharply reducing the risk to Japan of any attempt at leverage.

A related question concerns the desirability of enabling Moscow to enjoy autarky compared with maneuvering to increase Soviet dependence on external resources. This is an immediate policy issue in the case of oil. As noted earlier, in 1977 the CIA forecast that by 1985 Soviet production will have declined to the point where the USSR will become a net importer instead of a major exporter. This forecast triggered a widespread debate and was somewhat tempered in a 1979 CIA study. However, it enjoys sufficient support among some of the most informed specialists as to be taken as a serious contingency for the late 1980's or, given the necessary lead time for opening new reserves, the early 1990's.[57]

In purely economic terms, it makes sense to minimize Moscow's need for world resources and to maximize its utilization of indigenous reserves. The entrance of the USSR as a consumer in the OPEC market could be very disruptive, whether pursued by financial or political-military means. The likelihood of Moscow's adopting the latter course because of the lack of hard currency for oil purchases raises serious concern not only for Middle East countries adjacent to the Soviet Union but also for Western Europe, Japan, and America, all dependent on imports from the region. Therefore, any steps that can assure autarky for Soviet energy needs would seem to warrant high priority in the consideration of American policy.

The political and strategic consequences of autarky, however, are mixed. Much depends on the basic assumptions concerning future Soviet intent cited at the beginning of this chapter. If the Kremlin is bent on world domination, then the greater its economic self-sufficiency, the better will be its ability to wage war. From this perspective, autarky, especially in energy, is a danger to be obstructed by any means available to the West. But if peace is assumed to be a dominant Soviet objective, then the more Moscow can rely on its own resources, the lighter will be its demands on the world supply. This approach argues for the transfer of credits, knowledge, and technology to facilitate the explo-

234 UNITED STATES POLICY INTERESTS

ration and exploitation of otherwise inaccessible Siberian oil and gas.

Like the analysis of leverage from dependency, this debate depends on explicit contexts and cannot be resolved by simple generalization. If Soviet aggression should trigger nuclear war, Moscow's dependence on external energy sources will be irrelevant. The conflict will be of too short a duration to exhaust the available domestic supply, which presumably will be augmented by advance stockpiling. If the war is prolonged, the vulnerability of the West Siberian fields and transportation network to missile attack eliminates all prospects for domestic production. This poses a far more serious threat than the loss of foreign supplies. Only in a prolonged conventional conflict might dependence or autarky make an important difference in the Soviet ability to sustain a local conflict, as for instance with China.

As far as one specific EAS project is concerned, namely Yakutian natural gas, this question is only marginally relevant because Yakutia's output will be primarily for export rather than for domestic use. The abundance of hydro and thermal energy in East Asian Siberia assures a more than ample supply for at least the next two decades. Nor are the other EAS minerals surveyed above likely to be critical to Soviet needs, except for oil. Here much will depend on future discoveries, in view of the disappointing returns to date from the Sakhalin project. On balance, therefore, the strategic aspects of autarky and dependence weigh in favor of supporting the exploration and exploitation of EAS resources with whatever foreign capital and technology are required commensurate with a rational economic calculus of profitability.

The larger policy framework also raises the question of linkage between global aspects of Soviet-American relations and specific policy on technology transfer. Recent history shows that confrontation and friction between the two superpowers is inevitable in a rapidly changing world where internal political upheaval in Asia, Africa, and Latin America has an external impact on the perceived power balance. Two contending postures have emerged in U.S. policy in response to this situation. One urges continued cooperation in separate matters of mutual interest,

UNITED STATES POLICY INTERESTS 235

such as the limiting of strategic weapons, the use of outer space, and economic interchange. The second advocates linking such cooperation with political agreement on nonintervention in the affairs of third nations, human rights, and other issues in dispute between Moscow and Washington. This debate has existed within administrations as well as between the United States and its allies.[58] It is not likely to end in the near future. Twenty years of American export controls, reinforced by President Carter's partial embargo in response to the Soviet invasion of Afghanistan, establish a strong tradition of attempted linkage and leverage. But Western European and Japanese behavior challenges the assumptions underlying this effort and instead poses trade against linkage as the better instrument for influencing Soviet policy if used positively rather than negatively.

Chapter 7 explored the Soviet decision-making process and its implications for alternative courses of EAS development, which depend mainly on the nature and location of foreign participation. The nature of EAS development, and its political consequences for ongoing decisions that may be affected by the unequal bargaining influence of different regional and sectoral interests, can be shaped in part by the presence or absence of foreign participation. As an American specialist on the Soviet economy has remarked, "Regional development of modernization projects in Siberia may draw resources from the scarce pool of quality products and manpower usually reserved for the military, and reliance on western technology and systems may reduce the traditional role of the Party and the bureaucracy in planning and management."[59]

Expressing the point more broadly, Marshall Shulman, then special adviser to Secretary of State Cyrus Vance, noted that "the development of economic relations with the advanced industrial societies of the West is bound to have some influence on the directions that will emerge" in the post-Brezhnev period. Addressing the prospect of "a wholesale generational turnover at the upper levels," he cautioned, "Whether they will tend to move toward nationalism and orthodoxy, or toward Western-style modernization, we cannot now predict. All that we can say, perhaps, is that to the extent they see their interest in a responsible involvement of their country in the world economy and the world community, they should not feel from what we do or say that this option is closed to them."[60]

So far as East Asian Siberia is concerned, analysis of the strategic, economic, and political implications of its development as they apply locally, regionally, and globally reveals little risk and considerable gain for U.S. interests and those of its ally, Japan, in facilitating resource development. This is particularly true when the long-term considerations are juxtaposed with the short-term. The uncertainties are admittedly formidable, particularly on the Soviet side. The willingness and ability of Moscow to adopt the necessary technology, to allocate sufficient capital, and to rationalize its bureaucratic procedures so as to overcome the severe environmental and administrative obstacles that interpose remain in doubt.[61] The individuals and interests that will determine overall Soviet policy throughout the 1980's cannot be identified yet, so the returns from foreign cooperation, especially in political terms, are problematic. Yet unless action is taken in the near future to remove obstacles to the extension of U.S. Export-Import Bank credit and the transfer of technology, the opening of East Asian Siberia's natural resources will not occur in this decade, and may not be achieved in this century.

Notes

Notes

The following abbreviations are used in the Notes:
- AAG Robert G. Jensen, ed. Association of American Geographers Project on Soviet Natural Resources in the World Economy. Revised versions of the discussion papers will appear in Robert G. Jensen, ed., *Soviet Natural Resources in the World Economy* (Chicago, Ill., forthcoming).
- AS-USSR Academy of Sciences, USSR
- CDSP *Current Digest of the Soviet Press* (Columbus, Ohio).
- DSJP *Daily Summary of the Japanese Press* (U.S. Embassy, Tokyo)
- FBIS Foreign Broadcast Information Service (Washington, D.C.)

Chapter 1

1. Lach Szynna, ed., *Revelations of Siberia by a Banished Lady* (London, 1852), 1:5.
2. Alfred Max, *The Siberian Challenge*, tr. J. Harold Lesh (Englewood Cliffs, N.J., 1977), p. 38.
3. Leonid I. Shinkarev, *The Land Beyond the Mountains: Siberia and Its People Today* (New York, 1973).
4. E. Stuart Kirby, "The Pattern of Siberian Development: Actual and Potential," in NATO Directorate of Economic Affairs, *Exploitation of Siberia's Natural Resources*, Main Findings of a Round Table Held January 30–February 1, 1974 (Brussels, 1974).
5. Gerald L. Curtis, "The Tyumen Oil Development Project and Japanese Foreign Policy Decision-Making," in Robert A. Scalapino, ed., *The Foreign Policy of Japan* (Berkeley, Calif., 1977); interview with a Japanese official who stated authoritatively that the decision against Tyumen "at the highest level" was because of the Chinese protest, although "economic unfeasibility" was given as the public reason.

6. Central Intelligence Agency, *Prospects for Soviet Oil Production* (ER 77-10270; Washington, D.C., Apr. 1977), p. 9. For a more cautious forecast, see Central Intelligence Agency, *The World Oil Market in the Years Ahead* (ER 79-10327U; Washington, D.C., Aug. 1979), p. 37.

7. Bhabani Sen Gupta, *Soviet-Asian Relations in the 1970s and Beyond* (New York, 1976), p. 332, n. 126, offers a survey of Japanese study centers and scholars specializing in the USSR.

8. This portion draws on Haruhiro Fukui, "Policy-Making in the Japanese Foreign Ministry," in Scalapino, esp. pp. 8-18.

9. Paul Dibb, *Siberia and the Pacific* (New York, 1972); Violet Conolly, *Siberia Today and Tomorrow* (New York, 1976); Theodore Shabad and Victor L. Mote, *Gateway to Siberian Resources (The BAM)* (Washington, D.C., 1977).

10. Erich Thiel, *The Soviet Far East*, tr. Annelie and Ralph M. Rookwood (New York, 1957), p. 17.

11. E. Stuart Kirby, *The Soviet Far East* (London, 1971).

12. Conolly, p. 15.

13. Sergei P. Suslov, *Physical Geography of Asiatic Russia* (1956), tr. Noah D. Gershevsky, ed. Joseph E. Williams (San Francisco, 1961); see also A. Alpatiev, ed., *Fizicheskaia geografiia SSSR* (Physical geography of the USSR; Moscow, 1956).

14. J. P. Cole and F. C. German, *Geography of the U.S.S.R.* (London, 1970), p. 78.

15. Yu. Saushkin and T. M. Kalashnikova, "Basic Economic Regions of the U.S.S.R.," translated from *Voprosy geografii*, 47 (1959), in George J. Demko and Roland J. Fuchs, eds. and trs., *Geographical Perspectives in the Soviet Union: A Selection of Readings* (Columbus, O., 1974), p. 143.

16. B. P. Orlov, *Siberia: Achievements, Problems, Solutions*, tr. David Marks (Moscow, 1977), pp. 158-59.

17. Saushkin and Kalashnikova, pp. 156-58.

18. G. L. Tarasov, *Territorial'no-ekonomicheskie problemy razvitiia i razmeshcheniia priozvoditel'nykh sil vostochnoi Sibiri* (Territorial-economic problems of siting and developing the productive forces of eastern Siberia; Moscow, 1970), p. 179.

Chapter 2

1. George Kennan, *Siberia and the Exile System* (2 vols.; London, 1891).

2. Robert Conquest, *Kolyma: The Arctic Death Camps* (New York, 1978); Alexander Solzhenitsyn, *The Gulag Archipelago 1918-1956*, tr. Thomas P. Whitney (New York, 1974).

3. Michael Solomon, *Magadan* (Princeton, N.J., 1971).

4. Alfred Max, *The Siberian Challenge*, tr. J. Harold Lesh (Englewood Cliffs, N.J., 1977), p. 38.

5. "Siberia: The Soviet's Economic Quagmire," *Business Week*, Oct. 23, 1978, p. 71.

6. Victor L. Mote, "The Baikal-Amur Mainline and Its Implications for the Pacific Basin," Discussion Paper, 22 (July 1980), p. 5, in AAG.
7. "Soviet planners invest up to 20,000 rubles per migrant for wages, infrastructure, services, and other amenities," according to one source cited by Mote (p. 104), but another suggests that wage increases in 1979 should raise the figure to 30,000 rubles (p. 119, n. 146).
8. *Narodnoe khoziaistvo RSFSR, 1974: Statisticheskii ezhegodnik* (National economy of the RSFSR, 1974: Statistical yearbook; Moscow, 1975).
9. Paul E. Lydolph, *Geography of the U.S.S.R.* (3d ed.; New York, 1977), p. 439.
10. Ibid.
11. Sergei P. Suslov, *Physical Geography of Asiatic Russia* (1956), tr. Noah D. Gershevsky, ed. Joseph E. Williams (San Francisco, 1961), p. 150.
12. Ibid., p. 338.
13. Interview with informed official, AS-USSR, Akademgorodok, Sept. 20, 1978.
14. Theodore Shabad, *Basic Industrial Resources of the U.S.S.R.* (New York, 1969), p. 277.
15. Violet Conolly, *Siberia Today and Tomorrow* (New York, 1976), p. 166.
16. Lydolph, *Geography*, p. 442.
17. "262 mln., 442 tys.—Naselnie SSSR" (The population of the USSR: 262,442,000), *Izvestiia*, Apr. 22, 1979, pp. 1–3.
18. Lydolph, p. 406.
19. Suslov, *Physical Geography*, p. 128.
20. Lydolph, p. 406.
21. Suslov, p. 130.
22. Ibid.
23. Lydolph, p. 440.
24. Ibid., p. 334.
25. Ibid., pp. 442–43.
26. Suslov, p. 336.
27. Lydolph, pp. 333–34.
28. Ibid., p. 447.
29. Ibid., p. 443.
30. Suslov, pp. 133–50, has an excellent presentation from which this section is largely adopted.
31. Ibid., p. 134; Lydolph, p. 407.
32. Interviews, Permafrost Institute, AS-USSR, Yakutsk, Oct. 3–5, 1978.
33. Suslov, *Physical Geography*, p. 140.
34. Ibid., p. 139.
35. Ibid.
36. Ibid., p. 142.
37. Ibid., p. 144.
38. *Narodnoe khoziaistvo RSFSR za 60 let: Statisticheskii ezhegodnik* (National economy of the RSFSR after 60 years: Statistical yearbook; Moscow, 1977).
39. Ibid.
40. Theodore Shabad, "News Notes," *Soviet Geography*, 20 (Sept. 1979): 442.

41. *Ibid.*
42. Keith Bush, "The Infrastructure of Siberia," in NATO Directorate of Economic Affairs, *Exploitation of Siberia's Natural Resources*, Main Findings of a Round Table Held January 30–February 1, 1974 (Brussels, 1974); B. P. Orlov, ed., *Ekonomicheskie problemy razvitiia Sibiri* (Economic problems in the development of Siberia; Novosibirsk, 1974), p. 119.
43. A. G. Aganbegyan et al., *Razvitie narodnogo khoziaistvo Sibiri* (Developments in the national economy of Siberia; Novosibirsk, 1978), p. 89.
44. A. M. Ushakov, "Nekotorie voprosi rosta kulturno-tekhnicheskovo urovnia rabochikh novikh gorodov vostochnoi Sibiri" (Several questions in the growth of the cultural-technical level of workers in the new cities of eastern Siberia), in G. I. Mel'nikov, ed., *Sotsialnie problemy novykh gorodov vostochnoi Sibiri* (Social problems of new cities in eastern Siberia; Irkutsk, 1971), p. 84.
45. V. V. Vorobiev, *Naselnie vostochnoi Sibiri* (Population of eastern Siberia; Novosibirsk, 1977), p. 68.
46. Ushakov, p. 109.
47. S. Bogatko, "Comprehensive Development for the Eastern Regions: Along a Dotted Red Line," *Pravda*, Jan. 28, 1979, p. 2, in CDSP, 31 (Feb. 21, 1979): 22–23.
48. H. K. Kuznetsov, "Nauchno-tekhnicheskii progress i puti uskorenia obshchevo i professional'no-tekhnicheskovo obrazovania rabochikh" (Scientific-technical progress and ways of accelerating the general and professional-technical education of workers), in Mel'nikov, p. 69.
49. "BAM—stroika, opyt, idei" (Baikal-Amur Mainline—construction, experience, ideas), in *Ekonomika i organizatsiia promyshlennogo proizvodstva* (Economic and organizational industrial production; Novosibirsk), 4 (1978): 8.
50. V. M. Matveychuk, "Nekotorie voprosy zhilizhnogo stroitelstva v novykh gorodakh votochnoi Sibiri (1956–1965)" (Several questions of house construction in new cities of eastern Siberia), in Mel'nikov, *Sotsialnie problemy*, p. 36.
51. *Ibid.*; G. L. Tarasov, *Territorial'no-ekonomicheskie problemy razvitiia i razmeshcheniia proizvoditel'nykh sil vostochnoi Sibiri* (Territorial-economic problems of siting and developing the productive forces of eastern Siberia; Moscow, 1970), p. 37.
52. Vorobiev, *Naselenie vostochnoi Sibiri*, p. 71.
53. G. I. Mel'nikov and V. N. Sudakov, "Nekotorye voprosy adaptsii molodikh rabochikh" (Several questions of the adaptability of young workers), in Mel'nikov, *Sotsialnie problemy*, p. 63.
54. *Ibid.*, p. 149.
55. *Ibid.*, pp. 149–150.
56. *Ibid.*, p. 84.
57. *Ibid.*, p. 60.
58. *Ibid.*, p. 62.

59. Vorobiev, *Naselenie vostochnoi Sibiri*, p. 69.
60. Ibid., p. 70.   61. Ibid., p. 72.
62. Ibid., p. 73.   63. Ibid., p. 49.
64. Ibid., p. 48.
65. Orlov, *Ekonomicheskie problemy*, p. 119.
66. Interview with Academician A. G. Aganbegyan, Sept. 26, 1978.
67. L. Kostin, "Managing the Country's Labor Resources," *Planovoe khoziaistvo*, 12 (Dec. 1978): 16–27, in CDSP, 31 (Feb. 21, 1979): 1–4.
68. G. Tarasov and Z. Klyuchikov, "Comprehensive Development of the Eastern Regions: A Strategy for a Region," *Pravda*, May 16, 1978, p. 3, in CDSP, 30 (June 14, 1978): 11–13.
69. V. Sungorkin and V. Fronin, "Don't Just Put Up Fences, Build!— What Tynda's Architecture Should Look Like," *Komsomolskaia pravda*, Oct. 17, 1978, p. 2, in CDSP, 30 (Nov. 15, 1978): 10.
70. Ibid.
71. V. Yermolayev, Yu. Kazmin, and A. Starukhin, "Pravda Brigade at BAM: Cities Are Going Up," *Pravda*, July 5, 1978, p. 3, in CDSP, 30 (Aug. 2, 1978): 26, 32.
72. V. Brovkin and V. Yermolayev, "Comprehensive Development for the Eastern Regions: Greeting New Settlers," *Pravda*, May 29, 1978, p. 3, in CDSP, 30 (June 28, 1978): 10–11.
73. Ibid., p 11.
74. Yermolayev, Kazmin, and Starukhin, "Pravda Brigade."
75. Sungorkin and Fronin, "Don't Just Put Up Fences."
76. Ibid.
77. Ibid.
78. Brovkin and Yermolayev, "Comprehensive Development."
79. Ibid.
80. Ibid.
81. G. Podgayev, "Specialists and Khabarovsk Territory's Specific Features," *Izvestiia*, Nov. 19, 1977, p. 2, in CDSP, 46 (Dec. 14, 1977): 21–22.
82. Interview with A. G. Aganbegyan, Sept. 26, 1978.
83. Orlov, *Ekonomicheskie problemy*, p. 64.
84. John P. Cole and F. C. German, *A Geography of the U.S.S.R.: The Background to a Planned Economy* (London, 1961), chaps. 5–6.
85. Interviews, Geological Institute, AS-USSR, Yakutsk, Oct. 3, 1978.
86. Central Intelligence Agency, *USSR: Development of the Gas Industry* (ER 78-10393; Washington, D.C., July 1978).
87. Orlov, pp. 34–47.
88. Interviews, USSR, 1975 and 1978.
89. Interview with a leading Soviet geologist, Khabarovsk, Oct. 12, 1978.
90. John P. Hardt, Ronda A. Bresnick, and David Levine, "Soviet Oil

and Gas in the Global Perspective," in *Project Interdependence: U.S. and World Energy Outlook*, A Report by the Congressional Research Service, Library of Congress (Washington, D.C., 1977).

91. F. Salmonov and I. Nesterov, "The Geologists' Corrections," *Sovetskaia rossiia*, Dec. 8, 1978, p. 2, in CDSP, 31 (Feb. 21, 1979): 16–17.

92. Central Intelligence Agency, *Prospects for Soviet Oil Production: A Supplemental Analysis* (ER 77–10425; Washington, D.C., July 1977).

93. Hardt, Bresnick, and Levine, pp. 823–26.

94. Central Intelligence Agency, p. 30.

95. Hardt, Bresnick, and Levine, pp. 824–25; Donald A. Brobst and Walden Pratt, eds., *U.S. Mineral Resources* (Washington, D.C., 1973).

96. Interviews, Geological Institute, AS-USSR, Yakutsk, Oct. 3, 1978.

97. "Interview with Hiroshi Anzai," *Business Japan*, Feb. 1979, pp. 22–24.

98. Theodore Shabad and Victor L. Mote, *Gateway to Siberian Resources (The BAM)* (Washington, D.C., 1977), p. 44.

99. Interview with A. G. Aganbegyan, Sept. 26, 1978.

100. Central Intelligence Agency, pp. 11–12.

101. Interviews, Siberian Energy Institute, Irkutsk, Sept. 29, 1979.

102. Interviews, Geological Institute, AS-USSR, Yakutsk, Oct. 3, 1978.

103. Interview with A. G. Aganbegyan.

104. Hardt, Bresnick, and Levine, *Project Interdependence*, p. 823.

105. Central Intelligence Agency, *Prospects*, pp. 24–27.

106. *Ibid.*, p. 12.

107. Interview with an official of the Japan Petroleum Corporation, Washington, D.C., June 9, 1978.

108. *Transport i sviaz' SSSR, statisticheskiy sbornik* (Transport and communication in the USSR: Statistical collection; Moscow, 1972), pp. 74–75. The data given for 1970 are a conservative base for calculating later years.

109. Mote, "Baikal-Amur Mainline," pp. 41, 48–49.

110. Interviews with Soviet and Japanese specialists, 1978–79.

111. Shabad and Mote, *Gateway*, p. 81.

112. Pavel G. Bunich, "Economic Impact of the BAM," in Shabad and Mote, p. 137.

113. Interview with A. G. Aganbegyan, Sept. 26, 1979; interviews, Siberian Energy Institute, Irkutsk, Sept. 29, 1979.

114. Shabad, *Basic Industrial Resources*, p. 12.

115. Shabad and Mote, p. 51.

116. Shabad, pp. 8–9.

117. Conolly, *Siberia Today*, p. 82.

118. Shabad and Mote, p. 53.

119. *Ibid.*, pp. 50–53.

120. *Ibid.*, p. 80.

121. *Ibid.*

NOTES TO PAGES 54-58 245

122. Interviews, Institute of Geography of Siberia and the Far East, Irkutsk, Sept. 29, 1978.
123. Ye. Kozlovsky, "BAM's Raw Materials Complexes," *Pravda*, Nov. 15, 1978, p. 2, in CDSP, 30 (Dec. 13, 1978): 1.
124. Mote, "Baikal-Amur Mainline," p. 51.
125. Conolly, *Siberia Today*, pp. 96-97.
126. Interviews, Khabarovsk, Oct. 1978.
127. Conolly, p. 97.
128. Interviews, Economic Institute, Khabarovsk, Oct. 1978.
129. *Ibid.* 130. *Ibid.*, Oct. 12, 1978.
131. *Ibid.*, Oct. 13, 1978. 132. Conolly, p. 115.
133. Shabad and Mote, *Gateway*, pp. 81-83.
134. Interviews with geologists, Khabarovsk, Oct. 1978.
135. *Ibid.*
136. Shabad and Mote, pp. 55, 83; interviews, Economics Institute, Khabarovsk, Oct. 1978.
137. P. Shobogorov, "BAM is Hurrying the Geologists—The Raw Materials in the Earth of Buryatia Will Serve the Country," *Izvestiia*, June 8, 1978, p. 2, in CDSP, 30 (July 5, 1978): 19.
138. Interview with A. G. Aganbegyan, Sept. 26, 1978.
139. Shabad and Mote, *Gateway*, pp. 83, 131, 150.
140. *Ibid.*, p. 12.
141. Mote, "Baikal-Amur Mainline," p. 41.
142. *Ibid.*, p. 49.
143. *Ibid.*, p. 50.
144. Conolly, *Siberia Today*, pp. 127-29; Paul Dibb, *Siberia and the Pacific* (New York, 1972), pp. 98-113.
145. Kozlovsky, "BAM's Raw Materials Complexes."
146. Shabad, "News Notes," *Soviet Geography*, 20 (Oct. 1979): 511-12.
147. Interviews with Soviet specialists, Sept.-Oct. 1978.
148. Mote, "Baikal-Amur Mainline," p. 47.
149. N. P. Belen'ky and V. S. Maslennikov, "The Baikal-Amur Railroad: Its Area of Influence and Its Projected Freight Loads," *Zheleznodorozhnii transport*, 10 (Oct. 1974): 39-46, in *Soviet Geography*, 16 (Oct. 1975): 507-13.
150. V. V. Biryukov, "The BAM: Planning Aspects," in Shabad and Mote, *Gateway*, pp. 118-19.
151. Central Intelligence Agency, *The World Oil Market in the Years Ahead* (ER 79-10327U; Washington, D.C., Aug. 1979), pp. 37-39.
152. R. I. Vasilyeva, "Basic Problems of the Transportation Net in the Zone of the Baikal-Amur Mainline," in *Izvestiia akademii nauk SSSR, seriia geograficheskaia*, 3 (1979): 57-67, in *Soviet Geography*, 20 (Dec. 1979): 594. The author is associated with the Central Economic Research Institute, Gosplan USSR.

153. Shabad and Mote, *Gateway*.
154. Interview with A. G. Aganbegyan, Sept. 23, 1978.
155. Shabad and Mote, p. 67.
156. *Ibid.*, p. 80.
157. *Ibid.*, p. 93.
158. Mikhail M. Odentsov, "The Technogenic Factor in Engineering Geology," *Priroda*, 9 (Sept. 1977): 21–27, in CDSP, 30 (Feb. 22, 1978).
159. Mote, "Baikal-Amur Mainline," part 2.
160. Shabad and Mote, *Gateway*, pp. 98–104.
161. Yermolayev, Kazmin, and Starukhin, "Pravda Brigade." The same reporters claimed improvement the following year, citing completion of 86% of the 1978 tunnel plan, although progress still fell significantly short of the target; *Pravda*, May 7, 1979, in CDSP, 31 (May 30, 1979). They specifically noted, "The digging of the Northern Muya Tunnel is proceeding at an especially slow pace. Last year about 400 meters was dug, as against the plan figure of 800 meters. All this is causing alarm about the project's fate."
162. Interview with A. G. Aganbegyan, Sept. 23, 1978.
163. Interviews, Institute of Earth Kryology, Irkutsk, Sept. 29, 1978.
164. Robert N. North, "The Soviet Far East: New Center of Attention in the U.S.S.R.," *Pacific Affairs*, Summer 1978, pp. 195–215.
165. Vladimir N. Bandera and Z. L. Melnyk, *The Soviet Economy in Regional Perspective* (New York, 1973).
166. Tarasov and Klyuchikov, "Comprehensive Development," n. 68.
167. G. Tarasov, "Comprehensive Development of the Far East," *Planovoe khoziaistvo*, 11 (Nov. 1978): 46–53, in CDSP, 31 (Mar. 7, 1979): 11–12.
168. Mote, "Baikal-Amur Mainline," p. 12.

Chapter 3

1. This historical overview distills the findings of eminent historians, to whom reference may be made for a fuller account of specific events and topics. A standard text for an overview is Paul H. Clyde and Burton F. Beers, *The Far East: A History of the Western Impact and the Eastern Response (1830–1975)* (6th ed.; Englewood Cliffs, N.J., 1975). Superbly detailed analyses based on multiarchival research are offered in John J. Stephan, *Sakhalin: A History* (Oxford, 1971); and John J. Stephan, *The Kuril Islands: Russo-Japanese Frontiers in the Pacific* (Oxford, 1974). For a broader set of inquiries, also based on multiarchival research, we are indebted to the late George Alexander Lensen's works: *Russia's Japan Expedition of 1852 to 1855* (Gainesville, Fla., 1955); *The Russian Push Toward Japan: Russo-Japanese Relations, 1697–1875* (Princeton, N.J., 1959); *Japanese Recognition of the USSR: Soviet-Japanese Relations, 1921–1930* (Tallahassee, Fla., 1970); and *The Strange Neutrality: Soviet-Japanese Rela-*

tions *During the Second World War, 1941–1945* (Tallahassee, Fla., 1972). I am particularly grateful to Mr. Takehiro Togo, Japanese Ministry of Foreign Affairs, for access to his insightful study *Perception and Reality in Japanese-Soviet Relations*, Harvard University Center for International Affairs (Cambridge, Mass., 1979), mimeographed.

An excellent survey is offered by O. Edmund Clubb, *China and Russia: The Great Game* (New York, 1971). The Xinjiang story is recounted in Allen S. Whiting and Sheng Shih-ts'ai, *Sinkiang: Pawn or Pivot?* (East Lansing, Mich., 1956). Detailed analysis of the border dispute may be found in Dennis J. Doolin, *Territorial Claims in the Sino-Soviet Conflict: Documents and Analysis* (Stanford, Calif., 1965). A different perspective is presented in Morris Rothenberg, *Whither China: The View From the Kremlin* (Miami, Fla., 1977).

For a more direct statement of Soviet views, a number of recent publications are particularly illuminating for their use of archival and unpublished materials, albeit with a heavy overlay of propagandistic analysis. Among the more serious scholarly works are O. B. Borisov and B. T. Koloskov, *Sovetsko-Kitaiskie otnosheniia, 1945–1977* (Soviet-Chinese relations; 2nd ed., Moscow, 1977); E. M. Zhukov, *Mezhdunarodnie otnosheniia na Dal'nem Vostoke v poslevoennie gody* (International relations in the Far East in the postwar years; 2 vols., Moscow, 1978); M. S. Kapitsa et al., *Istoriia mezhdunarodnykh otnoshenii na Dal'nem Vostoke: 1945–1977* (The history of international relations in the Far East; Khabarovsk, 1978); and S. I. Verbitskii, ed., *SSSR-Iaponiia: K 50-letiiu ustanovleniia Sovetsko-Iaponskikh diplomaticheskikh otnoshenii* (Fifty-years establishment of Soviet-Japanese diplomatic relations; Moscow, 1978).

Chapter 4

1. Allen S. Whiting, *China Crosses the Yalu* (New York, 1960).
2. *Allocation of Resources in the Soviet Union and China—1978*, Hearings Before the Subcommittee on Priorities and Economy in Government of the Joint Economic Committee, Congress of the United States (Washington, D.C., 1978), part 4, p. 88.
3. Ibid., p. 239. According to an unofficial but well-informed source, by late 1979 this had increased to 46 divisions. See International Institute for Strategic Studies, *The Military Balance, 1979–1980* (London, 1979), p. 10.
4. John M. Collins, *Balance Between U.S. and Soviet Armed Forces* (Washington, D.C., 1980), pp. 28ff.
5. *Military Balance*, p. 60.
6. Raymond Garthoff, "Sino-Soviet Military Relations, 1945–66," in Raymond Garthoff, ed., *Sino-Soviet Military Relations* (New York, 1966), pp. 84–88.
7. Morton H. Halperin, *China and the Bomb* (New York, 1965).
8. *Allocation of Resources*, p. 240.

9. Mao Zedong, Speech to Japanese visitors, July 10, 1964, in *Mao Zedong sixiang wan sui* (Long live Mao Zedong thought; 1969 ed., Taibei, 1974), pp. 540–41. For a similar version, see Dennis J. Doolin, *Territorial Claims in the Sino-Soviet Conflict: Documents and Analysis* (Stanford, Calif., 1965), p. 44. The English version was translated from *Sekai shuho*, Aug. 11, 1964, which in turn was based on the original Chinese. No authorized transcript was issued by Peking.

10. Morris Rothenberg, *Whither China: The View from the Kremlin* (Miami, Fla., 1977), pp. 89–90.

11. *Pravda*, Sept. 2, 1964, in Doolin, pp. 47–52.

12. Based on the author's access to official U.S. data at the time. For a lower but incorrect estimate, see *Strategic Survey, 1969* (London, 1970); much higher figures were reported by Harrison Salisbury in the *New York Times*, May 24, 1969, and Aug. 31, 1969.

13. See n. 12 above.

14. Rothenberg, p. 91.

15. Edward E. Rice, *Mao's Way* (Berkeley, Calif., 1972), chap. 22, pp. 358–81.

16. The most careful reconstruction of the incident and examination of alternative hypotheses is Thomas W. Robinson, "The Sino-Soviet Border Dispute: Background, Development, and the March 1969 Clashes," *American Political Science Review*, 4 (Dec. 1972): 1175–202.

17. Neville Maxwell, "The Chinese Account of the 1969 Fighting at Chenpao," *China Quarterly*, 56 (Oct.–Dec., 1973):730–39.

18. Rothenberg, *Whither China*, pp. 91–92.

19. Information available to the author at the time. See also Lu Yung-shu, "Preparation for War in Mainland China," in *Collected Documents of the First Sino-American Conference on Mainland China* (Taibei, 1971), p. 907.

20. Henry Kissinger, *The White House Years* (Boston, 1979), p. 183.

21. Data from U.S. Army Map Service, 1:250,000, L-542, Sheet NL 53-7, *Hu-lin, China* (Washington, D.C., 1955). The particular point of proximity to China is above Lazlo. At Lazlo the distance is 5 km (3.1 mi.); see L-542, Sheet NL 53-4, *Pao-ch'ing, China*.

22. *The World Atlas* (Moscow, 1967), p. 44, shows the Trans-Siberian east-west route on this alignment; a slightly greater distance from China is depicted on another Soviet map, *Baikalo-Amurskaia zheleznodorozhnaia magistral* (The Baikal-Amur railroad mainline; Moscow, 1977), 1 cm:25 km, published by the Main Administration of Geodesy and Cartography, Council of Ministers, USSR. Both maps agree with the Army Map Service measurements for the north-south line to Vladivostok.

23. *The Times Atlas of China* (New York, 1973), p. xxix.

24. Ibid., pp. xvii, 22.

25. Yevgenii Yevtushenko, "On the Red Russian Snow," *Literaturnaia gazeta*, 12 (Mar. 19, 1969), in CDSP, 21 (Apr. 30, 1969).
26. The author visited the USSR in 1972, 1975, and 1978 to consult academic specialists in Moscow and other centers; in 1975 and 1978 he traversed Siberia between Novosibirsk and Khabarovsk.
27. In addition to those I encountered in private conversations, I have found a similar observation in Victor Louis, *The Coming Decline of the Chinese Empire* (New York, 1979), pp. 175–76.
28. *Military Balance*, p. 10. John M. Collins, *Imbalance of Power* (San Rafael, Calif., 1978), p. 130, notes that "about half of all Soviet divisions on the Chinese border are Category III. The Kremlin apparently anticipates no early aggression by either side in that area."
29. Interview with informed Soviet official, Sept. 1978.
30. Interview with Academician A. G. Aganbegyan, Sept. 27, 1978.
31. A "ship-day" registers the presence of a single naval vessel, regardless of size or function in a designated area. Thus, Soviet Far East naval movement to and from the Indian Ocean is counted in the Pacific Ocean en route and then in its destination on arrival. Data supplied from Barry M. Blechman and Robert P. Berman, eds., *Guide to Far Eastern Navies* (Annapolis, Md., 1978).
32. *Ibid.*, pp. 44–45.
33. *Ibid.*, p. 40.
34. Research Institute for Peace and Security, *Asian Security 1979* (Tokyo, 1979), pp. 45–49.
35. Blechman, p. 45.
36. *Ibid.*, pp. 46–47.
37. Paul E. Lydolph, *Geography of the USSR* (3rd ed.; New York, 1977), p. 439.
38. *Asian Security*, p. 55.
39. Sergei Gorshkov, "Navies in War and Peace," *Morskoi sbornik*, 11 (1972):26; my translation was supplied by Donald C. Daniel.
40. *Asian Security*, p. 49. Of course, these regiments could be supplemented with additional forces from the southern Kurils and Sakhalin.
41. Stephan S. Kaplan, "Soviet Risk-taking in Asian Countries," in Donald S. Zagoria, ed., *Soviet Policy in Asia*, Council on Foreign Relations (New Haven, Conn., forthcoming).
42. *Ibid.* Unless otherwise noted, the entire paragraph is based on Kaplan.
43. *New York Times*, Apr. 1, 1980.
44. Blechman, *Far Eastern Navies*, pp. 16–17.
45. *Ibid.*, p. 52.
46. Japan Defense Agency, *Defense of Japan, 1977 (White Paper)* (Tokyo, 1977), pp. 24–25.
47. David Walder, *The Short Victorious War* (New York, 1977), p. 80.

48. Alvin D. Coox, *The Anatomy of a Small War: The Soviet-Japanese Struggle for Changkufeng-Khasan, 1938* (Westport, Conn., 1977), p. 285; Hata Ikuhiko, "The Japanese-Soviet Confrontation, 1935–1939," in James W. Morley, ed., *Deterrent Diplomacy: Japan, Germany, and the USSR, 1935–40* (New York, 1976).
49. Hata, p. 131.
50. G. K. Zhukov, *The Memoirs of Marshal Zhukov* (New York, 1971), chap. 7.
51. M. V. Zakharov, ed., *Finale: A Retrospective Review of Imperialist Japan's Defeat in 1945*, tr. David Skvirsky (Moscow, 1972), p. 69.
52. Ibid., p. 74.
53. N. P. Belen'kiy and V. S. Maslennikov, "The Baikal-Amur Railroad: Its Area of Influence and Its Projected Freight Loads," *Zheleznodorozhnii transport*, 10 (1974): 39–46, in *Soviet Geography*, Oct. 1975, pp. 507–13. It is also included in Theodore Shabad and Victor L. Mote, *Gateway to Siberian Resources (The BAM)* (Washington, D.C., 1977), pp. 123–33.
54. Shabad and Mote, p. 72.
55. Ibid., p. 126.
56. *Baikalo-Amurskaia zheleznodorozhnaia magistral*.
57. Shabad and Mote, p. 79.
58. Ibid., pp. 74–76.
59. Ibid., p. 74.
60. E. V. Pinneker and B. I. Pikarski, *Podzemnie vody zony Baikalo-Amurskoi magistrali* (Underground water zone of the Baikal-Amur Mainline; Novosibirsk, 1977). Longitudinal graphs chart the subsoil conditions throughout the BAM zone.
61. Shabad and Mote, *Gateway*, p. 103.
62. Interviews, Permafrost Institute, AS-USSR, Yakutsk, Oct. 1978.
63. Victor L. Mote, "Environmental Constraints to the Economic Development of Siberia," Discussion Paper, 6 (Dec. 1978), in AAG. This and the following paragraph draw heavily on Mote's excellent synthesis of Soviet and western literature illuminating the complex interaction of human and natural hazards that confront BAM.
64. Interview with Soviet official, Sept. 17, 1978.
65. Mote, pp. 64–69; in subsequent correspondence with the author, he expanded the documentation cited here.
66. The estimate of BAM's cost as a proportion of total investment was offered by A. G. Aganbegyan in an interview, Sept. 27, 1978.
67. *Pravda*, May 5, 1979, in CDSP, 31 (May 30, 1979).
68. Interviews, Sept.–Oct. 1978.
69. "What Is the Soviet Union's Intention in Emphasizing Development of the East?" Beijing domestic service in Mandarin, Jan. 12, 1978, in FBIS, PRC, Jan. 13, 1978.
70. Interviews, Tokyo, July and Oct. 1978. In the fall of 1979, press

reports claimed that Komatsu, a major engineering firm involved with BAM, was negotiating the first Japanese joint-venture project in China; FBIS, PRC, Oct. 16, 1979.

71. Interviews with Japanese officials, Tokyo and Washington, 1978–80.

72. For an eyewitness account of Wrangel, see Stephen Uhalley, Jr., *The Soviet Far East: Growing Participation in the Pacific*, Field Staff Report, 21.1 (New York, Sept. 1977).

73. For specific examples in the Angolan and Ethiopian campaigns, see Robert F. Ellsworth, "Trends in International Maritime Transport," International Symposium on the Sea (Tokyo, 1978), p. 11, mimeographed.

74. Interview with A. G. Aganbegyan, Sept. 28, 1978.

75. Ibid.

76. Violet Conolly, *Siberia Today and Tomorrow* (New York, 1976), p. 97.

77. Interviews, July and Oct. 1978, Mar. 1979.

78. Richard L. Edmonds, "Siberian Resource Development and the Japanese Economy: The Japanese Perspective," Discussion Paper, 12 (Aug. 1979), in AAG.

79. Unpublished official report of the Japanese Ministry of Foreign Affairs, Tokyo, dated June 1978.

80. *Asian Wall Street Journal*, Sept. 7, 1979, reporting an official sixteen-year energy program.

81. Edmonds, p. 13.

82. John P. Hardt, Ronda A. Bresnick, and David Levine, "Soviet Oil and Gas in the Global Perspective," in *Project Interdependence: U.S. and World Energy Outlook Through 1990*, A Report by the Congressional Research Service, Library of Congress (Washington, D.C., 1977), pp. 798–801.

83. Central Intelligence Agency, *USSR: Long-Term Outlook for Grain Imports* (ER 79–10057; Washington, D.C., Jan. 1979).

Chapter 5

1. Akio Watanabe, "Japanese Public Opinion and Foreign Affairs, 1964–1973," in Robert A. Scalapino, *The Foreign Policy of Modern Japan* (Berkeley, Calif., 1977), p. 125.

2. Ibid.

3. Public Relations Office, Prime Minister's Secretariat, *Public Opinion Survey on Japan's Foreign Policy* (S–79–17; Tokyo, 1979), p. 10.

4. Watanabe, p. 125.

5. *Public Opinion Survey*, p. 13.

6. The author was in Japan during Deng's visit.

7. *Public Opinion Survey*, p. 12.

8. *Tokyo shimbun*, Jan. 6, 1979, in DSJP, Jan. 9, 1979; *Asahi* poll of March 1980, in *New York Times*, July 4, 1980.

9. Makato Momoi, public lecture at Asilomar, Calif., May 5, 1979. Momoi is a professor of the National Defense College, Tokyo, and an official of the National Defense Agency.
10. *Yomiuri*, Mar. 11, 1979, in DSJP, Mar. 15, 1979.
11. *Asahi*, Jan. 30, 1979, in DSJP, Feb. 2, 1979.
12. *Ibid*.
13. *Asahi*, Feb. 8, 1979, in DSJP, Feb. 14, 1979; *Yomiuri*, Feb. 15, 1979, in DSJP, Feb. 23, 1979. See also Research Institute for Peace and Security, *Asian Security 1979* (Tokyo, 1979), pp. 43–44.
14. *Nihon Keizai*, Feb. 5, 1979, in DSJP, Feb. 10–13, 1979.
15. *Nihon Keizai*, Feb. 5, 1979, in DSJP, Feb. 7, 1979.
16. Foreign Office statement of February 4, 1979, *Mainichi*, Feb. 5, 1979, in DSJP, Feb. 7, 1979.
17. *Asahi*, Oct. 2, 1979.
18. *Nihon Keizai*, Apr. 27, 1980. Answers were received from 112 Liberal Democratic Party members of the Diet (43.8% of the party total); 85 Japanese Socialist Party members (80.2% of the total); 47 Komeito members (81.0% of the total); 33 Democratic Socialist Party members (91.7% of the total); and 7 with no affiliation. The Japanese Communist Party members did not reply.
19. *Ibid.*, May 1, 1980.
20. *Asahi*, May 16, 1980.
21. *Ibid.*, June 7, 1980.
22. Interviews, 1978–79. See also Paul Langer, "Japanese Elite Assessments of the Regional Superpower Military Balance," in Donald C. Daniel, ed., *International Perceptions of the Superpower Military Balance* (New York, 1978), pp. 161–67.
23. *Asian Security 1979*, p. 41.
24. *New York Times*, July 4, 1980.
25. Interview, July 26, 1978.
26. Interviews with representatives of business, academic, political, and journalistic circles, Sapporo, July 20–21, 1978.
27. Interview, July 21, 1978.
28. Summary of Diet debates of February–March, 1980, *Asahi*, Apr. 1, 1980. The term was used earlier by Shin Kanemaru, director-general of the Self-Defense Agency, who suggested that the term "Sea of Russia" was justified by "such frequent appearances of Russian warships and other vessels"; see *New York Times*, May 14, 1978. As noted, a responsible military officer privately rejected this assertion to the author the following month.
29. *Asahi*, May 15, 1980, quoting Ichiro Nakagawa, former minister of agriculture and Liberal Democratic Diet representative from Hokkaido.
30. Excerpts from the Japan Defense Agency White Paper are quoted by Paul Langer, "Soviet Military Power in Northeast Asia and the Re-

gional Military Balance," in Donald S. Zagoria, ed., *Soviet Policy in Asia*, Council on Foreign Relations (New Haven, Conn., forthcoming).

31. For the Japan Defense Agency White Paper of July, 1979, translated by *Mainichi*, see *Survival*, Jan.–Feb. 1980, p. 32.

32. Langer emphasizes the impact of American strategic analysis on Japanese thinking.

33. Defense White Paper, in *Survival*, p. 33.

34. *Asahi*, May 16, 1980, quoting Foreign Minister Saburo Okita before the Committee on Foreign Affairs, Japanese House of Representatives.

35. *Asahi*, May 13, 1980.

36. Makamoto Momoi, "Basic Trends in Japanese Security Policies," in Scalapino, *Modern Japan*, p. 362.

37. Saeki Kiichi, "Comprehensive National Security and the Defense of Japan," *Asian Wall Street Journal*, Dec. 16, 1980.

38. Interviews with officials of the Ministry of Foreign Affairs, Tokyo and Washington, D.C., 1978–80.

39. For a useful survey with special emphasis on the genesis of these issues in the post–World War II years, see Rodger Swearingen, *The Soviet Union and Postwar Japan: Escalating Challenge and Response* (Stanford, Calif., 1978).

40. For an excellent history, see John J. Stephan, *The Kuril Islands: Russo-Japanese Frontiers in the Pacific* (Oxford, 1974), esp. chap. 4.

41. *Public Opinion Survey*, p. 12. This was a jump from 54% in August 1978, and undoubtedly reflects resentment over the military buildup on Kunashiri and Etorofu.

42. Interview, Ministry of Foreign Affairs, July 24, 1979.

43. Stephan, p. 247.

44. Bhabani Sen Gupta, *Soviet-Asian Relations in the 1970s and Beyond* (New York, 1976), pp. 288, 296–97.

45. *Mainichi*, Mar. 26, 1979; *Asahi*, Oct. 3, 1979.

46. Stephan, pp. 203–11.

47. Interview with M. S. Kapitsa, Sept. 13, 1978.

48. Compare, for instance, the accounts of M. S. Kapitsa et al., *Istoriia mezhdunarodnykh otnoshenii na Dal'nem Vostoke: 1945–1977* (The history of international relations in the Far East; Khabarovsk, 1978), pp. 14–15; and S. I. Verbitskii, ed., *SSSR-Iaponiia: K 50-letiiu ustanovleniia Sovetsko-Iaponskikh diplomaticheskikh otnoshenii* (50-years establishment of Soviet-Japanese diplomatic relations; Moscow, 1978), pp. 54–55.

49. Interview, Oct. 20, 1978.

50. Stephan, *Kuril Islands*, p. 146, n. 21.

51. *Ibid.*, pp. 185, 208.

52. Interview, Sept. 18, 1978.

53. Donald C. Hellman, *Japanese Domestic Politics and Foreign Policy: The Peace Agreement with the Soviet Union* (Berkeley, Calif., 1969), pp. 58–59.

54. *Ibid.*, pp. 61–62.
55. *Ibid.*, p. 60.
56. Stephan, *Kuril Islands*, p. 201.
57. *Ibid.*, p. 202.
58. Peggy L. Falkenheim, "Some Determining Factors in Soviet-Japanese Relations," *Pacific Affairs*, Winter 1977–78, p. 605.
59. Interview, July 21, 1978.
60. Falkenheim, pp. 608–14.
61. Interview, July 21, 1978.
62. Stephan, *Kuril Islands*, pp. 191–92; interviews, Sapporo, July 20–21, 1978.
63. *Public Opinion Survey*, p. 12.
64. *Ibid.* The actual figures were 65% for the fishery issue and 68% for the islands.
65. Falkenheim, "Determining Factors," pp. 610–16; see also Peggy L. Falkenheim, "The Impact of the Peace and Friendship Treaty on Soviet-Japanese Relations," *Asian Survey*, Dec. 1979, pp. 1215–16.
66. Interviews, Ministry of Foreign Affairs, Oct. 1978.
67. Interview, Tokyo, Oct. 15, 1978.
68. Interview, Washington, May 14, 1980.
69. Interviews, Moscow and Khabarovsk, Sept.–Oct. 1978.
70. *Ibid.*
71. *Public Opinion Survey*, p. 13. These figures changed from 62% to 26% respectively, in Aug. 1978.
72. Interview, Oct. 17, 1978.
73. Interview, Ministry of Foreign Affairs, July 24, 1978.
74. Interview, Oct. 19, 1978.
75. Interview with authoritative Soviet official, Sept. 1978.
76. M. Demchenko, "Is This in Japan's Interests?" *Izvestiia*, Feb. 16, 1980, in CDSP, 32 (Mar. 19, 1980).
77. M. Demchenko, "'Consultations' Beijing-Style," *Izvestiia*, Apr. 2, 1980, in FBIS, USSR International Affairs, Apr. 9, 1980.
78. *Beijing Review*, June 9, 1980, pp. 8–9; communiqué of May 29, 1980.
79. Interview, Soviet embassy, Tokyo, May 20, 1975.
80. See, for instance, Robert A. Scalapino, "Perspectives on Modern Japanese Foreign Policy," in Scalapino, *Modern Japan*, esp. pp. 404–6.
81. Robert Campbell, "Prospects for Siberian Development," in Zagoria, *Soviet Policy.*
82. Boris N. Slavinsky, "Siberia and the Soviet Far East Within the Framework of International Trade and Economic Relations," *Asian Survey*, Apr. 1977, pp. 325–28; Dmitri Petrov in Kapitsa et al., *Istoriia mezhdunarodnykh ostnoshenii*, pp. 468–75.
83. Falkenheim, "Impact," p. 212.
84. The following summary of Soviet-Japanese projects is based on

Richard L. Edmonds, "Siberian Resource Development and the Japanese Economy: The Japanese Perspective," Discussion Paper, 12 (May 1980), in AAG; and on Falkenheim, "Determining Factors," p. 615.
85. Interview, July 25, 1978.
86. Specific plant data are from Falkenheim, p. 616; the total amount was estimated by a former Japanese Export-Import Bank official in an interview, July 25, 1978.
87. Interview with Japanese company officer, Oct. 25, 1978.
88. Ibid.
89. For the fullest account in English, see Gerald L. Curtis, "The Tyumen Oil Development Project and Japanese Foreign Policy Decision-Making," in Scalapino, *Modern Japan*, pp. 147–73. The following section draws heavily on his information.
90. Ibid., p. 161.
91. Ibid., p. 169.
92. Interview, June 16, 1978.
93. Interviews, July and Oct. 1978; see also Falkenheim, "Impact," p. 1219, n. 38.
94. A different account was given publicly by the chief Japanese negotiator; see "Interview with Hiroshi Anzai," *Business Japan*, Feb. 1979, p. 23.
95. Ibid.
96. Interview, July 28, 1978.
97. Interview, June 11, 1978.
98. Interview, Oct. 15, 1978.
99. Interview, Mar. 15, 1979.
100. Interview, Ministry of Foreign Affairs, June 15, 1978.
101. Interview, July 18, 1978.
102. Interview, July 24, 1978.
103. Interviews, June–July 1978. For a succinct, albeit elliptical, summary of his views, see Takuya Kubo, "Security in Northeast Asia," in Richard H. Solomon, ed., *Asian Security in the 1980s: Problems and Policies for a Time of Transition* (R-2492-ISA; Santa Monica, Calif., Nov. 1979), p. 105. Professor Kubo is now director of the Research Institute for Peace and Security in Tokyo.
104. Curtis, "Tyumen Oil," p. 169.
105. Interview, Oct. 25, 1978. The Bohai Gulf contract was concluded in 1980.
106. Central Intelligence Agency, *The World Oil Market in the Years Ahead* (ER 79–10327U; Washington, D.C., Aug. 1979), p. 4; Arthur A. Meyerhoff, "Soviet Petroleum: History, Technology, Geology Reserves, Potential and Policy," Discussion Paper, 10 (June 1980), in AAG.
107. Authoritative Japanese study.
108. Japanese report of June 9, 1978.
109. Interview with member of the Sapporo Natural Gas Association, Chamber of Commerce, Sapporo, July 21, 1978.
110. Ibid.

111. Interview, Tokyo, Mar. 19-20, 1979.
112. *Ibid.*
113. Interview with American official, July 29, 1980.
114. Interview, Tokyo, June 25, 1978.
115. *New York Times*, Apr. 1, 1979.
116. "Interview with Hiroshi Anzai."
117. Interview with a member of the American consulting firm, Apr. 4, 1980.
118. "Interview with Hiroshi Anzai."
119. Interview, July 10, 1978.
120. Interviews, July 1978.
121. Official Japanese study, June 1978; the figures have been updated to include 1980 estimates.
122. "Interview with Hiroshi Anzai."
123. Interview, June 9, 1978.
124. J. Richard Lee and James R. Lecky, "Soviet Oil Developments," in *Soviet Economy in a Time of Change*, A Report by the Joint Economic Committee, Congress of the United States (Washington, D.C., 1979), 1: 586, 599. Lee and Lecky are CIA analysts.
125. Kathleen E. Braden, "The Role of Imported Technology in the Export Potential of Soviet Forest Products," Discussion Paper, 16 (Nov. 1979), in AAG; unpublished Japanese foreign ministry report, June 1978.
126. Interview, July 27, 1978.
127. Braden, pp. 37-42.
128. Paul Dibb, *Siberia and the Pacific* (New York, 1972), p. 112.
129. Braden, p. 9.
130. Interview, Mar. 19, 1979.
131. Alfred Max, *The Siberian Challenge*, tr. J. Harold Lesh (Englewood Cliffs, N.J., 1977), p. 88; Donald A. Brobst and Walden P. Pratt, *United States Mineral Resources* (Washington, D.C., 1973), p. 175.
132. John E. Tilton, *The Future of Nonfuel Minerals* (Washington, D.C., 1977), p. 28.
133. Campbell, "Prospects," pp. 29-30. Edmonds, "Siberian Resource Development," pp. 24-25.
134. Falkenheim, "Determining Factors," p. 620.
135. Campbell, p. 31.
136. *Ibid.*
137. Victor L. Mote, "The Baikal-Amur Mainline and Its Implications for the Pacific Basin," Discussion Paper, 22 (July 1980), p. 5, in AAG.
138. *Ibid.*, p. 15.
139. *Ibid.*, p. 14.
140. Falkenheim, "Determining Factors," p. 620.
141. Interview, Sept. 10, 1978.
142. John P. Hardt, Ronda A. Bresnick, and David Levine, "Soviet

Oil and Gas in the Global Perspective," in *Project Interdependence: U.S. and World Energy Outlook Through 1990*, A Report by the Congressional Research Service, Library of Congress (Washington, D.C., 1977), pp. 813–14.

143. Yoshimasa Matsunaga, president of Japan Aluminum Federation, in *Asian Wall Street Journal*, Aug. 5, 1980.

144. For example, see M. Demchenko, "Vote of No Confidence," *Izvestiia*, May 22, 1980, in CDSP, 32 (June 25, 1980); see also V. Tatarnikov, "Where the Threat to Japan Is Coming From," *Kraznaia zvezda*, Mar. 25, 1980, in FBIS, USSR International Affairs, Apr. 1, 1980. These themes emerged in the spring of 1980 as *Pravda*, *Izvestiia*, and Tass reported the growing political-military interaction of Beijing, Tokyo, and Washington.

145. *New York Times*, May 8, 1980.

146. *Asahi*, Apr. 1, 1980, quoting Prime Minister Ohira: "As to the credit and supplies for Siberian development, we continue to supply those projects which have already been agreed upon. However, for new projects we leave them undecided."

147. Saeki Kiichi, "Comprehensive National Security."

148. *Beijing Review*, Dec. 15, 1980.

Chapter 6

1. Allen S. Whiting, *Chinese Domestic Politics and Foreign Policy in the 1970s*, Michigan Papers in Chinese Studies, 36 (Ann Arbor, Mich., 1979).

2. Donald S. Zagoria, *The Sino-Soviet Conflict, 1956–61* (Princeton, N.J., 1961).

3. *Peking Review*, June 5, 1970; Mao's statement was issued May 20, 1970.

4. Whiting, *Domestic Politics and Foreign Policy*; Kenneth G. Lieberthal, *Sino-Soviet Conflict in the 1970s: Its Evolution and Implications for the Strategic Triangle* (R-2342-NA; Santa Monica, Calif., July 1978).

5. In June 1978 the author traveled widely as a guest of the Chinese People's Institute for Foreign Affairs.

6. *Wenyi baijia* (One hundred artistic schools; Harbin), 2: 254–56, in FBIS, PRC, Apr. 14, 1980; *Wen Wei Po* (*Wen Hui Pao*; Hong Kong), May 7, 1980, in FBIS, PRC, May 13, 1980.

7. Interview in German with Deng Xiaoping, Mainz ZDF Television Network, in FBIS, PRC, May 14, 1980; see also *Wen Wei Po* references in FBIS, PRC, to interviews granted by Deng and Hua Guofeng in late April and early May 1980.

8. *Allocation of Resources in the Soviet Union and China—1979*, Hearings Before the Subcommittee on Priorities and Economy in Government of the Joint Economic Committee, Congress of the United States (Washington, D.C., 1980), part 5, p. 53.

9. Ibid., p. 78.
10. John M. Collins, U.S.-Soviet Military Balance: Concepts and Capabilities, 1960–1980 (New York, 1980).
11. Allocation of Resources, p. 26. The same figures were cited to the author by a high Chinese official in October 1975.
12. Ibid., p. 54.
13. The interaction between West European countries and the People's Republic of China through military visits and statements concerning arms sales can be traced through the China Quarterly's "Quarterly Chronicle and Documentation" for this period.
14. Interview in Beijing, Oct. 13, 1975.
15. Allocation of Resources, pp. 120, 124.
16. This statement has been attributed to Mao under various circumstances, the earliest being a conversation with Prime Minister Nehru in 1954; another version was reported after Mao's visit to Moscow in November 1957. The only available Chinese text is an unauthorized rendition of his speech to the second session of the Eighth Congress of the Chinese Communist Party, May 17, 1958, in Mao Zedong sixiang wan sui (Long live Mao Zedong thought; 1969 ed., Taibei, 1974), p. 208. This is a collection of Mao's statements compiled during the Cultural Revolution by a faction that had access to confidential files. An informed official indicated its authenticity to the author on October 13, 1975. In this version Mao points out that "many times in China's past half the population has been wiped out." He notes that even if a third of the world perished, nearly a billion people would remain: "After several five year plans China will then develop and rise up. In place of the totally destroyed capitalism we will obtain perpetual peace. This will not be a bad thing."
17. Allocation of Resources, p. 123. The prepared statement of Lt. Gen. Eugene F. Tighe, Jr., U.S. Air Force, director of the Defense Intelligence Agency, forecast "an overall increase of about 15 percent" in China's tactical air force by 1989.
18. For example, a shooting incident on the Xinjiang border that occurred in the summer of 1977 was revealed by Chinese authorities to the author on June 22, 1978, and confirmed by a Soviet official in an interview in the Soviet Ministry of Foreign Affairs on September 15, 1978. However, neither side issued a public statement on the incident. Similarly, on May 1, 1980, a protest rally in the Xinjiang capital of Urumchi provided the initial account of a "premeditated ambush" that occurred on July 16, 1979; Beijing Xinhua domestic service, May 1, 1980, in FBIS, PRC, May 2, 1980.
19. Allen S. Whiting, The Chinese Calculus of Deterrence: India and Indochina (Ann Arbor, Mich., 1975), chap. 8; Stephen S. Kaplan, ed., Mailed Fist, Velvet Glove: Soviet Armed Force as a Political Instrument (Washington, D.C., forthcoming), esp. the concluding chapter by Kaplan.

20. Bhabani Sen Gupta, *Soviet-Asian Relations in the 1970s and Beyond* (New York, 1976).
21. Raymond L. Garthoff, ed., *Sino-Soviet Military Relations* (New York, 1967).
22. Zagoria, *Sino-Soviet Conflict*.
23. Chin O. Chung, *Pyongyang Between Peking and Moscow: North Korea's Involvement in the Sino-Soviet Dispute, 1958–1975* (University, Ala., 1978).
24. Victor Louis, *The Coming Decline of the Chinese Empire* (New York, 1979), surveys the entire range of possible anti-Chinese situations. Louis is a Moscow journalist, widely suspected of KGB ties, who has gained notoriety for his ostensible "leaks" from authoritative Soviet officials. For a thoroughly researched, scholarly study that virtually espouses the cause of Tibetan independence, see V. A. Bogoslovskii, *Tibetskii raion KNR* (The Tibet region of the PRC; Moscow, 1978).
25. Ye Jianying, speech of Sept. 29, 1979, *Beijing Review*, Oct. 5, 1979, p. 15.
26. *Beijing Review*, Apr. 28, 1980, pp. 14–17.
27. This was an important point of debate in the 1979–80 handling of the literary discussion in Heilongjiang; see *Wenyi baijia*. A left-wing Hong Kong periodical, *Wide Angle*, Apr. 16, 1980, carried the purported texts of two speeches addressing this issue: (1) Wang Yuping, deputy foreign minister, undated, and (2) Li Yimin, deputy director of the Foreign Liaison Department, CCP Central Committee, Oct. 9, 1979. I am indebted to Mr. James Tong for this reference.
28. FBIS, PRC, Feb. 26, 1973.
29. FBIS, PRC, Nov. 2, 1977.
30. Interview with Soviet official, Nov. 15, 1979.
31. Harry Gelman, "Outlook for Sino-Soviet Relations," *Problems of Communism*, Sept.–Dec. 1979, pp. 50–66. This is a useful overview and analysis of the recent relationship and its prospects by a longtime CIA specialist.
32. *Ibid.*; for an authoritative Chinese account, see Neville Maxwell, "Why the Russians Lifted the Blockade at Bear Island," *Foreign Affairs*, 57.1 (1978): 138–45. The overall question is examined in U.S., Department of State, Bureau of Intelligence and Research, Office of the Geographer, *China-U.S.S.R. Boundary*, International Boundary Study, 64 (revised; Washington, D.C., February 13, 1978). In an interview of December 5, 1977, a Soviet official remarked privately that "the Chinese made a major concession." No such comment appeared publicly.
33. *Beijing Review*, Apr. 6, 1979.
34. *Ibid.*, Sept. 28, 1979.
35. *Ibid.*, Jan. 28, 1980.
36. The demand for a Soviet withdrawal from Mongolia first appeared in the address given by Premier Hua Guofeng to the National People's Congress on February 26, 1978; *ibid.*, Mar. 10, 1978, p. 39. The

Afghanistan demand emerged with suspension of the Sino-Soviet discussions in January 1980.

37. Allen S. Whiting, *China Crosses the Yalu* (New York, 1960), chap. 4.
38. Whiting, *Calculus of Deterrence*, pp. 12-19.
39. *Ibid.*, chap. 2.
40. The only Chinese article of length and substance argued by analogy with the Trans-Siberian Railroad that BAM's purpose is to continue "the aggressive road opened up by the old tsar," and "to contend with the other superpower for the domination of northeast Asia and the entire Asia-Pacific region and secondarily to put pressure on Japan. This does not rule out other Asian countries." *People's Daily*, Mar. 26, 1977; Beijing domestic service in Chinese, Mar. 26, 1977, in FBIS, PRC, Mar. 29, 1977. The article had little detail, however, and no map.
41. Ai Shi, Heilongjiang Provincial Research Institute of Philosophy and Social Sciences, "The Purpose in Exploiting the 'Eastern Region' Is to Contend for Hegemony," *People's Daily*, Oct. 31, 1977, in FBIS, PRC, Nov. 3, 1977.
42. Beijing domestic service in Chinese, Jan. 12, 1978, in FBIS, PRC, Jan. 13, 1978.
43. A survey of *People's Daily* focused on articles that appeared during the ten-day period before and after the semiannual Soviet-Japanese joint economic meetings so as to evaluate the treatment of Siberian development. No reference to Siberia occurred in September 1977 or February-March 1979 other than simple factual reports on the meetings themselves. Only two brief commentaries mentioned Siberia in October 1979; see *People's Daily*, Oct. 4, 7, 1979. I am indebted to James Tong for research on this question.
44. Compare Xinhua correspondent Wu Xuewen's commentary, "Fierce Soviet-U.S. Contention Around Japan," Tokyo, Sept. 29, 1979, in *News from Xinhua News Agency*, London, Sept. 30, 1979, with the version in *People's Daily*, Oct. 1, 1979.
45. Beijing domestic service in Chinese, Aug. 22, 1980, in FBIS, PRC, Aug. 25, 1980.
46. Annual trade agreements facilitate the exchange, no credits being involved. Although the total grew from less than $50 million in 1970 to $500 million by 1979, no increase was projected for 1980 despite China's continuing expansion of trade with the West to an estimated total of $30 billion. See Richard E. Batsavage and John L. Davie, "China's International Trade and Finance," in *Chinese Economy Post-Mao*, A Compendium of Papers Submitted to the Joint Economic Committee, Congress of the United States (Washington, D.C., 1978), 1: 734-35; *Asian Wall Street Journal*, June 10, 1980.
47. M. I. Sladkovsky, *Istoriia torgovo-ekonomicheskikh otnoshenii SSSR s Kitaem, 1917-1974* (The history of trade and economic relations between the USSR and China; Moscow, 1977), p. 173.

48. Akademiia Nauk SSSR, Institut Ekonomiki, *Problemy razvitiia promyshlennosti i transporta Yakutskoi ASSR* (Problems of developing transportation and industry in the Yakut ASSR; Moscow, 1958), pp. 96-97.

49. Central Intelligence Agency, *China's Minerals and Metals Position in the World Market* (ER 76-10150; Washington, D.C., Mar. 1976), pp. 4-5.

50. Kathleen E. Braden, "The Role of Imported Technology in the Export Potential of Soviet Forest Products," Discussion Paper, 16 (Nov. 1979), in AAG; John S. Aird, "Population Growth in the People's Republic of China," in *Chinese Economy Post-Mao*.

51. N. S. Khrushchev, *Khrushchev Remembers: The Last Testament*, tr. and ed. Strobe Talbott (Boston, 1974), pp. 248-50.

52. Paul Dibb, *Siberia and the Pacific* (New York, 1972), p. 122.

53. *New York Times*, July 17, 1980. In the previous year China signed 40 contracts totaling nearly $100 million, and had 3,000 workers overseas, mostly in Iraq and Yemen. See also the interview with Zhang Enshu, deputy managing director of China Construction Engineering Corp., "Does China Export Labour?" *Beijing Review*, Oct. 27, 1980.

54. Servei Vasilievich Klopov, *Amur—reka druzhbi* (Amur—river of friendship; Khabarovsk, 1959); O. B. Borisov and B. T. Koloskov, *Soviet-Chinese Relations, 1945-70*, ed. Vladimir Petrov (Bloomington, Ind., 1975), p. 327.

55. Klopov, p. 31.

56. Ibid., pp. 14-15.

57. Ibid., p. 74.

Chapter 7

1. Jerry F. Hough, *The Soviet Union and Social Science Theory* (Cambridge, Mass., 1977), esp. introduction and chaps. 1, 2, 11.

2. F. E. Ian Hamilton, "Spacial Dimensions of Soviet Economic Decision-making," in V. N. Bandera and Z. L. Melnyk, eds., *The Soviet Economy in Regional Perspective* (New York, 1973), p. 244.

3. Brenton M. Barr, "The Changing Impact of Industrial Management and Decision-making on the Location and Behavior of the Soviet Firm," in F. E. Ian Hamilton, ed., *Spatial Perspectives on Industrial Organization and Decision-making* (New York, 1974), p. 419.

4. Jerry F. Hough and Merle Fainsod, *How the Soviet Union is Governed* (Cambridge, Mass., 1979); Alexander Yanov, *Detente After Brezhnev: The Domestic Roots of Soviet Foreign Policy* (Berkeley, Calif., 1977).

5. Irving Howe, ed., *The Basic Writings of Trotsky* (New York, 1963).

6. N. S. Khrushchev, *Khrushchev Remembers: The Last Testament*, tr. and ed. Strobe Talbott (Boston, 1974).

7. Morton Schwartz, *The Foreign Policy of the U.S.S.R.: Domestic Factors* (Encino, Calif., 1975), p. 173.

8. Hamilton, "Spatial Dimensions," p. 241.
9. Vsevolod Holubnychy, "Spacial Efficiency in the Soviet Economy," in Bandera and Melnyk, p. 32.
10. Barr, p. 421.
11. Hamilton, p. 246.
12. Hough, *Soviet Union*, chap. 3.
13. Paul E. Lydolph, *Geography of the U.S.S.R.* (New York, 1964).
14. Hough, *Soviet Union*, pp. 81–84.
15. Ibid., p. 83.
16. Ibid., pp. 74–79.
17. Jerry F. Hough, *The Soviet Prefects: The Local Party Organs in Industrial Decision-making* (Cambridge, Mass., 1969), chap. 12.
18. Ibid., p. 268.
19. Ibid., p. 266.
20. Yanov, *Detente After Brezhnev*, pp. 24–27.
21. Ibid., p. 24.
22. Ibid., pp. 26–28.
23. "Plenary Session of Province Party Committee," *Pravda*, Dec. 27, 1978, p. 2 in CDSP, 30 (Jan. 24, 1979): 16.
24. N. Bratchikov and S. Pastukhov, "Horizons of the Maritime Territory," *Pravda*, Jan. 25, 1979, p. 2, in CDSP, 31 (Feb. 21, 1979): 20.
25. Hough, *Soviet Prefects*, pp. 263–64.
26. "BAM—stroika, opyt, idei" (Baikal-Amur Mainline—construction, experience, ideas), *Ekonomika i organizatsiia promyshlennogo proizvodstva*, 4 (1978): 3–34.
27. Ibid., pp. 17–18.
28. Ibid., p. 20.
29. Ibid., p. 22.
30. Ibid.
31. Ibid., p. 10.
32. Ibid., p. 15.
33. Ibid., p. 16.
34. S. Shaidurov, "Comprehensive Development of the Eastern Regions: The Kolyma's Energy," *Pravda*, Dec. 13, 1978, p. 2, in CDSP, 30 (Jan. 10, 1979): 3–4.
35. Interview with Hiroshi Anzai, head of Tokyo Gas, Oct. 25, 1978.
36. Interview with Soviet official, Khabarovsk, Sept. 9, 1978.
37. Interview, Sept. 22, 1978.
38. "Interview with Hiroshi Anzai," *Business Japan*, Feb. 1979.
39. Interview, Khabarovsk, Oct. 10, 1978.
40. Interview, Sept. 22, 1978.
41. Victor L. Mote, "Environmental Constraints to the Economic Development of Siberia," Discussion Paper, 6 (Dec. 1978), in AAG.
42. Mark K. Bandman, "Content, Sequences, and Tools of Optimizing Creation of the Territorial Production Complexes," in Mark K. Bandman, ed., *General Questions of Modeling Territorial Production Complexes* (Novosibirsk, 1976), p. 18.
43. Interview with Mark K. Bandman, Akademgorodok, Sept. 27, 1978.

NOTES TO PAGES 198–208 263

44. Bandman, "Content," p. 16.
45. Ibid.
46. Interview, Economic Institute, Khabarovsk, Oct. 5, 1978.
47. Bandman, p. 17. 48. Ibid., p. 8.
49. Ibid., p. 38. 50. Interview with Bandman.
51. Bandman, "Content," p. 20. 52. Interview with Bandman.
53. Bandman, "Content," p. 14.
54. Hans-Jürgen Wagener, "Rulers of Location and the Concept of Rationality: The Case of the U.S.S.R.," in Bandera and Melnyk, *Soviet Economy*, pp. 66–67.
55. Holubnychy, "Spatial Efficiency," p. 25; Hamilton, "Spatial Dimensions," pp. 237–38; Alexander Woroniak, "Regional Aspects of Soviet Planning and Industrial Organization," in Bandera and Melnyk, pp. 273, 295.
56. Hamilton, p. 238.
57. Woroniak, p. 273.
58. Interview, Economic Institute, Khabarovsk, Oct. 12, 1978.
59. A. G. Granberg, "Sibir v narodnokhoziaistvennom komplekse" (Siberia in the national economic complex), *Ekonomika i organizatsiia promyshlennogo proizvodstva*, 4 (1980): 84–106.
60. Ibid., pp. 97–98.
61. Ibid., p. 99.
62. Robert Owen Keohane and Joseph S. Nye, *Power and Interdependence: World Politics in Transition* (Boston, 1977), pp. 26, 34.
63. Yanov, *Detente After Brezhnev*, p. 60.
64. For a disciplined but necessarily speculative reconstruction, see Arthur J. Alexander, *Decision-making in Soviet Weapons Procurement*, Adelphi Papers, 147–48 (London, 1978–79).

Chapter 8

1. Among the conservative writers holding this view, Richard Pipes became the most prominent during the 1970's; see his *International Negotiations: Some Operational Principles of Soviet Foreign Policy* (Washington, D.C., 1972); for a more recent statement, see Richard Pipes, "Soviet Global Strategy," *Commentary*, 69 (Apr. 1980).
2. The chief adviser on Soviet affairs to former Secretary of State Cyrus Vance, Marshall D. Shulman, is a leading exponent of this approach; see his *Beyond the Cold War* (New Haven, Conn., 1966).
3. For an extended analysis of this and related phenomena, see Morton H. Halperin, *Bureaucratic Politics and Foreign Policy* (Washington, D.C., 1974).
4. A balanced examination of the debate and its merits is offered in Connie M. Friesen, *The Political Economy of East-West Trade* (New York, 1976). See also *Issues in East-West Commercial Relations*, A Compendium of Papers Submitted to the Joint Economic Committee, Congress of the United States (Washington, D.C., 1979); *Technology and East-West Trade*,

Office of Technology Assessment, Congress of the United States (Washington, D.C., 1979).

5. The Atlantic Council, *East-West Trade: Managing Encounter and Accommodation* (Boulder, Colo., 1977).

6. *Technology and East-West Trade*, chap. 7.

7. *Ibid.*, pp. 148–49.

8. The director of the Sakhalin Maritime Oil and Gas Industry forecast an increase in annual oil production from 3 million tons in 1980 to 10 million tons "in the very near future"; S. Vtorushin, "Potential of the Sakhalin Land," *Pravda*, Aug. 16, 1979, in CDSP, 31 (Sept. 12, 1979).

9. Central Intelligence Agency, *U.S.S.R.: Long-term Outlook for Grain Imports* (ER-10057; Washington, D.C., Jan. 1979).

10. For a comprehensive expert assessment, see Arthur A. Meyerhoff, "Soviet Petroleum: History, Technology, Geology Reserves, Potential and Policy," Discussion Paper, 10 (June 1980) in AAG.

11. See, for instance, the Chinese government statement of May 7, 1980, *Beijing Review*, May 19, 1980, pp. 6–7. Working-level negotiations in 1980 failed to break the impasse between Chinese claims to the entire shelf and Japanese proposals for division along the median line; see Tokyo Kyodo in English, Nov. 22–23, 1980, in FBIS, PRC, Nov. 24, 1980.

12. Takuya Kubo to the author, June 25, 1978.

13. *Nihon keizai*, Feb. 8, 1980.

14. *New York Times*, Dec. 15, 1979; the hostages were seized on November 4, 1979, and not released until January 20, 1981.

15. *Nihon keizai*, Feb. 4, 1980.

16. *New York Times*, Dec. 16, 1979.

17. *Nihon keizai*, Feb. 17, 1980.   18. *Nihon keizai*, Feb. 22, 1980.

19. *New York Times*, July 4, 1980.   20. *Nihon keizai*, Apr. 3, 25, 1980.

21. *New York Times*, May 8, 1980.

22. John M. Collins, "The Military Balance Between the Superpowers in the Far East: A Study in Constraints," *Asian Perspective*, 2.2 (1978): 162–63.

23. *Ibid.*; the view is shared by the contributors to Donald S. Zagoria, ed., *Soviet Policy in Asia*, Council on Foreign Relations (New Haven, Conn., forthcoming).

24. For the 1970 Soviet population according to age, see *Demographic Yearbook 1978* (New York, 1979), pp. 204–5. Although no comparable data is available for China, I derive the inference from the frequent assertions that the majority of Chinese were born since 1949, and that the birth rate was high in the 1950's.

25. *Allocation of Resources in the Soviet Union and China—1979*, Hearings Before the Subcommittee on Priorities and Economy in Government of the Joint Economic Committee, Congress of the United States (Washington, D.C., 1980), part 5, p. 9.

26. Leslie Dienes and Theodore Shabad, *The Soviet Energy System: Resource Use and Policies* (Washington, D.C., 1979), p. 5.
27. Ibid.
28. Ibid., p. 264.
29. NATO Directorate of Economic Affairs, *Exploitation of Siberia's Natural Resources*, Main Findings of a Round Table Held in Brussels, January 30–February 1, 1974 (Brussels, 1974), p. 12.
30. Ibid., p. 16.
31. Ibid., p. 24.
32. *Asian Wall Street Journal*, June 2, 1980.
33. *New York Times*, July 5, 1980.
34. *Asian Wall Street Journal*, June 2, 1980.
35. Atlantic Council, *East-West Trade*, p. 18.
36. Ibid., p. 28.
37. Ye. Pinnecker, "Storehouses of Heat—How to Use Underground Water in the Vicinity of the BAM Route for Economic and Therapeutic Purposes," *Izvestiia*, Nov. 15, 1978, in CDSP, 30 (Dec. 13, 1978).
38. Atlantic Council, p. 30.
39. Arthur A. Meyerhoff, "Petroleum Basins of the Soviet Arctic," *Geology Magazine*, 17: 2.
40. John E. Tilton, *The Future of Nonfuel Minerals* (Washington, D.C., 1977).
41. Ibid., p. 4.
42. Information provided by Dr. Richard Sheldon, U.S. Geological Survey, July 10, 1979.
43. Tilton, pp. 6–7.
44. Interview with A. N. Voronov of the All-Union Petroleum Institute for Geological Exploration, *Oil/Gas Journal*, Mar. 12, 1979, p. 49.
45. Meyerhoff, "Petroleum Basins."
46. I. M. Mayergoyz, "The Unique Economic-Geographic Situation of the Soviet Far East and Some Problems of Using it over the Long Term," *Vestnik Moskovskogo Universiteta, geografiia*, 4 (1974): 3–9, in *Soviet Geography*, Sept. 1975, pp. 428–34.
47. Kiyoshi Kojima, *Economic Cooperation in a Pacific Community* (Tokyo, 1980), p. 35.
48. Theodore Shabad and Victor L. Mote, *Gateway to Siberian Resources (The BAM)* (Washington, D.C., 1977), p. 80; Donald A. Brobst and Walden P. Pratt, eds., *U.S. Mineral Resources* (Washington, D.C., 1973), p. 175.
49. *Oxford Economic Atlas of the World* (4th edition; London, 1972), p. 44.
50. Brobst and Pratt, p. 698.
51. Bureau of Mines, *Mineral Facts and Problems* (Washington, D.C., 1976), p. 107.
52. *Oxford Economic Atlas*, p. 48.

53. Council on Environmental Quality and the Department of State, *The Global 2000 Report to the President* (Washington, D.C., 1980), 1: 29.
54. *Ibid.*, p. 31.
55. Victor L. Mote, "Environmental Constraints to the Economic Development of Siberia," Discussion Paper, 6 (Dec. 1978), in AAG.
56. Interviews in USSR, Sept.–Oct. 1978; Ye. Kozlovsky, USSR minister of geology, "Behind the Decisions of the 25th CPSU Congress: BAM's Raw Materials Complexes," *Pravda*, Nov. 15, 1978, in CDSP, 30 (Dec. 13, 1978).
57. Meyerhoff, "Soviet Petroleum," pp. 103ff.
58. For an informed account of this phenomenon during the Carter administration, see Leslie H. Gelb, "Muskie and Brzezinski: The Struggle over Foreign Policy," *New York Times Magazine*, July 20, 1980.
59. John P. Hardt, "Military-Economic Implications of Soviet Regional Policy," paper prepared for a colloquium of the NATO Directorate of Economic Affairs held in Brussels, Apr. 25–27, 1979, p. 9, mimeographed.
60. Statement to House International Relations Committee, Oct. 26, 1978, cited in Hardt, p. 26.
61. An authoritative critique of these problems is offered in Meyerhoff, "Soviet Petroleum"; see also Dienes and Shabad, *Soviet Energy System*.

Index

Index

Afghanistan, Soviet invasion of: and Japan-Soviet relations, 118, 132, 157f; and China-Soviet relations, 171; and U.S.-Soviet relations, 209f, 235; and Japan-U.S. relations, 217
Aganbegyan, A. G., 37, 43, 48–49, 50, 202
Agriculture, 25–30 *passim*, 107
Aigun, Treaty of (1858), 71
Air routes, and Japan-Soviet Union relations, 156
Akademgorodok, 45
Aksai Chin plateau, 82
Aldan, 52, 54, 154–55, 192, 201
Allied antisubmarine warfare (ASW), 97
Aluminum production, 53, 157
Amur Oblast, 52, 54, 193
Amur River, 22f; China-Soviet Union relations and, 71, 73–74, 88–93 *passim*, 101, 170–71, 178–80, 214
Amursk, 154
Amurstal, 193
Angara River, 16, 52
Angarsk, 39–40, 41–42, 200
Angola, 168
Antimony resources, 55, 228–31 *passim*
Anzai, Hiroshi, 139–40
Arctic, Soviet exploration, exploitation of, 228

Arctic Ocean, sea route through, 92
Argun River, 178
Armco Incorporated, 217
Asbestos deposits, 56, 155, 228–31 *passim*
Atomic bomb, *see* Nuclear weapons
Autarky, dependence, and leverage, 232–36

Baibakov, N. K., 196
Baikal, Lake, 88
Baikal-Amur Mainline (BAM), 2, 3, 12, 16–17; implications of permafrost for, 30–31, 102f; Tynda and, 38–39, 40–41, 100; development of natural resources and, 51–56 *passim*, 231–32; and Soviet investment policy, 57–64, 104; scope of construction of, 58–61, 101–4; earthquakes and, 59, 102–3; strategic implications of, 81, 93–94, 99–107, 212; China's perspective on, 176f; location of iron and steel complex in zone of, 192–93; thermal springs along route of, 225–26
Beijing, Treaty of (1860), 71
Birobidzhan, 54–55
Black Sea, 92
Blagoveschensk, 100
Bolshevik revolution, 66f
Boxer riots, 67

270 INDEX

Bratsk, 52f, 192
Brezhnev, Leonid, 90, 202
Brucite deposits, 56
Bureaucratic practices: construction of BAM and, 60; in military budgeting, 98–99; Soviet-China-Japan relations and, 130–33; complications of working with Soviet, 138, 139–40, 141; and decision-making model, 184, 185–92; of Soviet provincial secretaries, 192–97
Bureya River, 53
Buryat ASSR, 54

Cadmium deposits, 228
Cape Krilov, 146
Cape Soya, 146
Carter, Jimmy, 210, 217, 235
Changkufeng (Lake Khasan), 99
Charo-Tokin region, 192
Chiang Kai-shek, 67, 173
China-India relations, 74, 82, 169
China-Japan relations, 3–5, 9–10, 66–69, 74–86 passim, 114–15, 151; Soviet policy and, 119, 130–34, 143–45, 159
China–Soviet Union relations, 2–5, 13, 77, 160–81, 204, 208, 214–16, 219–20; as factor in Soviet-Japan relations, 13, 119, 130–34, 143–45, 159, 174–76; territorial disputes in, 66–68, 71–76 passim, 81–82, 88–93 passim, 258; military security, capabilities, and, 78–79, 86, 88–94, 100–108 passim, 163, 164–65; in 1980's, and alternative futures for, 80–83, 162–74, 178–80, 219–20; and population densities along borders, 92–93, 180; U.S. policy interests and, 215
China–United States relations, 79, 161, 172–73
Chinese Eastern Railroad, 67
Chita-Irkutsk-Yakutia border, 54
Chita Oblast, 53–54, 194–95
Chukotka Peninsula, 49
Chulman, 51f, 154, 192–93, 201
Churchill, Winston, 68
Civil war, Russia's, 66f, 71, 75
Clay deposits, 195
Client states, in Sino-Soviet rivalry, 168–69

Climatic conditions and geography, 20, 21–26, 36–37, 107, 213. *See also* Earthquakes; Ice; Permafrost
Coal deposits, 51–52, 148–49, 154; Japan-Soviet relations and, 109, 137–38, 213; China-Soviet relations and, 179f; and transportation and pollution problems, 225; predicting supplies of, 227–28, 231
Cobalt deposits, 228, 231
Columbium deposits, 56
Commodity Control List, 210
Communist Economic Bloc (COMECON), 223f
Communist Party, Chinese, 169–70
Control Data Corporation, 148
Copper resources, 53–54, 55, 194–95, 230f; Soviet-Japanese relations and, 155; China's need for supplemental, 177, 230; prediction of, 228, 231; in Chile and Peru, 229
Cultural activity, Soviet, 35
Cultural Revolution (China), 90, 101, 115, 169

Damansky Island (Zhenbaodao), 73, 91, 93, 163
Daniel, Donald C., 95
Decision making: policy, and Soviet, 13–14, 57–64, 104, 121–22, 182–206, 207–9, 232–36; bureaucratic model of, 184, 185–92. *See also* Policy questions
Defense spending: in Japan, 118–23 passim; in NATO countries, 120; in Soviet Union, 121–22. *See also* Military capabilities; Strategic implications
Demographic factors, 31–37, 92–93, 180
Deng Xiaoping, 74, 115
Diamond mines, 52, 55, 228
Diaoyudao Islands (Senkaku), 74, 130
Dnieper River projects, 200
Dresser Industries, 210
Dulles, John Foster, 127

Earthquakes, 59, 102–3
East Asia: international relations in, 2–4, 11, 65–70; issues and stakes in, 70–79; in 1980's, 79–84; strategic implications of EAS development

INDEX   271

for, 85–111. *See also bilateral relationships among* China; Japan; Soviet Union; United States
East Asian Siberia (EAS): public's images of, 1–3, 12, 19–21; research experiences in, 6–8, 45–46; China factor in, 13, 119, 130–34, 143–45, 160–81, 214–16; terminology of, 14–18; geography, climate of, 21–26, 36–37, 107, 213; permafrost in, 26–31, 48, 102f, 107; demographic factors in, 31–37, 92–93, 180; recent developments and future prospects, 37–44, 218–22, 236; sea route serving, 92; Soviet decision making about, 182–85, 192–206, 219–22. *See also specific resources and aspects of by name*
East Turkestan Republic, 76
Economic factors, 16–18, 87, 106–8, 201–4, 222–32; Siberian development, and leverage of, 87, 108–11, 150–51, 232–36; in China-Soviet-U.S. relations, 167f, 172–73; suggesting symbiosis between EAS and China, 176–81. *See also* Export-import markets; Fishing issues; Interdependence
Electricity, *see* Hydroelectric power
El Paso Natural Gas, 137
Energy resources, EAS's, 3–5, 14, 16, 49–50; Japan's interests in, 4–5, 87, 108–11, 151–54, 156–57, 204, 213–14, 226–27; exporting of, 145–53; in world economy, 222–32; autarky in Soviet needs for, 233–34. *See also individual resources by name*
Environmental factors, 59, 150
Etorofu, 116–17, 123–26
European Economic Community, 223
European markets, for Siberian energy production, 223–26
Export Administration Act (1979), 209
Export Control Act (1949), 209
Export-Import Bank Act (1974), 210–11
Export-Import banks, role of, 4–5, 105, 137, 217–18
Export-import markets, 112f, 145–53, 209–11, 222–32. *See also* Energy resources

Far East, Soviet, 15, 18, 42, 97
Fevralsk, 201
Fishing issues, international relations and, 124, 127–33 *passim,* 216
Fluorspar, 228
Food, in EAS, 176–77, 225–26. *See also* Grain imports
Foreign policy, *see* Policy questions
Forest products, *see* Timber products
Formosa, *see* Taiwan
France, 224
Friendship, Alliance, and Mutual Assistance, Treaty of (1950), 68, 171
Friendship and Peace, Treaty of (1978), 74, 79, 115
Friendship Association, Sino-Soviet, 170
Fukuda, Takeo, 74

Gas, *see* Natural gas resources
Gas hydrate deposits, 228
Geography, *see* Climatic conditions and geography
Germany, West, 224f
Global 2000 Report to the President, The, 231
Gold deposits, 55, 228
Gorshkov, Sergei, 97
Gosplan USSR, 57–58, 186–93 *passim*
Gosstroi, 187
Grain imports, Soviet Union's, 213, 232–33
Granberg, A. G., 202–3
Graphite, 231
Great Leap Forward, 76, 179
Great Power game (in China), 77
Gromyko, Andrei A., 124
Gulf Oil Company, 137, 148

Habomais (archipelago), 98, 123–27
Hirohito, Emperor, 73
Hiroshima, 73
Hitler, Adolf, 66
Hogen, Shinsaku, 120
Hokkaido, 83, 98, 117–25 *passim,* 141, 146–47
Hua Guofeng, 134
Huang Hua, 170
Hydroelectric power, 52–54, 178–79, 180, 192

Ice, as obstacle to development, 29, 146f. *See also* Permafrost

Images: of EAS, 1–3, 12, 19–21; in international relations, 70; Japanese of Soviets, 12, 113–23, 128, 129–30; Chinese of Soviets, U.S., 160–62
India, 74, 82, 169
Indochina, see Vietnam
Inoki, Masamichi, 119
Interdependence, 12, 155–56, 167–68, 204–6, 213–14; and world's energy resources, 152–53, 213–14, 222–33
International relations: history of East Asian, 2–4, 65–70; issues and stakes in, 70–79; in 1980's, 79–84. See also bilateral relationships among China; Japan; Soviet Union; United States
Investment policy, Soviet, see Decision making; Policy questions
Iran, 225
Irkutsk (city), 45, 49, 107
Irkutsk Oblast, 16, 56
Irkutsk province, 54, 192, 194
Iron and steel complex, competition between provinces for, 192–94, 197, 201
Iron ore resources, 52, 54, 154–55, 179, 192, 228, 231
Italy, 224

Jackson-Vanik amendment (to Trade Act, 1974), 211
Japan, Sea of, 71, 77, 96–98
Japan-China relations, see China-Japan relations
Japan Defense Agency (JDA), 115ff, 122
Japan-Soviet Union relations, 2–12 passim, 109, 112–59, 226–27; historical perspective on, 2–5, 11, 100–101, 134–45; scholarly and government analysis of, 7–10; China factor in, 13, 119, 130–34, 143–45, 159, 174–76; conflict, cooperation, and interdependence in, 66–67, 69, 152–53, 214–15; U.S. role in, 69f, 77–84 passim, 118–24 passim, 132, 142, 144, 157–59; territorial disputes and, 72–75 passim, 98, 117, 123–29, 157; fishing disputes and, 124, 127–33 passim, 216. See also Strategic implications
Japan–United States relations, 69f, 112–13, 217–18
Japanese Socialist Party, 89

Kalashnikova, T. M., 16
Khabarovsk (city): development near and in, 55, 154, 193–94; China-Soviet relations and, 73–74, 93, 101, 170–71; strategic vulnerability of, 107
Khabarovsk Krai, 54, 56, 188
Khasan, Lake (Changkufeng), 99
Kholmsk, 201
Khrushchev, Nikita, 75, 88, 177–78, 184–85
Kirby, E. Stuart, 15
Klopov, S. V., 178–80
Kolyma hydroelectric station, 196
Kolyma River, 53
Komsomolsk, 100, 102, 108, 193, 201
Korea: China-Japan relations and, 68, 216; Soviet-Japan relations and, 75, 154; China-Soviet relations and, 169, 215; China-U.S. relations and, 172–73; workers for Siberia's forests from, 178
Korean War (1950–53), 75
Kosygin, A. N., 90, 138
Krasnoyarsk province, 16, 192
Kubo, Takuya, 142–44, 159
Kunashiri Island, 116–17, 123–26
Kuomintang, 67
Kuril Islands: Japan-Soviet territory disputes about, 72f, 124–27; strategic importance of, 82, 96, 98, 125–28
Kuznetsk, 148

Labor camps, Siberian, 73
Labor force, Siberian, 31, 32–37, 58; recent developments and future prospects, 37–44; productivity of, 203
Lead resources, 55, 155, 228–31 passim
Lena River, 22–23
Lenin, V. I., 90
Leningrad, 92

INDEX   273

Leverage, see Economic factors
Liaotung Peninsula, 177
Liberal Democratic Party (LDP) of Japan, 118, 125
Lignite resources, 231
Limestone deposits, 195
Lin Biao, 163
Liquefied natural gas (LNG), see Natural gas resources
Living conditions: out-migration caused by, 34–37, 38; in new cities, 38–42; in BAM zone, 107
Louis, Victor, 259

McKelvey, V. E., 48
Magadan, as port for natural gas, 139, 150, 196f
Magadan Oblast, 188
Magadan province, 195
Mamoru, Shigemitsu, 126
Manchukuo, 68f, 76, 84
Manchuria, Japan-Russia relations and, 75–76, 77, 99, 100–101
Manganese, 54–55
Mao Zedong: on land disputes with Russians/Soviets, 71, 75f, 89–90; and regularizing relations with U.S., 79, 161, 173; on Soviet revisionism, 160, 169–70; on U.S. imperialism, 161; on China's ability to survive a war, 164, 258
Maritime Krai, 88, 100
Media images, see Images
Merchant shipping, to Soviet Far East, 97
Mercury deposits, 55
Metallurgy factory (at Khabarovsk), 193–94
Meteorology, see Climatic conditions and geography
Mica deposits, 56, 155
Migration, internal (Siberian), 31, 32–37, 107
Military capabilities: development of EAS, and differences in, 77–79, 81f, 85–111, 112, 115–23, 157, 167, 204, 216–17; of U.S., 98, 120–21. See also Baikal-Amur Mainline; Nuclear weapons; Strategic implications
Mineral resources, 44–57, 227–28, 230–32. See also individual minerals by name
Minsk (Soviet aircraft carrier), 98, 141
Mirny, 55
Molybdenum deposits, 56, 155, 230
Mongolia, 74–75, 88, 99, 169, 171
Mongol invasion, 93
Mote, Victor, 59

Nagasaki, 73
Nakhodka, 106, 136, 156
Naledi (icing formations), 29
Nationalism, 74, 85
National power grid, 53
NATO countries: defense spending in, 120; and Siberia's energy resources, 223–25
Natural gas resources, 1–2, 14, 48–51, 137; exports of, 109, 139, 146–47, 149–53, 234; predicting supplies of, 228, 231
Natural phenomena, see Climatic conditions and geography; Earthquakes; Permafrost
Natural resources, 44–57; predicting supplies of, 227–31. See also individual classes of resources by name
Naval activity, Soviet, 94–99, 106, 116, 157
Nazi-Soviet pact (1939), 173
Neryungri, 51, 148, 154
Neutrality treaties, Japan-Soviet, 66, 72f
Nevelskoi, Strait of, 96f
Nickel resources, 155, 228, 231
Nippon Steel, 217
Nixon, Richard M., 79, 161, 173
Nomonhan (Khalkin-Gol), 99
Northeast Asian Triangle, see Triangle of tension; and bilateral relationships among China; Japan; Soviet Union
Northern territories, Japan's, and relations with USSR, 123–29, 157
Nuclear-powered ships, 92
Nuclear weapons: Japan and, 73, 118; Soviet-Chinese relations and China's, 88, 90f, 164

Occidental Petroleum, 137
Ohira, Masayoshi, 217

274 INDEX

Oil, 1–2, 14, 46–51 passim, 57–58, 146, 152; and Soviet-Japanese collaboration, 71–73, 87, 127–28, 137–40, 146–52 passim, 218; China's fields of, 180; policy issues relating to USSR production of, 233–34
Okhotsk, Sea of, 82, 88, 96–97, 117, 125, 139
Olga, 139f, 196f
Opium War (1839–42), 78
Orlov, Boris P., 17, 43

Pacific Fleet, Soviet, 94–98, 125, 212
Pacific Ocean: access to, 96–97; Soviet maritime presence in, 106, 252
Pakistan, 168–69
Pamir mountains, 82
Peace and Friendship, Treaty of (1978), 74, 79, 115
Pearl Harbor attack, 69
People's Liberation Army (PLA), 91
People's Republic of China, establishment of, 68. See also China-India relations; China-Japan relations; China–Soviet Union relations; China-U.S. relations
Permafrost, 26–31, 48, 102f, 107
Pescadores, 68
Petroleum resources, 46, 92. See also Natural gas; Oil
Petropavlovsk, port of, 95, 97
Phosphate resources, 55, 231
Pinchot, Gifford, 227–28
Platinum resources, 231
Policy questions, 3–5, 9–14 passim, 79–84, 207–9; recent developments in U.S., 207–12; economic factors in, 222–32; implications for EAS of West European and Japanese, 226–27; and Soviet-U.S. relations, 234–36. See also Decision making
Politburo, 185–86
Political factors, see bilateral relations among China; Japan; Soviet Union; United States
Population, 31–37, 92–93, 180
Port Arthur, 78
Portsmouth, Treaty of (1905), 72, 83
Potash fertilizers, 231
Potsdam agreement, 124

Power relationships, 76–79
Primoria, 193
Provincial interests, role of, 192–97. See also individual provinces by name

Quing empire, 67, 71

Racial issues, 134
Railroads, 3–4, 76. See also Baikal-Amur Mainline; Trans-Siberian railroad
Research experiences, and institutes, 6–8, 45–46
Rivers, 22–23, 52–53, 71, 73–74, 178–80. See also individual rivers by name
Roosevelt, Franklin D., 67–68, 84
Roosevelt, Theodore, 69, 83
Russian Soviet Federated Socialist Republic (RSFSR/Russia), 14, 38

Saeki, Kiichi, 119, 158–59
St. Petersburg, port and naval base of, 71
St. Petersburg, Treaty of (1875), 72
Sakhalin: oil and gas resources of, 51f, 110, 137f, 264; Soviet-Japanese relations and, 71–73, 87, 127–28, 137–40, 146–52 passim, 218; wood pulp mill proposed for, 154; Japan-U.S. relations and, 110, 217–18
Sakhalin Oil Development Cooperation Company (Sodeko), 148
Salt resources, 177
San Francisco Peace Treaty (1951), 124
Sapporo, 7, 147
Saushkin, Y., 16
Sayansk, 39, 41
Sea routes, see under Transportation
Self Defense Forces (SDF) of Japan, 115
Senkaku Islands (Diaoyudao), 74, 130
Shelekkov, 53
Shikotan island, 98, 117, 123–27
Shimanovsk, 201
Shimoda, Treaty of (1855), 72
Shniper, R. I., 203
Shulman, Marshall, 235–36
Siberia: images of, 1–3, 12, 19–21; subregions of, 14–18; geography

INDEX 275

and climate of, 20, 21–26, 36–37, 107, 213; demographic factors in, 31–37, 92–93, 180. *See also* East Asian Siberia; West Siberia
Siberian labor camps, Japanese prisoners of war in, 73
Sibgipromix, 193
Silver deposits, 55, 228, 231
Sino-Indian war (1962), 74
Sino-Japanese war (1894–95), 68
Sinophobia, Soviet, 93
Sino-Soviet Friendship Association, 170
Sino-Soviet relations, *see* China–Soviet Union relations
Sonoda, Foreign Minister (1979), 117
Sovetskaia Gavan, 95, 100, 201
Soviet Army Day, 170
Soviet Far Eastern Shipping Company, 155–56
Soviet Far East region, 15, 18, 42, 97
Soviet-Japanese Joint Declaration (1956), 124
Soviet Pacific Fleet, 94–98, 125, 212
Soviet Union, decision making and policy in, 13–14, 57–64, 104, 121–22, 182–206, 207–9, 232–36. *See also* China–Soviet Union relations; Japan–Soviet Union relations; Soviet Union–United States relations
Soviet Union–United States relations: energy resources in EAS and, 3–5, 148–51, 209–11; and Japan-Soviet relations, 69f, 77–84 *passim*, 118–24 *passim*, 132, 142, 144, 157–59; strategic implications of, 86, 95ff, 220–21
Soya (La Perouse) Strait, 96, 98, 126
Stalin, Joseph, 66, 67–68, 72, 75
Steel manufacturing, 54–55, 108, 193, 217
Stevenson amendment (to Export-Import Bank Act, 1974), 210–11
Strategic implications, 2, 3–5, 11–12, 85–111, 212–18; of BAM, 81, 93–94, 99–107, 212; of economic leverage, 87, 108–11, 150–51, 232–36. *See also* Military capabilities

Submarine-launched ballistic missiles (SLBM), 117
Submarines, Soviet, 82, 94–95, 96
Suez Canal, 92
Sulfur resources, 228, 231
Sungari River, 178, 180
Sun Yat-sen, 67
Suslov, Sergei P., 24–29 *passim*
Svobodnyy, 193, 201

Taiwan (Formosa), 68, 79, 172f
Talakan dam, 52–53
Tanaka, Kakuei, 115
Tantalum deposits, 56
Tarasov, G., 62–63
Territorial production complexes (TPC), 16, 197–201
Thailand, 173
Thermal springs, 225–26
Thiel, Erich, 15
Tibet, 169, 173
Timber products, 56f, 193–94, 231; and Japan-Soviet relations, 109–10, 136, 153–54; and China-Soviet relations, 177–78, 179
Tin resources, 55, 155, 228–31 *passim*
Titanium, 231
Tokyo Gas, 139, 151
Totalitarian model (of Soviet decision making), 184
Trade Act (1974), 211
Transportation: overland routes for, 91–94; sea routes for, 92, 96–97; Soviet-Japanese relations and, 140, 155–56. *See also* Export-import markets; *and individual railroads, rivers, and seas by name*
Trans-Siberian railroad, 2, 11, 17, 22, 40; vulnerability of, 77, 86–94 *passim*, 99–101, 103; Soviet-Japanese cooperation in use of, 155–56
Triangle of tension, 2–5, 9–10, 11, 65–84, 86, 181. *See also bilateral relationships among* China; Japan; Soviet Union; United States
Trotsky, Leon, 184
Tsugaru Strait, 96, 98
Tsushima Strait, 96ff
Tungsten deposits, 54, 228, 230f
Turkestan, East, 76

276 INDEX

Tynda, 38–39, 40–41, 100
Tyumen, 138f, 144f, 175, 239

Udokan, 53–54, 155, 194–95, 230
Ulan Bator, 75
Unemployment, and USSR's need for timber workers, 177–78
United States: policy options of, 14, 112–13, 207–36; role in East Asian triangle of, 69f, 77–84 passim, 144, 167f, 172–73; economic leverage of, 110–11; and Soviet-Japanese relations, 119–24 passim, 142, 157–59. See also China-U.S. relations; Japan-U.S. relations; Soviet Union–U.S. relations
Urtuiskii, 195
Ussuri, 54
Ussuri River, 71, 73–74, 90, 101, 170–71
Ust-Borzinskii, 195
Ust-Ilimsk, 52
Ust-Kut, 102

Vanadium resources, 231
Vanino, 100, 201
Versailles peace conference, 68
Vesna (Okean II), 96
Vietnam: invasion of Cambodia by, 79–80; and China-Soviet relations, 80f, 165–66, 170ff; Soviet relations with, 94, 165
Vladivostok, 45, 71, 77, 86, 91–94 passim, 100–101, 107
Volochayevka, 100
Vorobiev, V. V., 36

West Siberia, 1–2, 5–6, 14, 46–47, 92, 138–39, 145, 150–51; out-migration from, 32, 33–34

Wilson, Woodrow, 83
Wood chips, see Timber products
Working conditions, 35–36. See also Labor force
World War I, 68
World War II, 72–73, 75, 125
Wrangel, port of, 56, 106, 136, 154, 156, 181, 212–13

Xinjiang, 76, 91

Yakut ASSR, 16, 188, 192–93, 204
Yakutia: natural resources in, 48–55 passim, 108, 146–53, 177, 196–97; Soviet-Japanese relations and, 136ff, 139; China factor in, 181; foreign investment and, 203–4, 226–27; Soviet aggression, and future of, 234
Yakutsk, 45, 49–50
Yalta agreements (1945), 67–68, 69, 72, 76, 100, 124
Ye Jianying, 169
Yemen, 168
Yenisei River, 16
Yevtushenko, Yevgenii, 93
Young Communist League, 58
Yuzhno-Aldan region, 192

Zaire, rivalries of Communist countries in, 168
Zeya River, 52, 178, 180
Zeya-Shimanovsk, 201
Zhenbaodao (Damansky Island), 73, 91, 93, 163
Zhou Enlai, 89f, 168
Zhukov, G. K., 99–100
Zimbabwe, rivalries of Communist countries in, 168
Zinc resources, 55, 155, 228–31 passim

RAYMOND H. FOGLER LIBRARY
DATE DUE

BOOKS ARE SUBJECT TO
RECALL AFTER TWO WEEKS

NOV 0 6 1984

UA
770
W433

FEB 3 1982

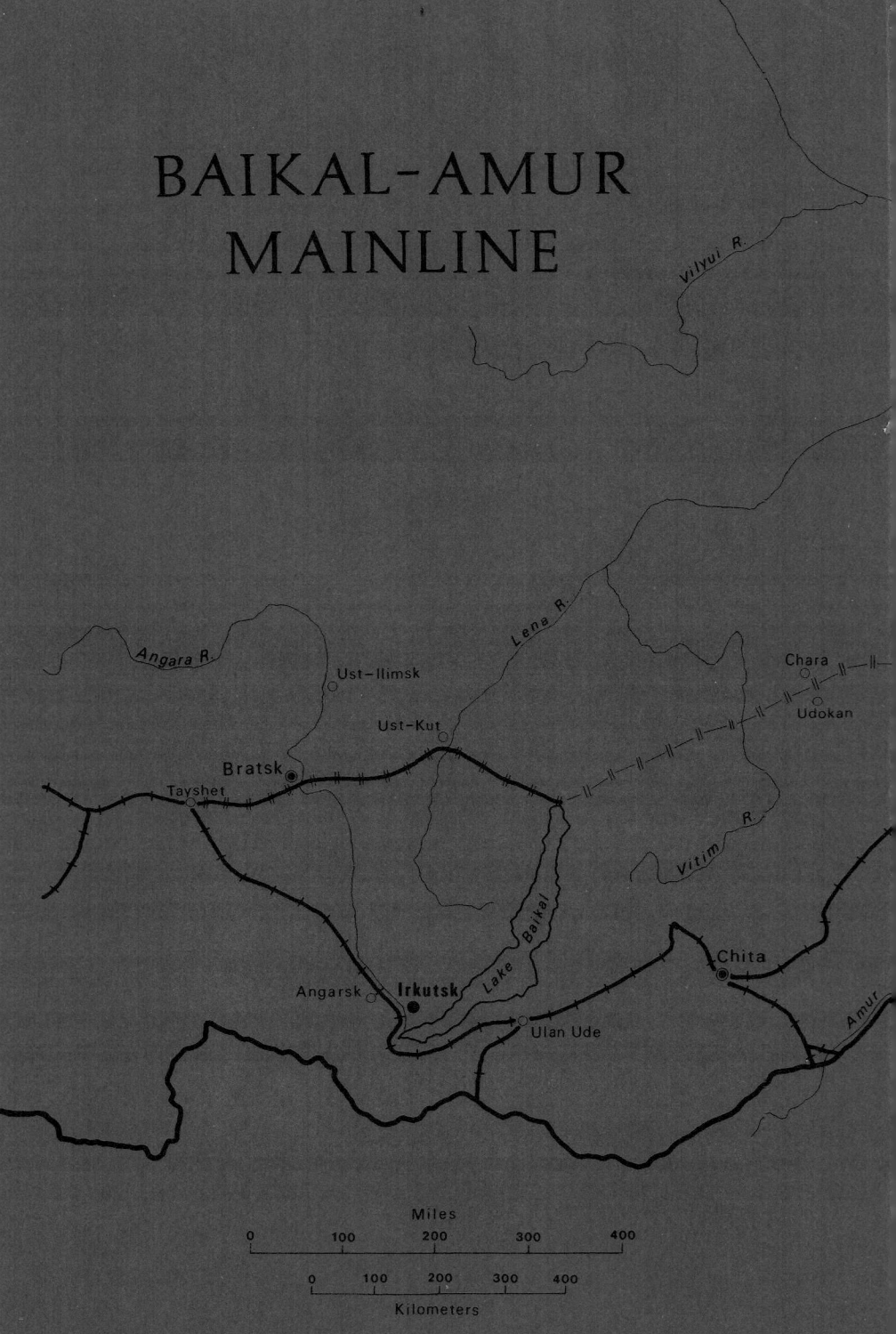